RACHEL

Testimony: Quakerism and Theological Ethics

scm press

© Rachel Muers 2015

Published in 2015 by SCM Press
Editorial office
3rd Floor
Invicta House
108-114 Golden Lane,
London
EC1Y 0TG

SCM Press is an imprint of Hymns Ancient & Modern Ltd (a registered charity)
13A Hellesdon Park Road
Norwich NR6 5DR, UK

www.scmpress.co.uk

All rights reserved. No part of this publication may be reproduced,
stored in a retrieval system, or transmitted,
in any form or by any means, electronic, mechanical,
photocopying or otherwise, without the prior permission of
the publisher, SCM Press.

The Author has asserted her right under the Copyright,
Designs and Patents Act, 1988,
to be identified as the Author of this Work

British Library Cataloguing in Publication data
A catalogue record for this book is available
from the British Library

978 0 334 04668 4

Typeset by Manila Typesetting Company
Printed and bound by
CPI Group (UK) Ltd

To Gavin

Contents

Acknowledgements		vii
Prologue: Oceans		ix
Introduction: Knowing Experimentally: Approaches to Quaker Testimony and Theology		1
1	Walking in the Light: The Bible and Quaker Testimony	29
2	'We do utterly deny . . .': Refusals, Silences and Negative Testimony	54
3	Speaking Truth to Power, and Other Holy Experiments	80
4	'Swear not at all': Oaths, Nonviolence and Conscience	105
5	Religious Freedom and Solidarity: Quaker Martyrs and their Communities	130
6	Being Witnesses: Marriage, Sexuality and Tradition	151
7	Sustainability and Simplicity	172
Afterwords		193
Bibliography		206
Index		216

Acknowledgements

> Reader; It is some time since I set about this Treatise, which makes me now think, that part thereof may seem to some to be unseasonable; for it swelled beyond my Intention, and took up more time in writing than I thought it would ... when I set about it, I saw a Field before me, which cost me some spiritual Travel before I got thorow.
>
> Elizabeth Bathurst, Preface to *Truth's Vindication*, 1683

The thinking reflected in this book has been shaped over time in many overlapping communities, both in the academy and among Quakers. While I take responsibility for every part of it, and especially for its manifold defects – and am fairly sure that nobody is going to agree with, or like, all of it – I am very conscious that I also owe whatever is good in it to others. It would take far too long to list here all the individuals who have left their mark on it or have helped it to take form.

So, my heartfelt thanks to all friends, and colleagues in the University of Leeds, and previously in the Universities of Exeter and Cambridge; in Jesus Lane (Cambridge), Exeter and Carlton Hill (Leeds); in the Society for the Study of Theology, the Society for Scriptural Reasoning and various groups at the American Academy of Religion; at Woodbrooke and at Yearly Meeting. I hope you all know who you are. Among those with whom particularly long-standing conversations have shaped and supported this book – and whose influence it has not always been possible to identify and acknowledge, however hard I have tried – are Mike

Higton, Julie Gittoes, Janet Scott, Rhiannon Grant and Ben Wood. I am also grateful to Jacqui Stewart and John Punshon for taking the time to share their expertise on Quaker testimony with me. Short papers that related closely to the book were presented at the Universities of Cambridge, Exeter, St Andrews and Aberdeen and at King's College London; I acknowledge with gratitude the helpful discussions on those occasions.

Natalie Watson has been an unfailingly patient and encouraging editor, and I am enormously in her debt for her continuing enthusiasm for the project even in the face of long delays.

As always, my greatest debts are to my family, and especially the family I live with. The book is dedicated to my husband, Gavin Burnell – because, even more than usual, he made it all possible. And in so far as time spent with Matthew and Peter Burnell has disrupted or changed the writing process, I would not have wanted it any other way.

I also thank Rhiannon Grant for her invaluable work on the Index.

Prologue

Oceans

I saw also that there was an ocean of darkness and death, but an infinite ocean of light and love, which flowed over the ocean of darkness. And in that also I saw the infinite love of God; and I had great openings.

George Fox, Journal for 1647

There's more than dark enough to drown us all,
pulls with strong currents though it's overflown.
Mostly, I drift; but sometimes catch the tide

and swept up, thrown between the waves of light
we splutter kingdomwards, make landfall, stumble
bedraggled and squint-eyed, a few steps on.

Introduction

Knowing Experimentally: Approaches to Quaker Testimony and Theology

Beginning with Quaker ethics

This book is about how Quaker theological ethics works, and about what Quakers contribute to theological ethics. I attempt to show how Quaker ways of living and acting – an *ethos*, a pattern of life – relate to theology, to ways of thinking and reasoning about God and all things in relation to God. In doing so, I also make some more general suggestions about how Quaker theology can be done, and about how theological ethics can be done. The modest hope is that both people who are interested in Quakers and people who are interested in the relationship between theology and ethics will find something worth thinking about, arguing with or developing further.

Most people with a limited knowledge of religious groups know Quakers, if not as people who wear large hats and make porridge oats, then as people who observe various slightly puzzling or unusual rules – like not fighting – along with puzzling or unusual religious practices – like silent worship. People who try to understand Quakers by understanding what they collectively believe are, notoriously, likely to end up more confused than before – confronted by an enormous diversity of expressed belief, diverse not only across time and space but even within the relatively small communities of Quakers in Britain or the USA. It is much easier to find patterns, consistencies and norms in Quaker practice than in Quaker belief – even though the porridge oats bit, for the record and once again, is not true.

So it might seem that ethics is the obvious way to approach Quaker thought. However, people who try to understand Quakers by understanding what they do – how these puzzling or unusual rules, or patterns of practice, fit together and constitute a community's identity – are equally likely to end up confused. Like Quaker theology, Quaker ethical reasoning is not often systematized. When we look more closely we find that in Quaker communities and in Quaker literature, the basis for a particular course of action is sometimes not explained; or it is explained in a way that does not obviously relate to other explanations; or it is explained in a way that does not obviously refer to God, or to conventional sources of theological authority or patterns of theological reasoning. This is true especially of contemporary 'liberal' Quakers in the West, but it is to some extent true elsewhere. As we shall see, from every era of Quakerism there are numerous examples of powerful and prophetic writing, articulating and advocating distinctive Quaker perspectives on the issues of the day; but there are fewer works that articulate any underlying coherence to these ethical positions.[1]

In twenty-first-century Britain Quakers are accustomed to being known and for the most part respected – grudgingly, confusedly or otherwise – for their sustained tradition of ethical and political activism. Quaker involvement in the anti-slavery movement, in humanitarianism, in peace work, in post-conflict relief work, and so forth, is often cited. It might be reasonable to think that Quakers often have something distinctive or important to contribute on ethical questions. Quakers themselves either claim or imply this when they devote, proportionally, a large amount of their available collective time and energy – in local, national and international

---

[1] An exception is the work of Jackie Leach Scully. See her article 'Quakers and Ethics', in Stephen W. Angell and Pink Dandelion (eds), 2013, *The Oxford Handbook of Quaker Studies*, Oxford: Oxford University Press, pp. 535–48. The collection of essays in Jackie Leach Scully and Pink Dandelion (eds), 2007, *Good and Evil: Quaker Perspectives*, Aldershot: Ashgate, draws together a range of meta-ethical perspectives.

INTRODUCTION

meetings – to producing major statements on contemporary ethical and political questions. Explicit claims such as 'In the Religious Society of Friends we commit ourselves not to words but to a way' (*Quaker Faith and Practice* 1994, hereafter *QF&P*, p. 17) are common in official and semi-official accounts of Quakerism.

Given that context, it seems to make sense in twenty-first-century Britain to write about Quaker ethics, and expect an audience beyond Quakerism to learn something from it. It is less obvious, however, that that exercise will end up being *theological*. What if Quaker ethics has nothing theological about it – or nothing that adds to existing work in theological ethics? What, for example, if Quakers are simply being rather more consistent about enacting a set of ethical principles that could be adopted by anyone? Or, what if the historical sources of Quaker ethics lie in some theological moves that are not particularly original or unusual – and have in any case been forgotten by contemporary Quakers? In that case, Quakers might be interesting as the source of several case studies in ethical reasoning, but not as the source of new ideas in theological ethics.

My claim in this book is that Quaker approaches to theological ethics – to the relationship between patterns of acting in the world, and patterns of thinking about God and the world-in-relation-to-God – are, in fact, distinctive and interesting in their own right. I do, however, think that in order to appreciate Quaker approaches to theological ethics, we have to suspend several common assumptions about how ethics works, and hence about what a distinctive contribution to theological ethics might look like. We have to refrain, at least temporarily, from looking for surprising new principles or rules, or even for surprising new interpretations of biblical or traditional texts. Rather, we have to pick up on the idea of 'not words but a way', and carry it through to its conclusion at least as far as Quakers do. We have not only to say that the primary form of response to God is in life and action but also to think through the implications of that idea for how both ethical reasoning and theology are done. To some extent, we have to avoid assuming that the ethical life of religious communities is about 'putting belief

TESTIMONY

into practice', and consider instead the implications of 'putting practice into belief'. Early in the book, I set out a framework for thinking about Quaker theological ethics along these lines. Later, I use it to examine some examples of key areas in which Quaker theological ethics might make a distinctive contribution.

As noted above, Quakerism is extremely diverse, not only historically and globally but even (in certain respects) within any given national or local group. My own ecclesial context, and the context on which I focus most of my reflection and from which I take most of my examples, is British Quakerism. British Quakers today – along with Quakers in numerous other parts of the world, although not the global majority – are categorized as 'liberal' in the standard taxonomies of world Quakerism.[2] They can be described as 'liberal', because they do not ordinarily use or require either confessions of faith or standardized rules of behaviour or dress, and also because they are the inheritors of the liberal turn in Quaker thought and theology in the late nineteenth century. Their style of worship is categorized as 'unprogrammed' – often, somewhat misleadingly, described as silent worship. In this book, I make frequent reference to British and North American examples, but I look back repeatedly to the history of Quakers and in particular to the earliest generations of the movement – to the 'single theological culture' (Dandelion 2007, p. 13) to which successive generations have looked to shape their understanding of Quaker identity.

At least some of the terminology I use, particularly in the early stages of the book, will however be unfamiliar or uncomfortable to large numbers of British Quakers today. I seek to relate characteristically Quaker terms and categories to a wider context of Christian theology, in a way that is rather seldom done by or for today's liberal Quakers. I do this not only because I want to make Quaker theological ethics accessible to a wider Christian audience,

---

[2] See Pink Dandelion, 2007, *An Introduction to Quakerism*, Cambridge: Cambridge University Press, Ch. 6, for an account of the contemporary 'Quaker family', focused on distinctions between 'Liberal', 'Conservative' and 'Evangelical' Quakers but incorporating discussion of programmed and unprogrammed worship.

INTRODUCTION

but also and more fundamentally because I think theology helps us to make sense of what Quakers do and say. In a tradition deeply suspicious of theology – particularly, the kind of theology done by those 'bred at Oxford or Cambridge' – this is a risky venture, but by no means unprecedented.[3] We shall see as we go along that I am not short of Quaker theological dialogue partners, either in the past or in the present.

At the heart of my account of Quaker theological ethics is a term that sounds through Quaker history and finds deep resonances in the wider theological tradition: testimony. I begin, then, with an initial orientation to the Quaker idea of testimony.

Characterizing Quaker testimony

> And this is our testimony to the whole world. (Fox, Hubberthorn et al. 1660)

When contemporary liberal Quakers speak about the distinctive or core features of Quaker identity – to each other or to non-Quakers – they often talk about testimony. 'Testimony' appears among Quakers as a component of individual and collective decision-making, a source of theological and spiritual reflection, and a focus for individual and collective self-examination. It also appears in outward-facing presentations of Quakerism, often as key to understanding what and who Quakers are. Testimony, then, seems to name something that is not merely important, but identity-defining and community-forming for Quakers. Testimony is not necessarily the only, or even the determining, facet of Quaker identity, but it is clearly – for contemporary Quakers – something that cannot be lost without changing Quakerism beyond recognition. (Any Quaker readers, or readers familiar with contemporary Quakerism, who are already irritated by my use of 'testimony' in

---

[3] The current edition of *Quaker Faith and Practice* includes a frequently quoted passage from the journal of George Fox that begins: 'Now after I had received that opening of the Lord that to be bred [i.e., *educated*] at Oxford or Cambridge was not sufficient to fit a man to be a minister of Christ...' (*QF&P* 19.02).

TESTIMONY

the singular, rather than 'testimonies' in the plural, are asked to be patient; I will try to explain this decision later in the chapter.)

It is usually clear, when testimony is mentioned among Quakers, that it relates somehow to ethics.[4] It relates to ways of acting and ways of life; and the ways of acting and ways of life to which it refers are not limited to defined contexts of worship or ritual. Beyond this, however, it can be hard to understand what Quakers mean by testimony – and what relationship the use of the word, or the reality to which it refers, might bear to its wider context in church and society, or to what other people say about ethics. When Quakers talk about testimony, do they mean general ethical principles to which they adhere? Or specific rules, sets of dos and don'ts? Or visions of what an ideal human life or an ideal human society would look like? And in any of those cases, why should we go on talking about 'testimony', other than to perpetuate a piece of quaint theological jargon?

Many Quakers would probably say that these questions, while possibly interesting and possibly even controversial, are not particularly important. The whole point about testimony, they might say, is acting and living in particular ways; arguing about words will not change lives, nor have very much impact on the community's identity. They would probably prefer – as some of my readers might prefer – to move straight on to the later chapters of this book, which deal with specific ethical, social and political issues and with specific examples from earlier and recent Quaker history. My argument in this Introduction does not directly contradict this response. I want to show, however, that thinking and talking about testimony as Quakers do is a useful and non-obvious way of doing ethics, and that understanding how testimony works could make a difference to ethics. It could make a difference to how we reason and act in relation to specific issues, and also to how we understand others' reasoning and action.

In order even to start discussing Quaker testimony, however, we need a preliminary definition. Perhaps surprisingly for a term that

---

4 See also on this Scully 2013, 'Quakers and Ethics', pp. 541–3.

INTRODUCTION

is so widely used, good and clear definitions – even preliminary ones – are hard to come by. I offer my own here as a starting point for discussion, not expecting it to be particularly controversial.

My initial proposal is that testimony for Quakers consists of patterns of action and behaviour:

- that are understood as an individual and collective response to God's leading and call;
- that are shared, intergenerationally sustained, communicated in stories and deliberated collectively, and that develop over time;
- that are located in everyday life, rather than (only) in specified liturgical contexts;
- and that work in communicative, challenging and transformative relation to a wider context.

In this book, I am not aiming to give a comprehensive history of Quaker uses of the term 'testimony', although I do discuss some key shifts in their historical context. Nor am I trying to provide a single definition of testimony that covers all its historical uses.[5] My account is deliberately constructive within a tradition, as well as descriptive. I aim to provide a theological account of Quaker testimony that attempts to be true to a broad range of historical and contemporary Quaker sources, comprehensible as Christian theology, and internally consistent. I am re-presenting Quaker thought – without claiming to be representative. I hope, incidentally, that my Quaker readers will bear this in mind if I say things with which they disagree; and I very much hope that my non-Quaker readers will bear this in mind before assuming other Quakers will agree with me.

---

[5] There have been many shifts over time in the use of the term 'testimony', but these rarely occur through explicit debates or through decisions that can be traced back. The story is more often one of subtle and often unmarked linguistic shifts across time and space; contrasting or contradictory uses of a term that pass without discussion; new assumptions made that are generally accepted but cannot then be traced back to their source; and, sometimes, remarkably creative theological developments presented as if they had always been uncontroversial. I am grateful to Jacqui Stewart for sharing with me an unpublished paper, prepared for the 'Testimonies Committee' of Britain Yearly Meeting, in which she traced the history of 'testimony' and in particular a significant theological shift in the second half of the twentieth century – a shift that I discuss further below.

TESTIMONY

Key features of the Quaker story

In presenting Quaker testimony I cannot tell the full story – either of Quakerism or even of any of its strands. Those looking for comprehensive overviews or detailed studies of Quaker history, thought and theology have many other options available to them, many from within the growing interdisciplinary field of Quaker Studies.[6] A handbook published in 2013 gives a full and detailed picture of the state of the field – and of the state of research on several key questions touching my discussion here, including specific areas of Quaker social action and witness. The origins of Quakerism in the seventeenth century have been extensively researched and discussed, both through individual figures, texts and incidents and in numerous excellent overviews; most other periods of Quaker history in the North and West have received scarcely less thorough treatment. The relative lack of research into the history and contemporary situation of Quakers in Africa and South America needs urgently to be redressed given the shifting global balance of Quakerism. Unfortunately, it is not one that I am myself competent to fill, and this book is also dominated by examples from the global minority.

Given that there are already plenty of histories of Quakerism, all that is needed here is a few comments about the origins and shape of the Quaker movement, enough to orient readers to key features of the contexts from which my examples are drawn – and in particular to aspects of Quaker history that continue to shape Quakers' communal self-understanding.

Quakers originated in the aftermath of the English Civil War, in a time of considerable social, religious and political upheaval.

---

6 Historical overviews include Thomas Hamm, 2003, *The Quakers in America*, New York: Columbia University Press; John Punshon, 2006, *Portrait in Grey: A Short History of the Quakers*, 2nd edn, London: Quaker Books. Studies of the early period include Rosemary Moore, 2000, *The Light in their Consciences: The Early Quakers in Britain 1646–1666*, University Park, PA: Pennsylvania State University Press; H. Larry Ingle, 1994, *First Among Friends: George Fox and the Creation of Quakerism*, New York: Oxford University Press; Hugh S. Barbour, 1985, *The Quakers in Puritan England*, Richmond, IN: Friends United Press.

INTRODUCTION

The core of the early movement is generally thought to have been groups of 'Seekers' in central and northern England. These were Protestants of broadly Puritan sympathies who for whatever reason had no secure ecclesial or spiritual home within the existing church structures – neither, as George Fox later put it, with the 'priests' nor with the 'dissenting people'. In a remarkably rapid process from the early 1650s onwards, these disparate groups became a national movement of worshipping communities and travelling preachers, with distinctive and publicly visible characteristics, a recognizable shared theology (or shared perspective on certain live theological debates), a strong organizational network and, inevitably, a range of internal arguments and power struggles.

Quakers were noteworthy for their mode of worship – with the minimum of fixed liturgical form, and involving both extended periods of silence and a range of more or less extreme spontaneous manifestations of 'the power of the Lord' – including, of course, quaking.[7] They were distinctive in the number and prominence of women among their public preachers and travelling ministers; particularly trenchant in their opposition to 'steeple houses', tithes and all signs of established ecclesial privilege; and relatively consistent in various practices that inevitably led to conflict with the authorities, including the refusal to swear oaths and the conspicuous refusal to acknowledge rank or privilege in modes of address.

Opposition to Quakers, official and public, was common from the early decades but shifted dramatically in scale following the restoration of the monarchy. Quakers encountered both the general penalties inflicted on Nonconformists under the series of Acts known as the Clarendon Code, and specific restrictions and penalties under Acts that singled them out as a group. Although there were periods of relative toleration, extended imprisonment and the loss of property and livelihood were common experiences for the first generation of Quakers. Persecution took its toll on

---

[7] The story is often told that the name 'Quakers' came from an incident when a leading Quaker told a judge to 'quake and tremble in the fear of the Lord'; be that as it may, it is now generally accepted that early Quakers quaked in meetings for worship.

the movement at a time when prison conditions were harsh; it is sobering to note how many of the best-known writers and preachers from the beginnings of Quakerism died at relatively young ages in the 1660s.

Neither the rapid rise and development of Quakerism as a movement nor the persecution of Quakers would cover many pages in a history of Britain. Even in the history of Quakerism they account for a relatively short period. However, in terms of Quaker imagination and self-understanding they are extremely significant. I would argue that Quakers carry with them not only the distinctive theological emphases of their seventeenth-century forebears, and not only many of the visibly and socially distinctive practices listed above, but also the experience of being first a gathered community, then a community on the wrong side of the law, and, eventually, a tolerated and 'peculiar' people.

It is worth paying some attention to the first of these terms, because it is easy to take for granted. I am suggesting that a formational Quaker experience is of the *gathering of seekers*, the bringing-together of scattered fragments, the emergence of coherence and community out of spiritual and social chaos. This is what seems to be pointed to by Francis Howgill, in a passage that continues to be widely read and quoted (normally in an abridged form):

> [We] were reckoned, in the north part of England, even as the outcasts of Israel, and as men destitute of the great knowledge, which some seemed to enjoy... The Lord of heaven and earth we found to be near at hand, and, as we waited upon him in pure silence, our minds out of all things, his dreadful power, and glorious majesty, and heavenly presence appeared in our assemblies, when there was no language, tongue nor speech from any creature; and the Kingdom of Heaven did gather and catch us all, as in a net, and his heavenly power at one time drew many hundreds to land, that we came to know a place to stand in and what to wait in; and the Lord appeared daily to us... And thus the Lord, in short, did form us to be a people for his praise in our generation. (Howgill 1672; see *QF&P* 19.08)

INTRODUCTION

Howgill, like a succession of Quaker writers at the time and since, locates the experience of 'being gathered' first and foremost in the practice of waiting upon God in worship – worship based on silence. He extends it, however, beyond the time of worship to characterize the daily life of the worshipping community – referring later to how 'our hearts were knit unto the Lord and one another'. The experience of being gathered leads to being formed as 'a people'.

This emphasis on gathering – on the calling to be 'a people' and the gift of being 'a people', over against appearances and expectations – both connects Quakers to, and makes them distinctive among, groups who espouse a 'gathered church' ecclesiology. Talking about a 'gathered church' does not necessarily imply or refer back to the situation of having *no church at all*, of being gathered up from scattered fragments; on its own it mainly emphasizes the particular shared commitment and calling of these people and this community. Quakers do, as I have already suggested, fit comfortably alongside church traditions that stress a common commitment to holiness, and to the shared responsibility and collective authority of the church members 'gathered' in obedience to divine guidance.[8] They add, to this tradition of the 'gathered' church, both a historical memory and a mode of worship that take them back, repeatedly, to the experience of being brought – as it were – out of nothing. Community emerges out of disunity. Sense emerges out of non-sense. God speaks and guides people when there is no given and present reason to suppose that this will happen – and every reason to suppose that it will not. Moreover, this experience of 'being gathered' out of nothing has visible, historical and social results.

The necessary coda to this account is, of course, that Quakerism does not emerge 'out of nothing'. It emerges out of the Reformation in the specific forms it took in England, the English Bible, the

---

8 On the importance of holiness in Quaker tradition and self-understanding, see Carole Dale Spencer, 2007, *Holiness: The Soul of Quakerism*, Milton Keynes: Paternoster Press. I am grateful to David Thompson for drawing my attention to the distinctive features of Quaker accounts of 'gathering' or of the 'gathered church'.

TESTIMONY

beginnings of the modern state, the English Civil War and the Commonwealth, Anabaptism, Puritanism, various strands of European mystical and heterodox thought, the specific social and economic histories of various regions of England, and so forth. It is perfectly possible, as many non-Quaker histories have shown, to narrate the origins of Quakerism non-theologically, without accepting or even entertaining any of the claims Quakers made about being gathered by the Holy Spirit.[9] That is, in itself, not particularly interesting – the same could be said about any history that is ever read or narrated theologically, including the life of Jesus and the origins of Christianity.

What might need more attention, though, is that Quakers' origins as a community, and the shapes that their worship and life now take, are linked to specific traumas of Christian history. In writing about distinctively Quaker perspectives and practices, I (or anyone else) must on some level recall the schisms, violence and breaches of communion from which Quakerism originates – and treat them as *in some sense* sources of genuine and continuing gifts, as well as sites of wounds. I must, in other words, be prepared to read the history of Christianity's divisions and conflicts in and through the Reformation, and in and through the origins of modernity, as something more than just a narrative of decline or failure. But, thinking from the perspective of a community that ended up – in more than one country – on the wrong side of the law, I must do this without losing sight of the suffering involved, and without turning the story of Reformation and modernity into a straightforward story of progress. This is very far from being a developed theory of the relationship between Quakerism and the wider Church – or even the basis for developing such a theory. It is, however, something to bear in mind as we examine Quaker testimony in its wider contexts.

---

9 The best-known example of a non-theological 'strong reading' of early Quakers is Christopher Hill's various accounts of their place in the political upheavals – the 'world turned upside down' – of the English Revolution. See Christopher Hill, 1975, *The World Turned Upside Down: Radical Ideas During the English Revolution*, London: Pelican.

INTRODUCTION

Putting Quaker testimony in context: contemporary theologies of witness

Readers familiar with recent work in ethics, particularly theological ethics, will probably have noticed connections between my initial account of Quaker 'testimony' and a set of recent developments in the field. The account I have given here of testimony seems to emphasize communities and their habitual and intergenerationally transmitted practices – rather than, say, the resolution of dilemmas or the application of general rules – as the main locus for theological ethics. In this it resonates with much recent work in the field, particularly though not exclusively in Protestant theological ethics, and particularly though not exclusively in English-speaking countries.[10]

Indeed, the language of testimony and witness is already prominent in contemporary theological ethics, thanks in large part to the widely read work of scholars drawing on Anabaptist traditions. 'Witness' is a key term in Karl Barth's exposition of the nature of the Christian vocation; it is picked up inter alia and importantly by John Howard Yoder, and then (from him or directly from Barth) by many of Yoder's most significant interpreters and conversation partners, including Stanley Hauerwas and James McClendon. The strong link between contemporary accounts of the 'ethics of witness', on the one hand, and theologians influenced by peace church and Radical Reformation traditions, on the other, in itself suggests grounds for potentially fruitful comparisons with Quaker testimony.

In most contemporary accounts, ethics as witness begins with Christology – with the story of Jesus Christ revealing and enacting God's truth in history. The ethical action of Christians and the

---

10 The full story of the late-twentieth-century 'turn to virtue, narrative and community' in theological ethics and the 'turn to practice' in theology has, as far as I know, yet to be told in detail. When it is told, it will almost certainly include the development of virtue ethics from the seminal work of Alisdair MacIntyre (for example, MacIntyre, 1991, *After Virtue: A Study in Moral Theory*, London: Duckworth); the postliberal turn in theology, associated with Hans Frei and George Lindbeck among others (see James Fodor, 2004, 'Postliberal Theology', in David F. Ford with Rachel Muers (eds), *The Modern Theologians*, 3rd edn, Oxford: Blackwell); and the work of Yoder and Hauerwas, see below. I am grateful to Mike Higton and Patrick McKearney for discussions of this.

TESTIMONY

Christian community witnesses to this story – interpreting it and pointing back to it, not repeating it exactly but always depending on it. Understanding Christian ethical action in terms of witness focuses attention on the historical location both of Jesus Christ and of Christian ethical action – without turning the historical gap between them into a problem. There is no need to turn Jesus' story into a set of rules or principles (that float above history and apply to all times and places) in order to be able to witness to it faithfully; the whole process is embodied, local, historical. This also implies that ethics as testimony is inevitably about ongoing or repeated interpretation – and thus, in a theological context, about the Holy Spirit as well as about Christ. The Spirit, as interpreting and communicating the reality of Christ, makes possible the action and patterns of life that truthfully witness to Christ.[11]

This existing and developing theological work on ethics as witness can help to illuminate the 'grammar' of Quaker testimony. In particular, the emphasis on the action of the Holy Spirit in truthful witness, and on the movement of testimony through history, will prove important as this discussion continues. This resonance between my provisional definition of Quaker testimony and a prominent strand of contemporary theological ethics is not a coincidence. Quakers historically have much in common with the Anabaptist tradition (the churches of the Radical Reformation, the (other) historic peace churches, or whatever label we might prefer); so we would expect the ethical categories that work well for talking about the latter to have relevance to the former.

So in what follows I draw extensively on this developing tradition in theological ethics to illuminate Quaker testimony. In particular, recent accounts of Christian ethics from an Anabaptist perspective that focus on the connection between witness and truthfulness – for example by Craig Hovey – are important

---

11 For an account of this view of theological ethics from one of its leading exponents, see Stanley Hauerwas, 2002, *With the Grain of the Universe: The Church's Witness and Natural Theology*, London: SCM Press.

INTRODUCTION

conversation partners.[12] As will become clear, I do, however, still want to argue that Quaker approaches to testimony are distinctive, and that Quaker ways of relating theology and ethics are distinctive. Even if Quaker theological ethics fits with a 'turn' to virtue, narrative and witness in theological ethics more generally, it adds an extra turn. For Quakers, as I interpret them, theological reasoning is primarily enacted; interpretation is primarily interpretation-in-practice; testimony, in the sense I have described it, just *is* what makes the community. Testimony is not the result, the application nor the 'putting into practice' either of theological reasoning or of (what would normally be described as) liturgy.

So, given the particular and complex history of Quakerism, how should Quaker theology, or theological ethics, be done? In the next section I introduce a thread of Quaker understandings of religious knowledge that will appear repeatedly in my discussion – an emphasis on 'experimental' knowing.

Knowing experimentally

> Then the Lord did let me see why there was none upon the earth that could speak to my condition, namely, that I might give him all the glory; for all are concluded under sin, and shut up in unbelief as I had been, that Jesus Christ might have the pre-eminence who enlightens, and gives grace, and faith, and power. Thus, when God doth work who shall let it? And this I knew experimentally. (Fox 1694/1952, p. 11; entry for 1647)

The last sentence of the passage from George Fox's journal is particularly often quoted by Quakers. In its seventeenth-century context, 'knowing experimentally' is knowing from experience – as opposed to simply from hearsay. The importance of 'experimental' knowing, in the passage quoted above, becomes clear when we note *what* is known in this way. What is known is the effective power of Christ – to

---

12 Craig Hovey, 2011, *Bearing True Witness: Truthfulness in Christian Practice*, Grand Rapids, MI: Eerdmans.

give 'grace, and faith, and power' to those who are 'concluded under sin and shut up in unbelief'. 'Experimental knowledge' of the salvific work of God in Christ is placed in implicit contrast to knowledge of the propositional content of Christian faith – the knowledge possessed by those whom early Quakers refer to disparagingly as 'professors', those who profess faith without practising it.[13]

A recurrent theme in early Quaker texts – particularly but not only conversion narratives such as this one – is the disjunction between hearing or understanding 'outwardly', from one or another authoritative source, and knowing through experience. The point is not that the content of the 'knowledge' is different in each case, because those who receive this knowledge (at least in most cases) have already heard the narratives of sin and salvation. Rather – and echoing, of course, other conversion narratives from other strands of Reformation tradition – it is the mode of knowledge that is radically different. The transition to knowing 'experimentally' is itself the result of the transformative action of God – and it allows the knower to perceive and respond to that transformative action. Knowledge of the effective and salvific power of God is often linked, in the various strands of Quaker tradition, to a single dramatic experience of conversion or 'convincement'. It is, however, also inextricably linked to visible patterns of everyday life – to what I have described as testimony.

Now, when I say that Quaker theology is linked to knowing experimentally, I do not mean to equate it with the conversion narratives – like this from Fox – and similar writings that form a key part of Quaker tradition. I mean, in fact, to place it one step back from those writings and from the lives and experiences on which they reflect. The work undertaken here is, to use a common description of academic theology in relation to the churches, a 'second-order' reflection on the primary matter of faith and practice.

---

13 For a further and complementary discussion of the meaning of 'knowing experimentally' for Quakers, see Jeffrey Dudiak and Laura Rediehs, 2013, 'Quakers, Philosophy and Truth', in Angell and Dandelion (eds), *Handbook of Quaker Studies*, pp. 507–19, here pp. 515–17.

INTRODUCTION

How is this still a matter of 'knowing experimentally', if I am not only or mainly writing about *my* 'knowledge from experience'? One clue might be taken from Howard Brinton, a biologist by training, a great communicator of Quaker thought and tradition, and probably the originator (in the first half of the twentieth century) of the modern Quaker understanding of testimony.[14] Brinton habitually described his writings on Quakerism using metaphors from the natural sciences. In summing up Quaker testimonies and Quaker practices, Brinton was trying, he said, to present the account that best fitted the mass of experimental data – that is, the community's lived experience and practice through the centuries. He acknowledged, as all writers of Quaker theology must, that the lived and written 'data' are confused, contradictory and open to multiple interpretations. The aim is, at best, to put forward *a* plausible reading of what is going on. Moreover, and importantly, Brinton, like the various other Quaker writers of Quaker history on whom he drew, never professed or pretended to be detached from his object of study – either experientially or practically. He was, like others before and since, explicitly searching for a *useable* and *habitable* account of Quaker tradition, a theology that would 'work' and continue to work for this particular ongoing community. Or, to put it another way and to avoid separating facts and evaluations, Brinton and others treat their own experience and practice, and that of their present communities, as part of the 'data' – a part that must not be disregarded.

Theology as 'experimental knowing', then, is neither disconnected from everyday experience, nor straightforwardly individual or private, nor interpretable without a linguistic and conceptual framework. Like the experimental investigations of a scientific community, it is, both in principle and in practice, subject to communal testing and reliant on an existing body of 'experimental' knowledge. The claims it makes are open to revision in the light of subsequent developments, including its own effects

---

14 For example Howard H. Brinton, 1943, *Guide to Quaker Practice*, Wallingford, PA: Pendle Hill.

and consequences, because it forms part of an ongoing series of experiments.

The comparison with science, however, does not quite meet the case. As we shall see, Quaker reflection on 'experiment' also incorporates the idea of active *experimenting* – venturing to act on the basis of what is already known or already believed, without being able fully to predict the consequences. We can experiment *with* what we know and thus move beyond it; we can set faith in action without being clear in advance about the consequences; we can apply existing claims and categories to new situations, not in order fully to predetermine what we will find but as starting points for an open-ended exploration. At several points in this book I experiment with detailed readings of texts, events and people from Quaker history, beginning from the concept of testimony and exploring what such a reading can yield. I do not claim to give a definitive or exhaustive account – still less the *only* plausible account – of any of the texts I read; the experiments are successful in so far as they make some kind of sense of the texts, enable others to relate to them and draw from them, and open up a conversation.

The idea of 'knowing experimentally' also invites reflection on particularity, on the perspective from which we speak and on the scope of the claims we make. The conversion narratives that talk about experimental knowing may seem to be irreducibly individualist, 'subjective' in a negative sense – able to tell us something reliable and trustworthy about *this* person and what he or she experiences, but not about anybody or anything else. Extending the discussion to a community's 'experiments' in practice, and experiences of the life of faith, breaks out of the circle of one person's experience and concerns. But it still might seem to limit the possible claim to truthfulness, and to set boundaries to knowledge and understanding; this is 'true for us', this will only make sense to you and only be recognizable to you as true if you are part of this group, if you worship in this way, if you live in this way. If that is as far as Quaker theology can get, it might seem to be simply serving an in-group – reinscribing a set of rather odd norms and ways of expressing things, in order to perpetuate a group identity.

INTRODUCTION

In response to this, it is important first to remember that what George Fox (for example) claims to 'know', in the passage I quoted above, is not something about himself but something about God. God is encountered, known and followed 'from where we are'; but it is God and not the self who is encountered, known and followed. To pre-empt a later discussion, I want to suggest that 'knowing experimentally' allows knowledge to be both particular – coming from somewhere and someone in particular, arising within particular practices and ways of life, historically contingent – and genuinely open to change, challenge and disruption from beyond our present particular circumstances. As people take the 'experiments' forward in further encounters with the presence, work and calling of God in the world, the shape of what they know experimentally will change.

So, doing Quaker theology, or Quaker theological ethics, is writing from a particular perspective and from within a particular set of assumptions, formative practices, stories and habits of mind and behaviour – in the terms I outlined earlier, a particular testimony or set of testimonies. It is making a claim about what can or must be said *from here* – acknowledging that not everyone is 'here', and that 'here' is not a privileged vantage point from which to make judgements or claims about the whole. But Quakers doing theology or ethics do still have warrant to speak about matters other than their own or their community's direct experience – because 'from here' we encounter realities and truths that are universal in scope.

Unsurprisingly, there are many similarities between my approach to Quaker theology and the approach taken by theologians from broadly Anabaptist/'peace church' traditions. Here also, there tends to be an emphasis on 'knowing by doing' and 'learning by following', and on the historical location and the particularity of 'knowledge' as it links to the particular call to discipleship. The traditions that draw on the Radical Reformation have tended if not to subordinate theology to ethics then to refuse to talk about theology in abstraction from ethics and from practice. James McClendon, for example, *began* his magisterial three-volume work of systematic theology from an Anabaptist perspective with a volume on ethics – deliberately prioritizing the aspect of theology that might more commonly be expected to come at the end (as the post hoc 'application' of theological claims).[15]

Structure and approach of this work

It is highly unlikely that a three-volume work of Quaker systematic theology will be written, but, if it were, the obvious place to begin would probably be not ethics but experience or convincement. The reasons for this will become clearer in the course of the book, but suffice it to say for now that Quaker theology, in my view, does not do justice to Quakerism if it simply starts from 'practice'. Both the practice and the theology rely on the foundational and continuing experience of being called, being gathered, having one's condition 'spoken to'. For this if for no other reason, a book focused on ethics risks distorting Quaker theology by overemphasizing the 'activist', and denigrating the 'quietist', the mystical, the theologically reflective components of Quaker experimental knowing. In my experiments in interpreting and representing Quaker testimony, I attempt to connect it – as others have done – with its 'ground and spring' in the encounter with God.[16]

In Chapters 1 and 2 of this book, I present two ideas that I think help to make sense of Quaker testimony and recognize its distinctive theological importance. In Chapter 1, I propose an account of Quaker testimony connected to a way of reading and inhabiting biblical testimony – one that anticipates the transformative effect of divine revelation in the 'here and now'. Testimony is, I suggest, action and speech at the 'leading edge' of revelation; it is the outworking of the promise that the Holy Spirit guides into all truth, and carries forward Christ's words and presence. One of its deep presuppositions in Quaker contexts is trust in the 'universal Light' – that Christ 'enlightens, and gives grace, and faith, and power' to all.

---

15 James W. McClendon Jr, 2002, *Ethics: Systematic Theology*, Vol. 1, 2nd edn, Nashville, TN: Abingdon Press.

16 The expression is from James Nayler, in a text to which I will return in later chapters; but in the sense I am using it here it appears most recently in Beth Allen, 2007, *Ground and Spring: Foundations of Quaker Discipleship*, London: Quaker Books.

INTRODUCTION

The implications of this are spelled out further in Chapter 2, where I explore the importance of *negative* testimony – bearing 'testimony against' – as a significant aspect of Quaker tradition. The key example of negative testimony in Quaker history, which I use as the lens through which to read others, is nonviolence or opposition to war. Looking at 'testimonies against' through the lens of nonviolence, I read them not as simple negations or denials, but as double negatives – denials of lies and denials of destruction. As double negatives or denials of lies, they open up space for a 'positive' future that they do not predict or control. This openness also connects nonviolence, or the testimony against war, with an even longer-standing distinctive Quaker practice – unprogrammed worship based on silence, itself both a form of testimony and a source and basis for other practices of testimony.

The subsequent chapters use these key ideas to engage more closely with specific examples of Quaker testimony – texts, themes, practices and stories. I begin in Chapter 3 with the interconnected practices of 'plain speech' and 'speaking truth to power', examining how Quaker understandings of truth and truthfulness extend beyond a concern for individual sincerity or purity to a public witness against systemic 'untruthfulness'. In order to show how this is not – in Quaker understanding – simply a battle of competing narratives, I look further at the implications of Quaker claims about the universal Light, in relation to the idea of 'answering that of God in every one' and to theologies of the Holy Spirit.

Chapters 4 and 5 examine an interconnected set of case studies relating to conscience, freedom and the state – and to questions of individualism and community in Quaker testimony. Looking at the now marginalized, although still extant, 'testimony against' swearing oaths, I use it as the starting point for understanding Quaker approaches to conscience and conscientious objection – as social, communicative and transformative, rather than simply as a matter of individual freedom. This leads on to a consideration of how to read, for theological ethics, the figure of the individual hero and martyr – Mary Dyer – or the divisive sufferer – James Nayler. In relation to both of these figures, and their lives and writings, I draw out the neglected theme of compassionate solidarity – arising in their lives as a consequence of 'denying lies' and responding to the truth.

Chapters 6 and 7, finally, examine two recent developments in Quaker testimony, in Britain and more widely, which have had a significant impact both on Quaker self-understanding and on Quakers' public voice and presence, and which both appear to be 'new departures'. Chapter 6 looks at marriage and sexuality, focusing on the recognition of marriages of same-sex couples; Chapter 7 looks at environmental concern. In both cases, I use the foregoing discussion to locate the supposed 'new development' within traditions of Quaker testimony, and also to argue for the distinctiveness of Quaker testimony on these issues within a wider context of public debate and concern.

This way of organizing the work might surprise those who are used to seeing short lists of Quaker testimonies, presented in introductions to Quakerism. Since these lists are so ubiquitous now in Quaker circles, in the final section of this introductory chapter I discuss how they work and how they fit with my account of Quaker testimony. Anyone who does not care that the book is not organized in terms of 'peace, equality, simplicity, truth' – or something like that – might wish to skip to the next chapter.

Quaker testimony lists

The everyday grammar of 'testimony' among Quakers is not straightforward. In general, contemporary Quakers talk more about 'the testimonies' than about a single body of testimony. Rather often, testimonies are enumerated or listed. Rather often, particularly but not only among 'liberal' Quakers, the lists appear both short and all-encompassing. In the USA a common list and acronym, used since at least the 1980s, is the five 'SPICE' testimonies:

- Simplicity
- Peace

INTRODUCTION

- Integrity
- Community
- Equality

'Spice' has the advantage that it can be, and often has been in recent years, extended to 'spices' – to accommodate

- Sustainability, or Stewardship.

In Britain, the 1994 revision of *Quaker Faith and Practice* lists and discusses four testimonies: peace, truth, simplicity, equality.[17] By contrast, the previous British Quaker Book of Discipline, from 1959, listed for the most part very specific and narrowly defined 'testimonies', that could not reasonably be taken as encompassing the whole of Quaker life and practice.[18] The switch to the use of short, wide-ranging and ostensibly comprehensive lists of 'testimonies' occurred at roughly the same time in Britain and the USA – and now appears to be well established. As commonly presented, the items on these lists are supposed to name themes, narratives or principles of historical and continuing Quaker testimony; but they are also very commonly referred to as 'the Quaker testimonies'.

How did this come about? I have already alluded briefly to the major, and now scarcely observed, work of theological creativity in the second half of the twentieth century that led to the widespread use and acceptance of testimony lists. The twentieth century, and particularly the period after 1945, saw a blossoming of social and political activism among Quakers in Britain and the USA. At a time in which there was great interest in the nature of Christian social teaching and Christian visions for society – and also considerable public interest in the exploration of new theological

---

17 There is no widely accepted acronym for the British list, although I have seen a children's book in which a dog and a cat demonstrate in a series of cartoons the importance of 'P.E.T.S.' (Peace, Equality, Truth, Simplicity).

18 London Yearly Meeting, *Christian Faith and Practice in the Experience of the Society of Friends*, 1960, London: Headley Brothers. The index entry for 'Testimonies' starts with the subheadings: 'betting and gambling; capital punishment; conscription; hat honour; integrity in business; oaths; peace; penal reform . . .'. It is followed, encouragingly, by an entry for 'Theology, value of'.

TESTIMONY

ideas – many people were drawn to Quakers as a result both of their theological searching and of their ethical and social concerns. In Britain, the work done during the First World War on Quakers' social witness that produced the seminal document 'Foundations of a True Social Order' (London Yearly Meeting 1918) gained further momentum in the period after 1945.

In this context, 'testimony lists' began, and continued, as a useful way of reading Quaker tradition in order to understand what it might look like to be faithful to that tradition and creative within it. The development was pushed forward by the widely read writings of key individuals – most notably Howard H. Brinton in the USA and John Punshon in Britain.[19] It rapidly found widespread acceptance, coming to form part of the ordinary vocabulary of a community looking for ways to express its distinctive vocation in a rapidly changing world.[20] It was a bold rereading and reformulation of Quaker tradition within a wider context of Christian theology, historical and contemporary.

However, Quakers' development of lists of testimonies, and the rise to prominence of testimony as a community-defining idea for Quakers, did not have extensive consequences for theology beyond Quakerism. It was not, *as theology*, a contribution to Christian (or other) ethical debate. Talk about 'testimonies' was primarily a way of giving an account of an aspect of Quaker identity, rather than itself a way of entering wider theological discussions. Quakers entered the wider discussions not through their theological or conceptual innovation but through the specific ways in which they responded to, and carried forward, their traditions of life and action – through speaking, writing and acting for peace; through

---

[19] Brinton, 1943, *Guide to Quaker Practice*; John Punshon, 1987, *Encounter with Silence: Reflections from the Quaker Tradition*, London: Quaker Home Service. See also John Punshon, 1980, *Testimony and Tradition*, London: Quaker Home Service.

[20] The speed with which the vocabulary spread was in part due to the immense popularity of Brinton's and Punshon's introductory books on Quakerism. The adoption of lists of testimonies, broadly following Punshon and Brinton, into Quaker Books of Discipline in the second half of the twentieth century is an important marker of the wide currency of these lists. I am grateful to John Punshon for conversations about the reception and development of new accounts of testimony in the post-war period.

INTRODUCTION

responses to economic injustice; through interactions with the women's movement and with movements for racial equality; through new thought about sexuality, and so forth.

So how can we assess or analyse the presentation of Quaker testimony in a list – 'simplicity, peace, integrity, community, equality, sustainability' – and what use might it be for theology? There are, undoubtedly, many obvious ways to criticize the lists (besides the necessary and important point that, contrary to what at least some contemporary Quakers seem to assume, they are of very recent origin and in no way immutable or indispensable). We could say that the words used are so vacuous as to be acceptable to all – or rather, so obviously good as to be impossible for anyone to oppose. This would also make it impossible for anyone meaningfully to affirm them as a *distinctive* aspect of their belief and practice – 'Everybody agrees with these, so what's special about Quakers?' We could say that they are equally capable of being used to describe a very wide range of actions, practices and communities, some of them mutually antagonistic or contradictory. We could, alternatively, say that they are so idealistic as to be impossible to instantiate in the real world. Most problematically for the present work, we could say that they are, as stated, entirely non-theological, indistinguishable from 'secular' ideals – and arguably, in the case of 'equality' at least, indistinguishable from specifically modern and Western secular ideals that simply reflect the tendency of liberal religious groups to move uncritically with the winds of the times.

All of these criticisms are to some extent fair. Many of them, or at least those that focus on the vagueness or generality of the words, miss the point. There is a reason why Quakers have not written much about 'the testimonies'. The testimonies are not the words, nor the 'notions' that the words call to mind; the testimonies are certainly not (as Brinton was at pains to point out when he enumerated them, and many others have emphasized since) a social programme or a set of policies to be implemented. The words only make sense if they are connected, not to theories of social organization or ethical decision-making but to specific things people have done and continue to do, or specific ways people live or continue to live. The words only make sense because of what they describe and where they lead.

If this is so, the exercise of naming or listing 'the testimonies', and then thinking about the list, is a way into engagement with faithful action and faithful lives. It is a way of tracking the footsteps of predecessors and companions in discipleship in order to walk as they walked. It does not constitute the primary activity of ethics or the primary form of testimony, even though writing and speaking about faithful life and action is itself testimony. The collective testing and development of Quaker theological ethics is not primarily a matter of reflecting on the meanings and implications of forms of words. It is a matter of reflecting on a complex, rich and internally conflicted historical inheritance – a process that is significantly helped by the constructive theological work of successive generations of readers and interpreters of testimony.

Quakers do, moreover, recognize particular summaries (like the list testimonies) of this complex historical inheritance as provisionally normative. There are agreed accounts of historical testimony that carry, for the time being, a certain authoritative weight, and that orient – without fully constraining – reflection about the community's present and future. At its best, Quaker thinking about testimony calls members of this community to read their past as a preparation for discerning their present and future calling. The point is not to tell a story of 'where we have been' or to dwell on past greatness, but to tell a story that makes sense of where we are now – and enables the next few steps to make sense.

One of the most influential interpreters of contemporary liberal Quakerism, Pink Dandelion, has described its development towards an implicit or explicit 'behavioural creed'.[21] By this Dandelion means that certain forms of behaviour (both in worship and in everyday life) are prescribed as community-defining, boundary-forming and determinative of historical continuity, while the interpretation and motivation of these behaviours is left

---

21 See Pink Dandelion, 1996, *A Sociological Analysis of the Theology of Quakers*, Lewiston, NY: Edwin Mellen.

INTRODUCTION

entirely open. He tells a story of how this came about – which, in his work, comes across as a narrative of decline. Particular behaviours initially adopted as a consequence of transformative religious experience, he argues, have shifted into a prescribed set of behaviours to which both experience and reflection on the theological significance of the experience and the behaviour are optional.

When I say that testimony lists work a bit like creeds, I do, like Dandelion with his 'behavioural creeds', want to draw attention to their character as community-defining and determinative of historical continuity. But – having perhaps fewer negative assumptions about creeds than some Quaker writers do – I also want to draw attention to their openness and generativity. At least in some of their applications, the testimony lists *open up* spaces for reflection, interpretation and action, even as they define the form and shape of a community – in the same way that the historic Christian creeds open up the broad space of theology, prayer and practice.

Seen in this way, the vagueness of the terms in the lists of testimony makes them more, rather than less, useful. Like the dense summary formulations of the creeds, they demand thought, application, debate and development over time. They are obviously and necessarily incomplete without interpretation, the interpretation that comes from individual and collective action and reflection. Looked at as aspects of a person's or a community's life, they set out not a closely specified plan for interacting with the world but a way of orienting oneself to the world, a set of habits or dispositions.

Talking about 'simplicity', for example, among contemporary Quakers opens up a whole range of discussions about right relationships and action in the context of globalization, late capitalism, rapidly developing technology, global disparities of wealth and anthropogenic climate change. 'Simplicity' comes into play in small-scale individual decisions about lifestyle and patterns of consumption, and in responses to large-scale political movements. Using the term in a Quaker context invokes a complex history of discernment and action, and enables people to reread the present situation in the light of that history. It does not prescribe an answer, any more than creeds prescribe answers to specific challenges to theology; but it sets up questions, or invites experimentation along certain lines and within certain necessary parameters; 'See what can be done from here, see how this situation looks in the light of what we already know.'

I have chosen to pay attention to Quaker testimony as a whole – rather than a series of discrete and identifiable parts – and to Quaker testimony as action or process – rather than a set of 'findings' or established principles. I do this because it makes sense, as I see it, of how Quaker life and practice actually works; because, for reasons I shall discuss in the next chapter, it makes sense theologically; and because it seems important in order to redress the balance, both in Quaker self-description and in wider public understanding of ethics. I treat testimony primarily as a single complex whole, and only secondarily as a set of discrete 'testimonies' that can be discussed to some extent independently of one another and related separately to different aspects of life. I also treat testimony as something that is done and lived, as a 'verbal noun' that draws attention to an ongoing process rather than just to the results of a completed work.

'Testimony' as a theological and ethical term, however, has far deeper roots than those within Quaker tradition. In the first chapter, I set Quaker testimony – both the term and the reality to which it refers – in the context of biblical interpretation.

1
Walking in the Light: The Bible and Quaker Testimony

Approaching the Bible

In this chapter, I introduce a framework of biblical interpretation within which Quaker testimony might be read and interpreted by a wider Christian community, and which can also offer Quakers a way of understanding what testimony is about. I think that my interpretation of testimony – here and in the rest of the book – is a plausible development from existing Quaker readings and uses of biblical texts. It should, I hope, be clear by now that I am not claiming to give the *only* possible reading, either of any biblical texts or of the history of Quaker testimony. In particular, for this chapter I am not interested in finding a 'biblical justification' for Quaker practice, nor in imposing on contemporary Quakers frameworks of belief that many of them do not accept. To put it baldly, many contemporary Quakers in 'liberal' meetings with unprogrammed worship (like Britain Yearly Meeting) do not read or refer directly to the Bible very much, and do not see this as a problem. I have no interest in denying this fact, and I do not write with the purpose of changing it.

I do, however, want to suggest that the ongoing tradition of Quaker testimony carries with it, and enables, distinctive uses of biblical images, themes and categories, as well as a distinctive approach to reading the Bible. At the very least, this means that in conversations about Quaker testimony with a wider Christian audience, the Bible can be a point of connection, rather than a source of division. In making this case, I begin by saying something first about Quaker approaches to the Bible – in the early years of Quakerism, and then as these initial moves continue to shape Quakers' relationship to the Bible.

Biblical settlements, biblical unsettlements

Mike Higton has coined the expression 'biblical settlement' to refer to the pattern of accepted readings and interpretations of the biblical texts by which a particular community lives – a way of reading the Bible that makes it habitable for this community.[1] Higton argues that any given community that reads and interprets the Bible forms over time a set of 'resilient and coherent' judgements about the Bible that cohere not only with each other but with the community's practices and way of life. Very importantly, components of a biblical settlement will include not only readings of particular texts but assumptions about the interrelationships and relative importance of different texts, and about the governing principles for reading any and every text. Different communities find and sustain, through their specific histories and ongoing conversations, different resilient and coherent ways of inhabiting the Bible; and the differences encompass assumptions about what the Bible is and how it works, as well as about specific readings. Many features of a biblical settlement will rarely be argued for or even thematized – to those who inhabit this settlement they seem obvious, natural, the only possible way to read.

In order to think about Quaker testimony and the Bible, I need to entertain the possibility – which goes somewhat beyond Higton's argument – of a communal 'settlement' in which the role of biblical texts and their interpretation is largely implicit. While the obvious application for this is contemporary liberal unprogrammed Quakers, it is in fact quite common for the distinctive characters of local, national or global church communities

---

1 Mike Higton, 2008, *SCM Core Text Christian Doctrine*, London: SCM Press, pp. 364–71.

to be described without explicit reference to biblical interpretation. In this situation, there is reason to think that paying explicit attention to the biblical settlements that have helped to shape any given community's pattern of life – uncovering the various 'settled results' and habitual readings that operate – might be useful. It can help to resolve apparently intractable problems or conflicts that are symptoms of problems in the underlying settlement. It can make space for conversations across perceived binary divisions – for example, by reframing the choice between accepting and rejecting 'the Bible', or specific 'biblical' language, as a discussion about the different readings and interpretive assumptions with which people are working. It can make space for faithful innovation, creative rereading and reinterpretations, by drawing attention to the contingent assumptions with which we are working – and inviting people to ask whether these assumptions still hold. Moreover, it can connect *this* particular community to any number of other readers and groups of readers trying to find habitable places with these texts – and give them some sort of common space in which to meet and establish reciprocal understanding and ongoing conversation, even if they still agree on more or less nothing. Thinking about processes of interpretation, rather than carrying on assuming that we know all about what the Bible says (for good or ill), helps to turn the Bible from a defended boundary into a meeting place, and that should, on the face of it, appeal to Quakers.[2]

But does it actually make sense to talk about 'biblical settlement' in relation to Quakers? Even a cursory reading of early Quaker writings – let alone the many detailed studies in recent years – suggests that the metaphor of 'inhabiting' the biblical texts is particularly

---

2 I am drawing here on a growing body of theory around Scriptural Reasoning as a process for developing 'better quality disagreement' among and between Jews, Christians and Muslims, and also on the theology and practice of conversations within the global Anglican Communion around issues of sexuality. See, inter alia, David F. Ford and C. C. Pecknold, 2006, *The Promise of Scriptural Reasoning*, Oxford: Blackwell; Nicholas Adams, 2006, *Habermas and Theology*, Cambridge: Cambridge University Press, Ch. 11; Mike Higton and Rachel Muers, 2012, *The Text In Play: Experiments in Reading Scripture*, Eugene, OR: Wipf and Stock Cascade.

appropriate, and also particularly complex in its application. As several scholars of early Quakerism have noted, Quaker writings are characterized – distinctively although not uniquely in their time – by a proliferation of biblical allusion, quotation and imagery, applied with immediacy to the contemporary situation at the individual, the social and the political levels.[3] The detailed discussion of specific texts as a tool for theological argument (for example) plays a secondary role. It is as if the Quaker writer or preacher is *too close* to the biblical texts to argue about them; and this rhetorical feature can be directly linked to claims about the presence of Christ, the Word of God, as inward teacher, instructing and guiding the speaker. The Word, as it were, was closer than the book.

The problem with calling early Quakerism a biblical 'settlement', though, is that it was not very settled, and not very settling. It makes more sense to talk about the Quaker movement as a biblical un/settlement. It was a rereading of the Bible for the mid-seventeenth century's 'world turned upside down' – or a rereading of the world turned upside down, in the words of the Bible. Much Quaker writing from this early period has the un/settling characteristics of apocalyptic, both in the texts it uses and in its approach to biblical texts as such. The breakings-apart and transformations *in* the Bible are echoed in the breakings-apart and transformations *of* the biblical texts in Quaker speech and writing; and this in turn seems the only appropriate way of reading and speaking the Bible in a world that is itself in the middle of chaotic breaking and transformation.[4]

---

3   Rosemary Moore, 2000, *The Light in Their Consciences*, University Park, PA: Pennsylvania State University Press, p. 53, notes the frequent presence in early Quaker writings of 'a continuous flowing paraphrase in which biblical phrases from different sources were run together along with the authors' own comments'. For an older account of the distinctive style of early Quaker writings, and its connection with the approach to biblical interpretation that emphasized 'living inside' or 'reliving' the biblical texts, see Jackson I. Cope, 1956, 'Seventeenth-Century Quaker Style', *PMLA* 71/4, pp. 724–54.

4   Douglas Gwyn's work on early Quakers and the apocalyptic imagination is well known; see for example Gwyn, 1986, *Apocalypse of the Word*, Richmond, IN: Friends United Press.

WALKING IN THE LIGHT

The move in the early generations of Quakerism from apocalyptic un/settlement to some kind of communal settlement – while maintaining a strong sense of continuity with the earliest unsettling texts and actions – has been charted and evaluated by numerous historians, often in competing ways, and it appears again at various points in this book. To pre-empt the discussion that follows, I want to argue that there is strong continuity between the biblical un/settlement and operative hermeneutic of early Quakers, on the one hand, and the implicit and enacted theologies of contemporary Quakers, on the other. This continuity is not mainly carried in texts, but it *is* to some extent carried in terminology, and how that terminology is used. One example of this is testimony. Talk of testimony connects Quakers to a way of reading and inhabiting the Bible that is still of relevance and importance today.

Generations of Quakers were deeply immersed in the Bible as a whole, reading their world through its narratives and symbols, weaving the language and phraseology of the Bible both into their preaching and into their everyday speech. One of the striking features of contemporary liberal Quakerism is that biblical terminology and phraseology remains part of Quaker 'everyday speech' – and carries at least some of its theological weight even without the frequent rereading and recalling of the texts from which it is drawn. It is easy to condemn this as a sign of decay, or the dilution of Quaker witness, or the loss of heritage. I think it is not so simple.

Early Quakers' distinctive style of preaching and writing generally eschewed the use of proof-texts. They performed the unity between the prophetic word and the scriptural text – interpreting the scriptures in 'the same Spirit that gave them forth', collapsing the distance between text and interpreter. Being able to say exactly where an idea came from, and being able to defend one's interpretation against opponents, was a useful skill for the Quaker controversialist. There were Quaker biblical scholars, applying critical approaches to the canon and text of scripture, from remarkably early in the movement – among the most notable being Samuel Fisher, who engaged in extended controversy with the Puritan

TESTIMONY

divine John Owen.[5] But these uses of scripture in theological debate appear to be secondary – both in quantity and in the weight accorded to them – to other modes of interpretation, which are closer to creative re-performance than to detailed citation.

Listen, for example, to Hester Biddle's polemical-prophetic appeal, *Wo To Thee Town of Cambridge,* in 1655:

> And now see in you and search in you whether you are in *Cain's* ways, murdering and killing the just in you, and whipping and stocking them that the Lord hath sent to you; therefore repent and do so no more, take heed and do so no more, lest I render my plagues double upon thy head; and when the book of conscience is opened then shalt thou witness this to be true ... sit down and bethink thee what thou art, that thou art but dust and ashes; and cannot I kill and make alive, cannot I cast down and bring up, cannot I scatter and bring together? yea, my hands have done all these things; I am gathering all my sheep together where they have been scattered in the dark and cloudy day, I will bring them out from under *Pharaoh* that they may have one Master, one Shepherd, and one sheepfold I. The true Shepherd will lay down his life for the sheep, but the hireling will flee when persecution comes, and therefore will I gather my sheep out of their mouths, and he that hath an ear let him hear.[6]

A quick glance at this – slightly abridged – passage by anyone familiar with the biblical texts reveals criss-crossing references to

---

5 Samuel Fisher, 1660, *Rusticus ad Academicos.* The title is a rather tongue-in-cheek attempt to downplay Fisher's own scholarship – he was educated at Oxford. There is a brief overview of Fisher's life and his debate with Owen in Timothy W. Seid, 2001, 'Samuel Fisher: 17th-Century Quaker Biblical Scholar', *Quaker Religious Thought* 97, article 7. Fisher often has more prominence in histories of biblical interpretation than in histories of Quakerism.

6 Hester (Ester) Biddle, 1655, *Wo To Thee Town of Cambridge.* See the short biography of Biddle by Elaine Hobby, in Marion Ann Taylor and Agnes Choi (eds), 2012, *Handbook of Women Biblical Interpreters: A Historical and Biographical Guide,* Grand Rapids, MI: Baker, pp. 69–72; see also the Introduction to Paul Salzmann (ed.), 2000, *Early Modern Women's Writing: An Anthology 1560–1700,* Oxford: Oxford University Press, pp. xxiii–iv. Biddle also wrote a companion 'Wo' piece addressing the 'City of Oxford'.

(at least) Genesis, Exodus, Deuteronomy, John and Revelation. There are shifts in 'voice' from referring to 'the Lord' in the third person to speaking the first-person words of God; there are tropes of commonplace scriptural interpretation (the 'book of conscience' for the book in Revelation 20.12), swept along with direct scriptural quotation and near-quotation and with additions and paraphrases from the author's own voice. There are biblical narratives of past events (Cain and Abel, Pharaoh and the children of Israel), 'intercut' with eschatological visions (the book in Revelation) and with the perspective of eternity. And all of this is applied, layer upon layer – like a series of translucent overlays, or perhaps optician's lenses – to the 'whipping and stocking' (i.e., putting in the stocks) of travelling preachers in a small English town in the 1650s.

The preacher and polemicist shows herself – in this representative, not exceptional, example – highly literate in the English Bible. She clearly relies on similar literacy in her audience. They would need it in order, for example, to supply the reference to John 11 that makes sense of '[I will] gather my sheep out of their mouths' (the hireling abandons the sheep to the wolves, John 11.12); and they would need it in order to hear the context that each quotation or near-quotation draws with it, to feel the force of the words and the scope of the claim they represent. Her writing is directed to a community of readers, and is intended, as it were, to teach them how to read both the Bible and the world. But the new 'reading' proposed collapses the distance between texts, readers and world; different biblical narratives, along with the readers and speakers and their world, are brought together in a single point of recognition or changed perception.

What is going on behind this kind of scriptural interpretation or application? One important aspect of it is that early Quakers could quote scripture without, as it were, adding the quotation marks, because the claim behind all their proclamation was that the Spirit that inspired the scriptures was now poured out on all flesh (Joel 2.28–29; Acts 2.17–22). Preaching or proclamation in this context was not primarily the correct application or interpretation of inspired text, but rather speech in inspired conformity to God's truth – which might be expected to echo the similarly inspired words of the biblical writers.

One of the best-loved (and most selectively quoted) accounts of early Quaker teaching on the Bible reflects this attitude. This is Margaret Fell's account (written many years later) of what George Fox said when he interrupted a service at Ulverston Church:

> And then he went on, and opened the Scriptures, and said, 'the Scriptures were the prophets' words and Christ's and the apostles' words, and what as they spoke they enjoyed and possessed and had it from the Lord'. And said 'Then what had any to do with the Scriptures, but as they came to the Spirit that gave them forth. You will say, Christ saith this, and the apostles say this, but what canst thou say? Art thou a child of Light and hast walked in the Light, and what thou speakest is it inwardly from God?' (Fell 1694, p. ii)

'What canst thou say?' is a favourite Quaker saying, but what is interesting to me here is that the context of the whole discussion is biblical interpretation – or, to be precise, preaching on a text, speaking authoritatively into a contemporary situation on the basis of the biblical witness. '*You will say*, Christ says this, and the apostles say this, but *what canst thou say?*' calls not for the speaker's own experience as opposed to, or in addition to, the words of Christ and the apostles (which is the sense in which it is most often used these days) but rather for the speaker's 'credentials' as an interpreter of the words of Christ and the apostles. The question is – on what basis can anyone claim the authority to tell people what 'Christ says and the apostles say' to the current situation? And the first answer suggested refers the hearers to the unity of Christ (as the 'Light'), the prophets and apostles, and the present community of preachers and hearers – through the Spirit that 'gave forth' the prophetic and apostolic word.

When Margaret Fell describes her reaction to the challenge, however, she provides a subtly different answer to the question about authority:

WALKING IN THE LIGHT

> I cried in my spirit to the Lord, 'We are all thieves, we are all thieves, we have taken the Scriptures in words and know nothing of them in ourselves'. (Fell 1694, p. ii)

Knowing the Scriptures 'in ourselves' rather than (merely) 'in words' is, she suggests, the key criterion for authoritative preaching and proclamation – perhaps, the basis on which someone can be said to 'enjoy and possess', rather than to 'steal', the power of the canonical text. If the precondition for good interpretation is the presence of the Spirit that 'gave forth' the scriptures, this will have consequences for the interpreter. The scriptures will be, as it were, internalized, known 'in ourselves'.

Now, as Fell's own writings show, she was herself more than competent to argue a case from the detailed interpretation of biblical texts. She does this most notably in her account of *Women's Speaking [i.e. preaching] Justified, Proved, and Allowed of by the Scriptures* (1666). However, the decision to argue from scripture does not mean that, for Fell, truthful speech was supposed to originate from, or rely on, familiarity with the word of scripture. It would be more accurate to say, looking at Fell's writings in the context of early Quaker thought, that the authentic leadings of God, proclaimed and lived by a faithful people, would be found to be 'justified, proved and allowed of' by the scriptures – because their origin was the same Spirit of God.

So far I have suggested, following various other commentators, that early Quaker interpretation of the Bible was shaped by a view of biblical authority centred on the one Holy Spirit as the giver of revelatory, and in particular prophetic, speech – both to the biblical writers and to contemporary readers and hearers. It produces a mode of interpretation that 'unsettles' both the biblical text and the present order by collapsing spatial and temporal distances – focusing all the biblical images and narratives on to a single point, the present situation to which the interpreter addresses herself.

This move of bringing the text into the present, collapsing distance, has of course many parallels beyond Quaker writings and practice. One interesting articulation from another tradition –

because its closeness to the Quaker situation helps to show how the latter is distinctive – is in James McClendon's systematic theology from a 'baptist' context. McClendon sums up the vision that grounds a distinctive baptist hermeneutic, thus: 'the church now is the primitive church and the church on judgement day' (McClendon 2002, p. 30). At key points in his later discussion, he returns to the basic hermeneutical moves that also embed claims about the church community – saying 'this is that' and 'then is now', seeing and enacting the convergence between the given and defining past, the lived present, and the hoped-for future.

The identity thus expressed – between the church now, the primitive church and the eschatological church – is, McClendon comments, 'mystical and immediate; it might be better understood by the artist and the poet than by the metaphysician and dogmatician' (2002, p. 32). For McClendon's believers' church, then, the present tense of the Bible's readers – reading or hearing the biblical word here and now – draws in and encompasses the Bible's past and future tenses. The called and sanctified community of which the Bible speaks – in both the past and the future tense – *is* the present community of readers.

This has obvious similarities to the Quaker hermeneutic outlined above. There is, however, a difference of emphasis – which McClendon implicitly acknowledges, elsewhere in the book, by not confidently including Quakers within his 'baptist vision'. For Quakers the collapse of identities is not so much between the *church* 'here and now' and the church 'there and then', as between the *world* 'here and now' and the world 'there and then'. The prophetic and apocalyptic emphasis in Quaker action and speech points beyond a focus on reviving or restoring apostolic Christianity, and towards a focus on the global/cosmic transformation that apostolic Christianity heralded and proclaimed. 'Primitive Christianity', the life and witness of the first disciples of Jesus, is important not as a pattern for individual discipleship or church order but rather as an example – the clearest 'known case' after Jesus' life, death and resurrection – of what faithfulness to the direction and inspiration of the Spirit of Christ looks like.

WALKING IN THE LIGHT

William Penn's famous account of Quakerism as 'primitive Christianity revived' – written mainly as an apologetic tract, 'because the prejudices of some are very great against this people and their way' – locates Quakers' 'primitive Christianity' not in their practices but in their proclamation of a divine 'principle' available to all (Penn 1696). Arguably Penn, for his apologetic purposes, goes too far – even for his contemporaries, and certainly for the Quakers of many subsequent eras – in the direction of identifying 'primitive Christianity' with certain beliefs or claims, and inviting readers to judge Quakers' 'Christianity' by their doctrinal conformity. The interesting point for my purposes, though, is that he does not claim that Quakers have restored the form and the practice of the earliest Christian communities. He claims, rather, that they have entered into the kind of relationship with the risen Christ that transformed the lives of 'primitive Christians'. As was the case for the first Christians and as for the promised eschatological community – Penn claims – Christ is the 'principle' or source of this people's life and of their understanding of the world.[7] So being 'primitive Christianity revived' is not about reflecting an earlier *form* of Christianity, but about re-vival – new or restored life – in the spirit from which the apostolic church lived.[8]

All of this, however, makes it clear that there are significant and understated theological moves, or 'settled results' of biblical interpretation, underlying Quakers' approach to the Bible – and, more importantly for our purposes, their life and testimony as a community.

---

[7] David L. Johns discusses Penn's tract in more detail, and with a particular eye to its relevance for contemporary debates among Quakers, in Johns, 2013, *Quakering Theology: Essays on Worship, Tradition and Christian Faith*, Aldershot: Ashgate, pp. 123–37.

[8] T. L. Underwood, in a deliberately provocative expression that captures this point very well, draws the contrast between seventeenth-century Quakers and their Baptist contemporaries (as it relates to 'primitivism') thus: 'Baptists tried to replicate the New Testament church as fully as they could. However . . . early Friends in the height of their enthusiasm seem to have believed that they *were* the New Testament church.' T. L. Underwood, 2001, *Primitivism, Radicalism and the Lamb's War: Baptist–Quaker Conflict in Seventeenth-Century England*, Oxford: Oxford University Press, p. 4.

TESTIMONY

Quaker un/settlements: (1) Light

I have suggested that Quakers had, and have, an 'unsettling' relationship with the Bible – a tendency to read it against the social and political (and ecclesiastical) grain, to hear and voice it as urgent prophecy for the times. In order to see how this shapes Quaker approaches to theological ethics, and Quaker uses of testimony, we need to look more closely at how this unsettled and unsettling relationship with the Bible can itself make sense from and through biblical texts.

It is often said, with much justification, that the Gospel of John is the 'Quaker' Gospel.[9] The point is not that Quaker theology and practice is the obvious or only plausible response to the Gospel of John, nor that all Quakers, now or in the past, know and like the Gospel of John. The point is, more modestly and fairly uncontroversially, that many features of Quaker theology and practice drew and still (implicitly or explicitly) draw on a particular reading of John and the Johannine literature. Understanding that connection can illuminate Quaker theology and practice – particularly in the context of other communities' lived and written interpretations of John.

The most obvious place to look for signs of Quakers' Johannine theological framework is in their core theological vocabulary; and the most obvious place to start is with 'light'. Famously, John 1.9, as translated in the King James Version, was a treasured text for early Quakers: 'That was the true light that enlightens every man that cometh into the world.' It provided one of the clearest examples of how the intense experience of conversion and transformation could be found reflected, confirmed and explained in the Bible. The universal gift of the Light of Christ grounded the experience of finding, individually and collectively, the loving and revelatory presence of God in a 'world turned upside down' and in a situation

---

9 Two recent works from different places on the theological spectrum of world Quakerism that indicate in different ways the centrality of John for Quaker thought and practice are Douglas Gwyn, 2011, *Conversation with Christ*, Philadelphia, PA: Quaker Press, and Paul Anderson, 2013, *Following Jesus*, Newberg, OR: Barclay Press.

of social collapse. To speak of light was to speak of revelation and transformed understanding – 'pure openings' – in intimate connection with the gift of divine love.

Thus George Fox:

> Now the Lord God opened to me by his invisible power how that every man was enlightened by the divine light of Christ . . . This I saw in the pure openings of the Light without the help of any man, neither did I then know how to find it in the Scriptures; though afterwards, searching the Scriptures, I found it. (Fox 1694/1952, entry for 1648; quoted *QF&P* 19.04)

It is striking, as Melvin Endy and others have pointed out, how clear and consistent Quakers were – and still are – in their belief in the *universal* gift of 'light', that *everyone* was 'enlightened by the divine light of Christ'.[10] It was not – contrary to what some subsequent writers assume – something that their experience straightforwardly compelled them to assert; all that you need to conclude from a series of conversion experiences (or similar) is that *many* people are 'enlightened by the divine light'.[11] Nor was it the only or obvious way to read the text; the extended debates between Quakers and their contemporaries around this very issue demonstrate that there were plenty of alternatives available.

I will suggest in a later chapter that the trust that 'every [person is] enlightened by the divine light of Christ' underlies Quaker testimony as 'experimental' practice. For the moment, the main point to note is that this text and the related Johannine passages on 'light' have a central place in the Quaker biblical settlement. In Quaker

---

10 Melvin B. Endy, 1973, *William Penn and Early Quakerism*, Princeton, NJ: Princeton University Press. Setting Penn (specifically) in his wider intellectual context, Endy demonstrates particularly clearly that the decision to affirm the universality of the light of Christ was a conscious and a controversial one that – in its apparent reliance on a single proof-text and the lack of an 'experimental' basis – ran somewhat against dominant patterns in Quaker theology.

11 Janet Scott, 1980, *What Canst Thou Say? Towards a Quaker Theology*, Swarthmore Lecture 1980, London: Quaker Books, does claim that the universal Light is known from experience; but the *experiential* arguments that she briefly puts forward can, I think, only get as far as 'many' or 'most' or even 'all we have come across so far', not 'all'.

accounts of their experiences, their worship and their practice in terms of light, and specifically the divine Light of Christ, we see another aspect of their mapping of 'then and there' on to 'here and now'. With the focus on John 1.9, 'light' gave Quakers a starting point from which to speak about the saving work of Christ as both individual and universal, both fully God's work and fully effective in human life. The *same* light was given to all in their diverse circumstances; it was 'found' in the scriptures but not given *by* the scriptures.

There is a long history of debates about how to interpret this core symbol of light within Quakerism. Rufus Jones, one of the intellectual giants of liberal Quakerism, identified the light with a universal principle of divine immanence known to mystics of all traditions through the ages; and Maurice Creasey, in a more recent classic re-articulation of early Quaker Christology, identified it uncompromisingly with the presence of the risen Christ.[12] Those interpreters who want to link Quakers to the liberal Anglican theology of the later seventeenth century emphasize the connection of the light with human reason; those who want to locate Quakers more solidly with their Puritan forebears emphasize its divine origin, and its effects in judgement and condemnation. But the ambiguity and multiplicity of the metaphor of light is not a scholarly creation; it is really there in the writings and experience of Quakers through the centuries. The light *was* (and is) both 'convicting' and loving, both innermost to human experience and thoroughly beyond the human, both particular and universal, both reasonable and exceeding reason. In other words, the plurality of Quaker theologies of light is closely connected to the complexity of the core experiences to which they relate. This in turn is not surprising if we take seriously the central claim to which all this Quaker talk about 'light' refers – that God is present and revealing God's self in and through a particular history.

---

12 Maurice A. Creasey, 1956, 'Early Quaker Christology', PhD thesis, University of Leeds. An overview is available online via Woodbrooke: https://www.woodbrooke.org.uk/data/files/CPQS/Summaries/Maurice_A_Creasey.pdf.

WALKING IN THE LIGHT

The continuing force of the 'light' metaphor is explained partly by its biblical roots but partly also by its wider symbolic power. We might be cautious about claiming that light is a universally comprehensible symbol, but it is certainly one that, in Paul Ricœur's words, 'gives rise to thought' in diverse religious and cultural contexts (Ricœur 1967, p. 352). 'Light' makes sense outside a Christian context and outwith biblical narratives. Indeed, the non-specificity of the symbol both encouraged the development of Quaker beliefs in the universal saving presence of God – the light could be present even where Christ was not named – and encouraged one of the most common criticisms levelled against them, that they paid insufficient regard to the historical Jesus Christ.

But what is the connection between testimony and Quaker talk of the universal Light? It is relatively easy to separate the two terms if one begins from a common set of assumptions about the relationships of religious belief and practice. We might assume that Quakers talked about light to explain what they believed or knew about themselves, God and the world; and that they then acted on those beliefs. We might think that 'the light' is something you know, see or believe in, and that action is subsequent to prior enlightenment. I have already suggested, however, that the separation of belief and practice, that prioritizes the former over the latter, does not work for Quaker theology. In the striking expression of a contemporary Rwandan Quaker that echoes numerous older convincement narratives, 'I got this light that pushed me' (Sizeli Marcellin, in British Yearly Meeting 2014, p. 38). Quakers picked up and focused on the texts, in John and the Johannine literature, in which the light demands response, movement, action. Those who 'do what is true come to the light' (John 3.21); those who follow Jesus have the light rather than walking in darkness (8.12); the time when light is given is the time to 'walk... so that the darkness may not overtake you' (12.35); and, in a verse quoted almost as often by Quakers as John 1.9, the people of God walk in the light (1 John 1.7).

Crucially, also, thinking about light in relation to the Johannine literature places it in a dramatic and conflictual narrative – both

TESTIMONY

the narrative of Jesus' life and the narrative of the people he calls his friends. In Jesus' life, a particular human history enacts the confrontation of God's truth with the 'prince of this world'; that confrontation persists in the story of those whom Jesus calls his friends. And all of this happens at the point of encounter between the 'light' that has come into the world and the 'darkness' that dominates the world.

It has been both widely held and widely debated in recent scholarship on John that the text is structured as a two-level drama, in which the story of the community who are the audience of the Gospel narrative is explicitly mapped on to the story of Jesus himself.[13] Whether or not this holds good as a historical claim about the origins of the Gospel, or as a useful lens through which to interpret specific passages, the idea of the two-level drama does draw attention to core aspects of John's theological world. In particular, the disciples' participation in Jesus' life is linked to participation in his work and encountering the world in similar ways. What Quakers seemed to find, in their scripturally saturated religious context, was the experience of being pulled into the middle of John's central drama – the confrontation between the saving and revealing work of God and the world's implacable opposition to that work. The dramatic encounters that structure the Gospel – between 'light' and 'darkness', between truth and lies, between Jesus and the 'prince of this world' – can be perceived and engaged with 'here and now' as much as 'then and there'. This is where the core idea of testimony comes in.

Quaker un/settlements: (2) testimony

My suggestion is that Quaker testimony – both the things that are done and the ways they are talked about – emerges in the

---

13 The enormously influential theory of the Johannine two-level drama was set out in J. L. Martyn, 1968, *History and Theology in the Fourth Gospel*, Louisville, KY: Westminster John Knox. For an overview of recent debates, see William M. Wright, 2009, *Rhetoric and Theology: Figural Reading of John 9*, Berlin: de Gruyter, Ch. 1.

dramatic 'here and now' of the inbreaking of God's light into the world. Testimony happens, as it were, at the leading edge of the history of salvation and revelation. The task of testimony is the task of speaking and doing God's truth, of coming to the light and walking in the light – in a situation where the truth is not easily apparent and the light is not immediately obvious or attractive. Testimony, thus understood, is in continuity with the testimony of 'Christ and the apostles', not only or mainly in the sense of replicating their words and actions or of reproducing accurate information about them, but in the sense of 'standing where they stand', or of being caught up in the movement of testimony that they inaugurate.

In taking this sort of account of testimony from the Johannine literature, I am following various recent interpreters – Paul Ricœur, Andrew Lincoln and others – in associating Johannine testimony primarily with legal, as opposed to historical, testimony.[14] Historical testimony – to summarize an extended discussion in Ricœur – is the narrative account of what happened; it is assessed on whether and how it does justice to a past event, and it bears authority or trustworthiness through its relation to that event. Legal testimony, while also having an aspect of 'saying what happened', has a stronger aspect of advocacy. It emerges in an adversarial context – paradigmatically, a court of law – as 'evidence for' or 'evidence against', and it is assessed in the context of a wider overall judgement on a present controversy.

John and the Johannine literature are full of testimony – the testimony of Jesus (John 3.32; 7.7; 8.13–14), and of the works Jesus does (5.36; 10.25), of John the Baptist (John 1.8; 1.15), of the Father (5.3; 8.18), of the scriptures (5.39), of the disciples individually and collectively (John 3.11; 15.27; 19.35; 21.24) and of those who encounter Jesus (4.39; 12.17). Testimony is contested or refused; its validity is argued; the acceptance or non-acceptance

---

14 Paul Ricœur, 1980, *Essays on Biblical Interpretation*, ed. Lewis Mudge, Minneapolis, MN: Fortress Press, Ch. 3; Andrew T. Lincoln, 2000, *Truth on Trial: The Lawsuit Motif in the Fourth Gospel*, Grand Rapids, MI: Baker.

of testimony, and especially of Jesus' testimony, is a focus of controversy. Now, it is at least possible – as Lincoln most recently demonstrates – to read the whole narrative of John's Gospel, with its multi-layered building up of testimonies, as a single adversarial trial.[15] It culminates in the historical trial of Jesus, but also points forward to the various trials of his followers. Jesus is on trial, *and* 'the world' – in the person of his accusers – is on trial; testimony is brought forward and tested in a precarious and open-ended situation in which the truth struggles to be received or to find a hearing. Testimony is located at the point of confrontation between the truth of God and the paradoxically dominant *un*truth of the world-opposed-to-God.

The book of Revelation – another favourite with early Quakers – brings out a further implication of this multi-levelled 'trial of the truth'. The early Christian communities are described as holding and suffering for 'the testimony of Jesus' (12.17; 19.10). What is 'the testimony of Jesus'? Partly prompted by the even more puzzling claim that 'the testimony of Jesus is the spirit of prophecy' (19.10), one possible interpretation is that these communities suffer and are rewarded not only for giving testimony *about Jesus*, but for giving *Jesus' testimony*. They are caught up in the movement of revelation both summed up and inaugurated in Jesus' history – and, like Jesus, they provoke violent opposition which they suffer without violent resistance.[16]

---

15 This is a plausible reading, but of course not an uncontroversial one. For a contrasting approach to 'testimony' in John, one that places much more evidence on the historiographical character of Johannine testimony and hence sees far more discontinuity between the testimony of the 'eyewitnesses' and that of subsequent generations, see Richard Bauckham, 2007, *The Testimony of the Beloved Disciple: Narrative, History and Theology in the Gospel of John*, Grand Rapids, MI: Baker. Bauckham notes that the word-group for testimony (*martureo*) is not normally associated with historiography, but wants to emphasize that an account of 'what happened' is still a feature of legal testimony.

16 On this reading of the 'testimony of Jesus' in Revelation, see Allison Trites, 1977, *The New Testament Concept of Witness*, Cambridge: Cambridge University Press, pp. 155–9; J. P. M. Sweet, 1981, 'Maintaining the Testimony of Jesus: The Suffering of Christians in the Revelation of John', in William Horbury and Brian McNeil (eds), *Suffering and Martyrdom in the New Testament*, Cambridge: Cambridge University Press, pp. 101–7.

WALKING IN THE LIGHT

John's account of the promise of the Paraclete, the 'Spirit of truth', is key to articulating this relationship – of continuity that is deeper than simply imitation – between Jesus' life, death and resurrection and subsequent testimony; and, as we shall see in later discussion, it is also key to understanding Quaker claims about corporate testimony. The Paraclete not only calls to mind the teachings of Jesus, sustaining the testimony *about* him (14.26), but also continues the process of adversarial testimony – testifying on Jesus' behalf (15.26) and convicting the world in relation to sin, righteousness and judgement (16.8). The Spirit's presence with the disciples is linked both to their capacity to remember and follow Jesus – to enact historically their faithfulness to him – and also to their sharing in Jesus' own life.

It is essential in this and in subsequent discussion to recognize the close connections in Quaker thought – shaped, as I have suggested, by a particular un/settlement with the Bible and in particular with the Johannine literature – between truth spoken and truth 'done'. Truth appears in lives and actions; testimony is lived and done; but this lived and enacted testimony also 'makes sense', lends itself to rereading and reinterpretation. Truth, moreover – as we shall see further in the next chapter – is intimately connected with the breaking apart of structures and patterns of life associated with *un*truth. As William Edmundson put it, in the context of (what is thought to be) the first direct Quaker attack on the system of slavery, 'Truth is that which works the remedy, and breaks the yoke' (Edmundson 1676/1834, p. 9).

The practices of biblical interpretation I discussed in the first section – bringing *all* the biblical witness into the present, voicing it in a single contemporary voice that redescribes and 'unsettles' a particular historical situation – can from this perspective be seen as, itself, an example of testimony. The speaker who – as it is claimed – is empowered by the Spirit both recalls and re-voices the paradigmatic testimony and continues its movement, speaking and enacting the particular challenge that the situation requires.

TESTIMONY

Un/settling questions: introducing the Nayler case

Thus far, I have tried to sketch a reading of Johannine testimony that helps to make sense of Quaker testimony, in *something like* the way early Quakers made sense of it, and something like the way in which it continues to operate among Quakers – whether or not the interpretive moves that support it are made explicit. From the point of view of theological ethics, some important challenges to this account of Quaker testimony need to be raised here. One very pressing critique – of Quakerism in at least some of its manifestations, of the Johannine literature read in this way, and of the whole idea of mapping the 'here and now' in conflictual terms – is that it is dangerously sectarian. It invites a mapping of human groups and societies in terms of the saved and the lost, the drawing of clear and non-permeable boundaries between 'us' and 'them', the escalation of relative differences into a cosmic battle of good and evil, and a hypocritical and/or hyper-critical insistence on the perfection of one's own community.

As we shall see when we look closely at some Quaker examples, there is a genuine challenge here that needs to be faced – and for which there are in fact plenty of theological resources within the very texts and interpretations I have outlined. To anticipate, the problem of sectarianism is addressed first by acknowledging just how local, present and open-ended the 'here and now' of testimony is. What I have called, above, the leading edge of salvation history runs through all individuals, communities and situations. It calls for continuing discernment and risky decision, rather than self-congratulation and satisfaction with achieved results. Its 'advances' are more than likely to appear as loss, failure and moral ambiguity – as, paradigmatically, in the execution of a convicted criminal in a backwater of the Roman Empire. Second, and probably more importantly – because the sectarian impulse could turn everything I have just said to its advantage – it is enormously important that truth and lies, or light and darkness, are not equivalent and balanced forces. They are not two sides of the same coin, or two armies on the same field. Their confrontation is not a mutual struggle for annihilation; it is, from the perspective of 'Jesus' testimony', a struggle *against* annihilation, a struggle to save whatever might be lost or destroyed. This is the core point with which I engage in the next chapter.

Another significant critique – which has been advanced, in different contexts, against a 'testimony'-focused reading of John – is that it tends to marginalize or downplay the historical life, death and resurrection of Jesus, particularly its unique salvific significance, and hence in fact to misrepresent the testimony of Christians through the ages. Unlike the previous critique, this is not directly a challenge to theological ethics. It does, however, have major implications for theological understandings of what it means to be human, how salvation is to be understood in relation to particular human lives and histories, and other issues that bear on theological ethics. The challenge 'What are you saying about the unique significance of Jesus' life, death and resurrection?' is linked to challenges like 'Are you attributing salvation to your own actions rather than to Jesus'?' or 'Are you making Jesus into nothing more than an example to be followed in general terms?'

Quakers' response to the charge of neglecting historical 'testimony' concerning Jesus, and particularly concerning Jesus' death – which has been brought against them since the earliest years of the movement – has varied considerably. One typical approach has been to affirm the core articles of Christian faith concerning Jesus' history – and then to question the importance of these affirmations in and of themselves. There is a question, we might say, about the importance of the historiographical testimony concerning 'there and then' without the movement to make it significant 'here and now'. Attempts in the early Quaker literature fully to refute the charge that Quaker teaching made 'Christ that died at Jerusalem' insignificant, or insufficiently central, rarely satisfied Quakers' opponents.[17] The

---

17 See on this, Moore, *The Light in their Consciences*, pp. 109–10. Katharine Evans' answer when interrogated at Malta is a good example of a Quaker approach to questions about the importance of Jesus' history: 'They asked her, Whether she did own that Christ who died at Jerusalem; she answered, we own the same Christ, and no other, he was the same yesterday, today and for ever.' Katharine Evans and others, 1715, *A Brief History of the Voyage of Katharine Evans and Sarah Cheevers*, London: Sowle.

TESTIMONY

Quakers had a habit – rather irritating to their opponents – of shifting the ground in debates about Jesus' history; asked about the sufficiency of Christ's death for atonement, they might affirm it rather cursorily and then ask what was really meant by atonement within a person's life, or what it meant to say that sin was overcome. They might draw attention to what they saw as the pernicious effects of (as Fox put it) 'preaching up sin', downplaying the possibility of the effective transformation of people's lives 'here and now' by emphasizing the historical event of atonement.

The related critique, that an emphasis on continuity with the 'testimony of Jesus' makes Jesus mainly a historical example of good speech and conduct, is rather easier to answer. Locating testimony at the 'leading edge' of salvation history means that it is not about imitating what has been done before. Jesus' history does not exhaustively *demonstrate*, or serve as the blueprint for, all future ways of living faithfully. Jesus' 'there and then' is 'here and now', not simply through remembering and replication, but through the continuity of God's presence in human histories – through the gift of the Spirit. This opens up the possibility of new forms of truthful speech and action that can genuinely be said to be truthful, or to be of God – without in itself, of course, deciding whether any specific example of speech or action can be thus described. As with Margaret Fell's examination of how women's preaching was 'justified, proved and allowed of' by the scriptures, reference to the history of Jesus and the histories that surround it will be an important part of assessing a new claim or a new development; but this is not about following a blueprint.

This latter point raises the wider question about the discernment process that accompanies testimony. If testimony occurs in contested spaces, in situations where the truth is not obvious or where something is 'on trial', how are decisions made about what constitutes right testimony? Calling testimony the continuing movement of divine truth in the world not only risks turning everything into an all-out conflict, it seems to make it extremely, even unbearably, important to make the right call. Appeals to the communal, intergenerational and storied nature of testimony – and hence to a shared and ongoing practice of discernment and testing – partly answer the concern but do not fully resolve it in any given case.

For anyone seeking evidence of the risks of Quaker approaches to testimony, the famous or notorious case of James Nayler serves as a particularly stark illustration of the controversies caused by the claim to 'continue Jesus' testimony'. It also presented the best-known of many instances in which Quaker testimony was literally placed 'on trial'.[18] Nayler, a prominent preacher and theologian in the early Quaker movement, was tried for blasphemy, convicted and punished with mutilation and imprisonment; he later died in prison. He was found guilty of having assumed to himself both 'the gesture, words, honor, worship, and miracles of our blessed Saviour. Secondly, the names and incommunicable attributes and titles of our blessed Saviour'.[19] The occasion of this conviction – and also of a major crisis within the nascent Quaker movement – was an incident at Bristol. Nayler rode into the city accompanied by a few companions (most notably the preacher and writer Martha Simmonds) who 'spread their garments' in front of his horse and sang 'Holy, holy, holy' – in what was recognizably a re-enactment of Christ's entry into Jerusalem.

The accounts of his examination at Bristol and subsequent trial by Parliament show Nayler responding to question after question, designed to elicit an openly blasphemous self-identification with Jesus Christ, with answers that both avoid saying that he *is* the same person as Jesus Christ, and refuse to put any 'space' between his story and Jesus' story. Asked in Bristol, 'Art thou the unspotted Lamb of God that comes to take away the sins of the world?', Nayler answers, 'If I were not a lamb, my enemies would not come to devour me.' Asked repeatedly (amid some confusion) whether

---

18 For a detailed account of the Nayler case that sets it in both historical and theological context, see Leo Damrosch, 1996, *The Sorrows of the Quaker Jesus: James Nayler and the Puritan Crackdown on the Free Spirit*, Cambridge, MA: Harvard University Press. I am grateful to Jon K. Cooley for introducing me to Damrosch's work.

19 *A Complete Collection of State Trials and Proceedings upon High Treason and Other Crimes and Misdemeanours*, Vol. 2, 1730, London, p. 265.

he is the 'King of Israel', he answers before the Parliamentary committee 'I have no kingdom in this world, yet a kingdom I have; and he that hath redeemed me hath redeemed me to be a king forever.' It is hard, in fact, to avoid the conclusion that the final outcome – which was not unanimously agreed – was exactly what Nayler wanted, or at least what he deliberately set his path towards, namely, that he would be convicted and punished for blasphemy, having said nothing that was obviously blasphemous.[20]

In many ways James Nayler looks like the disturbing limit case of 'continuing the testimony of Jesus' and 'collapsing distances of time and space' in the sense I have described. For various reasons, at the time and since his actions were taken, even by the majority of Quakers, to have gone *beyond* the limit – perhaps to constitute a catastrophic loss of discernment, a wrong call with devastating consequences. In Chapter 5, below, I return to Nayler's case and read him alongside the stories of uncontroversially acclaimed Quaker 'martyrs', in an attempt to reintegrate his testimony into a shared – though complex and conflicted – history of responses to religious persecution. For now, however, the key point to note is that the *theological* risk of claiming to continue Jesus' testimony (the risk of following a delusion, forgetting the history of Jesus, denying Jesus' uniqueness) is matched or counteracted in Nayler's testimony by a *lived* risk that he deliberately takes. He takes the risk of refusing to evade the consequences of the claim he is making, refusing to give up the 'experiment' of living as one redeemed into a kingdom – and also the risk of ending in failure and disgrace.

The more obvious concern that readers might raise about the Nayler case, though, is that his action does not look 'ethical'. On the terms most of us are used to, it looks either ethically neutral – just a rather puzzling expression of crazy but harmless views – or downright *un*ethical, in so far as it puts himself and his fellow Quakers at risk for no good reason, and/or risks misleading the

---

20 Much more frivolously, it is also hard to avoid the conclusion that the inability to give a simple answer to a straight yes–no question – well known as a Quaker trait by anyone who has ever tried to conduct a survey of any kind among Quakers – was a very early development.

people. If Nayler is in some respect a 'limit case' of Quaker testimony, he also seems to overstep the limits – the ethical framework – within which testimony is now usually understood. I suggested in the previous chapter that Quaker thought and theology does not (quite) begin with 'ethics' – and both Nayler himself, and the patterns of thought and interpretation that accompany his action, help to show what this means. Quaker thought and theology begins with being caught up in the movement of God's truth; being gathered and drawn in by the Kingdom of Heaven, as Howgill put it; being impelled by the 'light that pushes me', as Marcellin puts it. So it starts somewhere rather more deep-seated, more disturbing and more comprehensive than what we normally call 'ethics'. The kind of Quaker testimony on which I mainly focus in this book – shared community-defining traditions of practice – arises from, and is grounded in, the claim and experience to which Nayler points. In the next chapter, I suggest how this turns into something that looks more like 'ethics' as we know it.

2

'We do utterly deny . . .': Refusals, Silences and Negative Testimony

Conflict and nonviolence

In the previous chapter's account of testimony, I returned several times to ideas and images of conflict – locating testimony in adversarial situations, in the confrontations between light and darkness or between truth and lies. Since Quakers are known for pacifism and for peace work, this seems to call for some explanation. Indeed, the prominence of military images and biblical references in early Quaker writings – and in particular the very widespread portrayal, based on Revelation, of the movement as engaged in the 'Lamb's War' – has frequently been noted by historians, together with the tension (if such it is) between this imagery and the relatively early commitment to nonviolence.[1] This early 'war' imagery – which, we should note, does not appear in *all* early Quaker texts – makes most sense if we place it in a wider context: the dramatic and conflictual framing of testimony, described in the previous chapter,

---

1 For a recent discussion of the relationship between the early 'Lamb's War' and Quaker pacifism, see Gene Hillman, 2002, 'Quakers and the Lamb's War: A Hermeneutic for Confronting Evil', *Quaker Theology*, issue 7. For a discussion of recent debates over the gendered implications of 'Lamb's War' imagery (and especially of the claim that it was predominantly used by Quaker men), see Pam Lunn, Betty Hagglund, Edwina Newman and Pink Dandelion, 2009, '"Choose Life!" Quaker Metaphor and Modernity', in Elaine Graham (ed.), *Grace Jantzen: Redeeming the Present*, Aldershot: Ashgate, pp. 91–110.

and the significant weight accorded throughout Quaker history to negative testimony, 'testimonies against'.

Not only in the seventeenth century, but at most periods before the late twentieth century, most of the widely recognized distinctive Quaker practices could be expressed as testimonies *against* something. Quakers had a wide range of traditions of refusal, some dating from the earliest decades of Quakerism and some of more recent origin: refusing to swear oaths, to pay tithes, to observe practices that reinforced social distinctions, to own slaves or to support the institution of slavery, to fight, and so forth. These traditions of refusal were not simply traditions of 'objection in principle'; as we would expect, they were traditions of action, or perhaps of non-action. Consider, for example, the famous declaration by a group of leading Quaker men to Charles II in 1660, subsequently labelled the 'Peace Testimony'. At its heart is an uncompromising refusal:

> All bloody principles and practices, we, as to our own particulars, do utterly deny, with all outward wars and strife and fightings with outward weapons, for any end or under any pretence whatsoever. And this is our testimony to the whole world. (Fox et al. 1660)

For much of the eighteenth and nineteenth centuries, various negative testimonies were 'peculiarities' of the Quaker community. They marked Quakers out as different; they made a clear boundary between this group and the rest of the world. Already by being made 'special cases', exempt under law *as a community* from swearing oaths or paying tithes, Quakers were established as a 'peculiar people' within British society. Over many years, Quakers enjoined one another to maintain the 'ancient testimonies' against swearing oaths, or paying tithes, or observing various public festivals, or – most conspicuously – against various ornaments and 'vain' forms of dress. In such injunctions, reasons were generally given for the 'ancient testimonies', but it is hard to avoid the impression at least some of the time that what matters most is the maintenance of a clear boundary. The boundary is between Quakers as a group and the rest of the world; but it is also in the individual's life, between 'the world' and the things of God.

I argue in this chapter that the negative character of historic Quaker testimony is neither accidental nor incidental. It is theologically and ethically important – and, as we shall see, it corresponds in important ways to the practice of silent worship. Negative testimony is comparable, in important ways, to apophatic theology – to modes of speech about God that emphasize un-saying or the failure of speech, systematically denying that God possesses the attributes of created things or can be directly compared to created things. It is also comparable to traditions of asceticism – that is, to sustained disciplines of the mind and body of which a key component is self-denial in various forms.[2] Neither of these quite works as a framework for understanding Quaker negative testimony – but their presence and prominence within Christian tradition does provide a starting point for understanding the importance of negation, denials and refusals.

The overarching context within which my reading of negative testimony is possible is the account of truth that underlies the discussion of testimony in the previous chapter. One of the implications of prioritizing the legal account of testimony, and the Johannine focus on Jesus as the one who is, does and reveals the truth, is that truth can be understood theologically as something done, performed or 'lived in' – and as something that emerges precariously in and through history. Testimony – enacting or speaking truth – enters into and engenders conflict, not because truth and falsehood are somehow equal and opposing forces, but because the drama of revelation, or of the making-real of God's truth, is

---

[2] Max Weber accorded Quakers a distinctive place among the Protestant groups who brought asceticism into the marketplace – and whose ethic engendered the 'spirit of capitalism'. It is not my intention here either to rely on or to critique Weber's account – which I also discuss in the next chapter. However, it is worth noting that his 'asceticism' includes a discipline of daily life, but not the expectation of change or transformation; and this does not fit Quakers particularly well, however it might work for some of the other groups he discusses. Max Weber, 1905/1930, *The Protestant Ethic and the Spirit of Capitalism*, trans. Talcott Parsons, London: Unwin Hyman.

as yet unfinished. Knowing in broad terms how the story works out – or knowing and trusting in the character of the God whose story it is – does not allay or short-circuit the dramatic tension of any particular moment.[3]

Expecting testimony to be conflictual or embroiled in 'dramatic tension', however, is not the same as expecting it to be formulated in negative terms. In fact, on the face of it that seems rather odd. We might expect the enacted proclamation of God's revelation to be resoundingly positive. The truth that Jesus Christ is and speaks, we might think, is the truth that does not have to prove something else wrong in order to make itself right, that does not have to enter the sphere of denials and contradictions. A negative statement – we might think – relies on and is secondary to the positive statement it negates; and the truth that Christians live and proclaim is prior to whatever opposes it, and does not rely for its power on having something to oppose.

In fact, Quaker theologians and historians can be rather embarrassed by the negative history of Quaker testimony – by the sheer amount of effort that was put into (for example) refusing to swear oaths, refusing to pay tithes, maintaining 'peculiarities' of dress that began as refusals of unnecessary ornament, or agonizing over what activities in a time of war were compatible with the witness against war. It can lead the suspicious reader, Quaker or otherwise, to believe that what we have here is a group anxious to preserve its peculiarity at all costs, and finding that the easiest way to do so is through a series of pointed and stubborn refusals – refusals that are maintained and insisted on out of all proportion to their theological content. In later chapters of this book, I consider specific examples of these sustained refusals – such as 'hat honour', the refusal to swear oaths, and various objections to religious

---

3 I draw here on the work of J. Ben Quash and Samuel Wells, among others, in using 'drama' as a key analogy for understanding the relationship between givenness and freedom – or between divine providence and human agency – in theology and in theological ethics. See J. Ben Quash, 2005, *Theology and the Drama of History*, Cambridge: Cambridge University Press; Samuel Wells, 2004, *Improvisation: The Drama of Christian Ethics*, Grand Rapids, MI: Brazos.

'forms' – in an attempt to uncover their continuing theological and ethical relevance. First, however, I need to make the case that negative testimony – the sustained refusal to do, say or accept certain things – can be positively important.

On not doing things: the double negative

> What you ought to do to remedy the evil is *not* clear. What you must *not* do is clear in particular cases [*von Fall zu Fall*]. (Wittgenstein 1980, p. 74e)

What does it mean that Quakers have historically refused (with varying degrees of consistency) to swear oaths, to engage in gambling or speculation, to respond to violence with violence, to follow conventions of dress or speech associated with differential social status, and so forth? What is interesting about persistently saying 'no'?

I propose that Quakers' negative testimony is in fact a double negative. It is a negation of the 'no', a refusal of destruction, a denial of a lie. It is sustained enacted opposition, 'case by case' (as in the striking aphorism quoted above), to some power or structure of thought that claims to shape and uphold the world but in fact destroys it. It says 'no' to the claim or the practice or the structure that itself says 'no' to life. Put in simple terms, the 'no' of negative testimony is a refusal to be, or to remain, part of the problem.

This is easiest to see, and most extensively theorized, in the case of nonviolence – taken up as a collective Quaker commitment in the 1660 Declaration. Commitment to nonviolence says that violence is the problem and refuses to be part of it; it is an attempt to break the destructive cycle rather than perpetuate it. I want to suggest that the claim to be doing or acting *in truth*, to be taking the side of truth over against falsehood, makes a link between nonviolence and other sorts of negative testimony. But it is probably easiest to start with nonviolence (in 1660 and subsequently); violence is a negative, *non*violence is a double negative.

Now, the first thing to say is that a double negative, a 'negation of negation', is not just the same as an affirmation. This is obvious enough in real life, but occasionally becomes less obvious in print. Various features both of contemporary public (including ethical) 'debate' and of our intellectual inheritance tempt us to think that the normal form of a controversy is a simple binary. 'Debates' about any controversial public issue are often set up on the assumption that there are two roughly equivalent sides. The message is that every issue presents two and only two well-defined alternatives, each of which is the negation of the other.

I do not need, or want, to argue against all uses of binary patterns of reasoning, or of the principles of non-contradiction and the excluded middle. For innumerable purposes, including theological purposes, these principles are crucial. We often need to be able to say, 'This statement is either true or false, and to deny that it's false is to affirm that it's true.' But with Quakers' negative testimony – as indeed with apophatic theology *and* with ascetic practice – we are not working with two equivalent and known alternatives, the one of which is the negation of the other. On one side we have something we *do not fully know or understand yet* – the reality of God and of the world reconciled to God, the full flourishing of created and reconciled life. On the other side we have some existing 'evil' that is only too familiar, and that prevents us from seeing the reality of God, of the world as it is or of the world as it will be.

As the quotation from Wittgenstein at the head of this section suggests, the confrontation – between the familiar or obvious thing now judged to be 'evil', and the as-yet-unknown alternative course of action – does not occur in the abstract to be resolved once and for all, but occurs 'case by case'. (Wittgenstein, as it happens, was discussing the 'evil' of anti-Semitism – which he recognized as something that affected his own actions and responses, as much as it affected his external environment.) On each given occasion, denying or refusing the familiar evil is not quite the same as making a specific positive claim, or committing oneself indefinitely to a specific course of action. There is no way to know, in advance, what the denial or refusal 'means' or what it brings about. This is because – and this is the next crucial point – the act of denial or refusal is what moves us from what is known and taken for granted to something that is not yet fully known. The moment of denial or refusal interrupts our established patterns and assumptions, breaks the circle, and allows, on however small a scale, a glimpse of alternative possibilities.

Truth and the negative

If we think about negative testimony as 'denying lies', it becomes even clearer that it is not simply the equivalent of a positive claim or affirmation. Truth and lies are asymmetrical. On the one hand, there are always many different lies that can be told in the attempt to avoid acknowledging one truth; lies can multiply indefinitely. But on the other hand – and this is my main focus here – a lie once adopted and maintained keeps things artificially simple; it prevents people from seeing real current complexities or real future possibilities.

Two examples – one literary and one historical – from non-Quaker sources help to convey the implications of this asymmetry. Christopher, the autistic narrator of Mark Haddon's novel *The Curious Incident of the Dog in the Night-Time*, points to the first asymmetry of truth and lies as he explains why he is incapable of lying:

> A lie is when you say something happened which didn't happen. But there is only ever one thing which happened at a particular time and a particular place. And there are an infinite number of things that didn't happen at that time and that place. And if I think about something which didn't happen I start thinking about all the other things which didn't happen. (Haddon 2003, p. 37)

Christopher is disturbed by the infinite number of equally possible 'things that didn't happen' that lie on the other side of each single, fully known, available 'thing that happened'. This looks, on the face of it, like the opposite of what I have just suggested – it looks as if the truth is clearer and more obvious than the lie.

'WE DO UTTERLY DENY...'

The irony in the novel, however, is that for most of the story Christopher is being lied to systematically – and the reader knows this long before he does. The 'one thing' that Christopher thinks defines the current shape of his life (his mother's death) did not in fact happen; and there is a very large – but *not* infinite or random – number of 'things that happened' that he never knew about, and things that *could* have happened differently had he not been deceived. The latter part of the novel shows his precarious attempts to reorient himself to the real complexities of his and his family's situation, after he finds out what is going on, and the brittle stability established by the coherent deception falls apart. The (eventual) denial or collapse of the lie opens up a more complex and unpredictable world – but a world in which all of the characters in the novel can gradually rebuild functional relationships.

The philosopher Edith Wyschogrod, in her account of history-writing after the Shoah (Holocaust), brings the ethical import of 'denying the lies' into sharper relief. Wyschogrod's *An Ethics of Remembering* (1998) asks how it is possible to write histories of the Shoah in an age when historians cannot claim to know and tell the 'objective' and unbiased truth. On the one hand there is a deep ethical responsibility to speak about what happened, to testify on behalf of the dead; on the other hand, there is the impossibility of being certain, the inability of the historian to pin down the 'one thing that happened' from among the many possibilities. The response from the 'heterological historian' is what Wyschogrod calls the negative deictic statement:

> [T]he historian need not claim that she presents absolute truth, 'It has to have been X, it could not have been otherwise'. But she can claim a kind of certainty, grounded in a non-event: 'It might have been X or Y, but I am sure it could not have been Z'... 'Here I stand. It could not have been thus.' (Wyschogrod 1998, pp. 168, 208)

It is very important that the non-event, the 'could not have been', to which Wyschogrod alludes here is not just some random thing that did not happen, one of the infinite series of random and bizarre 'things that didn't happen' contemplated by the boy in *The Curious Incident*. Her work is centrally concerned with lies such as 'the Shoah was invented', or 'only a few Jews were killed' or 'they deserved it' – specific lies that need to be contested because they threaten the memory of the dead.[4] The urgency of the historian's testimony about the Shoah, the ethical force of the 'Here I stand', comes from the present risk of denial, falsification or forgetting. So the historian's commitment to the declaration 'it could not have been' is not simply an exercise in eliminating ridiculous hypotheses. It is, rather, an act of putting oneself on the line against the power of a specific lie, as the first step in allowing the truth to emerge. It is the first step towards writing the lives of the nameless others and the history of the Shoah.

Wyschogrod's primary interest in truth, as a historian, relates to the past – although her reflections on the writing of history gain their ethical significance from present struggles over the past. However, what she applies to the past, and narrates in relation primarily to the question of historical certainty, the nature of historical knowledge, and so forth, can be applied in the case of negative testimony to the present and the future. The rejection of retaliatory violence, for example, might say, 'The true means by which conflicts are resolved in history may take many forms but it *cannot take this one.*'

All of this, however, seems to have rather little to do with theology. What is the relationship between denying lies about God, and denying lies about 'things that happened'? Or, what is the relationship between testimony as 'being caught up in the movement of divine truth' and testimony as an ethical decision for nonviolence?

One resource for answering this question comes from Dietrich Bonhoeffer's essay on truth-telling – which has been taken up more recently by Stanley Hauerwas in a discussion of Christian 'living in

---

4 Of course, in most of the contexts in which they are used, lies like this also threaten the living and promote distorted and destructive ways of life; but Wyschogrod, as a historian, wants to say that they would need to be opposed even if there were no contemporary 'relevance' – because the historian has a responsibility to bear witness for the dead.

truth'.[5] Bonhoeffer relates the question of 'what it means to tell the truth' – in the ordinary sense of the word – to the larger question of how one reads the whole situation of self, other and world before God. Telling the truth becomes a matter of truthfully affirming the world as it is before God – which includes, as Bonhoeffer argues in the article, acting (through one's speech as part of one's wider self-commitment) for the preservation of the world loved and preserved by God, rather than for its destruction. 'The lie is the negation, denial, and deliberate and wilful destruction of reality as it is created by God and exists in God' (Bonhoeffer 1943/2010). The question 'What does it mean to tell the truth?' becomes a question about how the truth can be *done*, in context and through speech and action – or, more urgently, how one is, in speech and action, to avoid serving the 'father of lies'. Truthfulness, if we read with and beyond Bonhoeffer in a Johannine mode, is not one among many moral dilemmas (although it does arise in specific situations *as* a moral dilemma); it is the basic question of self-orientation. This is another way into the ethical significance of testimony; testimony is a collective, learned and storied process of 'doing the truth'.

Bonhoeffer's essay suggests that this is more than a formal claim, about the status of testimony as enacted response to divine truth; it implies substantive claims about what that response will look like. Testimony for God's truth will involve the attestation of the truth of and about the world-before-God, and opposition to whatever seeks to destroy it. In other words, ethical testimony is concerned with historical and worldly as well as ultimate realities. It is set against any and every kind of 'big lie' – any structure or pattern of life that systematically conceals, suppresses or silences some aspect of the complex reality of the world-before-God. And, as Hannah Arendt recognized, the 'big lie' was and is inevitably caught up with violence and destruction – destroying the things of which it denies the existence.

---

5 Dietrich Bonhoeffer, 1943, 'What is Meant by "Telling the Truth"?', English translation 2010, *Conspiracy and Imprisonment* (*DBWE* 16), trans. Lisa Dahill, Minneapolis, MN: Fortress Press. Stanley Hauerwas, 2004, *Performing the Faith: Bonhoeffer and the Practice of Nonviolence*, Grand Rapids, MI: Brazos.

TESTIMONY

This is why it makes sense to talk about testimony as a double negative, a negation of negations, a denial of lies. 'Testimony against' – such as nonviolence – is about the deliberate rejection of practices, structures and patterns of life that deny or destroy specific aspects of 'reality as it exists in God'. It lives the truth through denying lies.

But what is the relationship, in negative testimony, between the denial of lies and the emergence of truth – to continue with our example, between nonviolence and peace? Does the act of negation need to give rise to some (initially) vague new positive outcome in order for it to be valid?

The obvious initial answer is 'no' – at least if we think about some well-established patterns of theological reflection on the claim that 'all are concluded under sin'. A moment of prophetic critique, a 'no' spoken against the powers of the world – 'breaking the circle', interrupting established patterns – is in itself truthful testimony. It truthfully reflects and responds to the judgement of God on all the attempts people make to set themselves up as the judges and shapers of the world. With this in mind, many recent theological discussions of Christian witness focus on *repentance*.[6] They see repentance, enacted as well as spoken, as a primary form of Christian testimony – the necessary and the only possible first response to God from people embedded in sinful structures. The first move – which is already a response and already dependent on God's action – is to recognize evil and turn away from it – 'confession unto repentance', as Jennifer McBride expresses it in a powerful account of contemporary Christian political and social witness.[7]

---

[6] A key voice in this discussion is that of Karl Barth – for example in his famous articulation of the 'great negative possibility' for Christians in politics, the refusal to take part either in the affirmation of state authority or in the revolutionary act against it, as a testimony to God's 'no' to *both* sides of the struggle for power. For an extended discussion of Barth on repentance, see Randi Rashkover, 2005, *Revelation and Theopolitics: Barth, Rosenzweig and the Politics of Praise*, London: T&T Clark.

[7] Jennifer M. McBride, 2011, *The Church for the World: A Theology of Public Witness*, New York: Oxford University Press.

'WE DO UTTERLY DENY...'

Repentance can plausibly be understood as a move of interruption, denial or refusal, abjuring what has gone before, without knowing yet what the 'alternative' might look like – just because the one who needs to repent is so deeply embedded in false and death-dealing structures that she simply cannot see or imagine, let alone plan, what an alternative might look like. In a telling and often-quoted public exchange directly relevant to the question of nonviolence, H. Richard Niebuhr set out the particular Christian case for 'doing nothing' rather than engaging militarily in the Sino-Japanese conflict. Niebuhr argued for a specific form of 'inactivity' in the face of multiple and complex evil, rooted in '[what] the old Christians call repentance'. His appeal to 'the grace of doing nothing', and his careful distinguishing of Christian approaches from other calls for non-intervention, centres on the belief that 'there are no non-combatants, that everyone is involved, that China is being crucified (though the term is very inaccurate) by our sins and those of the whole world' (H. R. Niebuhr 1932).

There is, then, Niebuhr suggests, no readily available possibility of 'righteous' action, no right thing waiting to be done. It is not clear, to return to an earlier quotation, what one *should* do to remedy the evil – but there is, by grace, the opportunity to do nothing. It is possible, Niebuhr argues, to recognize and repent of one's unrighteousness, and to await patiently the outcome of a story over which we can claim no control; this possibility arises from grace and manifests continuing dependence on grace.

Repentance on its own, though, as a moment of critique or refusal, does not necessarily look like the basis for new social and political possibilities. The denial, the refusal, the 'no' to evil, might rightly call into question the goodness or self-evidence of a present course of action – but just because of how seriously it takes the distortion of *all* human action and self-assertion by sin, it does not seem to provide the next step. The response to H. Richard Niebuhr's article by his brother Reinhold took the debate into this relatively familiar territory – familiar, at least, in debates about pacifism and the use of force. Reinhold agreed with the basic point made about the need for repentance, and the implication of everyone in evil – and

TESTIMONY

then questioned the 'responsibility' of refusing to intervene with force in a situation where injustice is being done. It might be important – Reinhold Niebuhr suggests, in a vein familiar from many debates over nonviolence inter alia – to make or to accept the prophetic critique, to note the objection, and then, for want of better alternatives in an imperfect world, to carry on.[8] Quakers, and others adopting a principled stand of nonviolence, become accustomed to being told that their point is important, that their message has been heard, even that they need to continue making their point – and that nothing is going to change.

This is where it becomes important that 'negative testimony' in Quaker tradition is enacted and sustained over time. At first glance an extended exercise in doing nothing is not particularly interesting if it is simply a *repeated* exercise in doing nothing – giving the same answer over and over again to the same question. Nonviolence or pacifism has, in fact, often been examined and debated as if it were a series of repeated discrete moments of refusal. It has frequently been evaluated in terms of action or inaction in a single situation – 'What do you do when the maniac with the gun is about to open fire on the crowd?' It is in fact quite hard to represent the sustained negative – from the outside and perhaps even from the inside – as anything other than a repeated negative, since it appears in each case as an interruption or challenge.

There is, in any case, something to be said for the repeated negative, the repeated interruption, the repeated protest; in any given situation it might be the best or the only thing to do. To appreciate Quaker negative testimony in practice we do have to give due weight and respect to the veterans of decades of peace vigils, who keep turning out with the same banners and posters (which remain depressingly relevant) to protest against whatever is the latest most prominent manifestation of the same problem. But an extended exercise in not-doing, or an intentionally sustained pattern of not-doing, is not the same as a repeated act of critique, interruption or refusal. To give what might serve as a very concise

---

8   Reinhold Niebuhr, 1932, 'Must We Do Nothing?', *Christian Century*, 30 March 1932.

summary of Quaker history and liturgy – if you do nothing for a while, things happen.

Now, there are good practical reasons – reasons one could 'know experimentally' without much theological discussion – for thinking that sustained practices of refusal, such as commitment to nonviolence, might not just operate as a repeated critique of how most of the world works but might actually change things. It is a matter of everyday experience – even, of management cliché – that deliberately giving up an established pattern of action, with its associated ways of categorizing and perceiving the world, enables possibilities to emerge that would otherwise be literally unthinkable. We are all frequently exhorted to 'think outside the box' – however large the box really is, and however few opportunities there really are to escape from it.

More seriously and more to our purpose, a common defence of pacifism against charges of unrealistic optimism is that it is highly unlikely that good alternatives to militarism will be developed, or even imagined, while militarism is still deeply embedded in our social and economic structures. Of course, pacifism is currently unrealistic; the point, some would say, is to change the current reality. The history of nonviolent protest movements suggests that people do, in fact, find numerous imaginative and unexpected alternative ways of furthering a cause or opposing injustice once they rule out violent means. Moreover, these alternative approaches are, in many cases, associated with shifts in perception of the conflict situation, of those involved in it, and of the meaning of success. It is not just a case of continuing the war by other means, but of learning, through the deliberate and sustained eschewal of certain destructive actions and ways of life, to see the world differently. Something that was unthinkable, not-yet-knowable, not clear – the positive counterpoint to whatever one 'must *not* do' in this particular case – emerges over time.

How can this effect – the surprising and contingent emergence, over time, of new possibilities for action and perception – be interpreted theologically? Two answers emerge from a reflection on Quaker negative testimony – one affirming the unpredictable 'effectiveness' of negative testimony, the other adding a note of caution about setting too much store by this effectiveness.

The Declaration to Charles II, as we have seen, puts forward an indefinitely extended communal commitment to a particular form of negative testimony – to 'utterly deny . . . all outward wars and strife and fightings with outward weapons'. The basis for this commitment to nonviolence, however, is a more fundamental and implicit commitment – and an affirmation of faith. As the Declaration continues, after the 'utter denial' to which I have referred:

> the Spirit of Christ, by which we are guided, is not changeable, so as once to command us from a thing as evil, and again to move unto it; and we certainly know, and testify to the world, that the Spirit of Christ, which leads us into all truth, will never move us to fight and war against any man with outward weapons, neither for the kingdom of Christ, nor for the kingdoms of this world.

The fundamental commitment, then, is to be guided by the Spirit of Christ which 'leads us into all truth'. Grounding negative testimony in the guidance of the Holy Spirit – rather than primarily in the command and example of Jesus, although the two are presented as fully coherent and entirely inseparable – gives it a distinct and distinctive orientation to the future. The promise is not simply to continue to obey a call and command already given, but to continue to be guided by the one who gave the command. And this in turn connects negative testimony with the wider commitment to be 'led into all truth', to do truth, to walk in truth. Faithfulness to the guidance of the Spirit encompasses *both* the denial of lies and the disclosure through time of truthful ways of living.

At the same time, the grounding of negative testimony in the guidance of the Spirit blocks any attempt to instrumentalize negative testimony – to use 'thinking outside the box' as a method for success, to expect the commitment to nonviolence to generate good alternatives quickly. Following the guidance of the Holy

'WE DO UTTERLY DENY . . .'

Spirit is not – as was clear enough to Quakers in 1660, if not before – a particularly good or secure way to get what you want, or even to get what you think is best for everyone else. As John Howard Yoder and those influenced by his Anabaptist theological ethics are particularly clear in saying, Christian nonviolence is not a strategic move, not a survival tactic and not a political programme. Nonviolence may be aligned 'with the grain of the universe' (Hauerwas 2002), but there is no reason to suppose that this will produce results on any predictable timescale. That is one of the many reasons not to discount the 'grace of doing nothing'.

Even with that qualification, though, there is a distinctive emphasis in Quaker 'negative testimony' over against its near-equivalents in the Anabaptist traditions – an emphasis that places it in many ways closer to older traditions of ascetic practice. The focus on the guidance of the Holy Spirit, rather than only on the teaching of Jesus – on present, future-oriented guidance rather than on obedience to a given command – means that the positive 'outcomes' are more clearly in view, or are harder to exclude from consideration. These negations and refusals are going somewhere. Rejections of death-dealing structures of power are *for the sake of* abundant life, even if we cannot imagine from here what abundant life looks like.

The spiritual traditions of asceticism also aim at future 'outcomes' – the reorientation of human loving and willing towards God. The ascetic's repeated acts of denial confront, in different ways, the things that, in this particular situation, stand in the way of rightly ordered desire. The point is not that anyone can control or predict the outcome. The negative and the positive are not equivalents, the truth is not obvious even when the lie is obvious. The point is that there is an outcome; if you do nothing, over time, things happen. The 'experimental' knowing – embodied, local, self-involving, grounded in practice and issuing in practice, open to change – that arises from and sustains Quaker testimony might begin from refusals and negations but does not stop there.

It is clear enough, in fact, from Quaker history that negative testimony is not a place to stop – and, again, the relationship

TESTIMONY

between nonviolence and peace is the clearest example. There are numerous examples of sustained and shared commitment to nonviolence – by Quakers and others, in particular the 'historic peace churches' inheriting Anabaptist traditions – being linked to practical peacemaking activities with positive effects. The stories of this practical peace work – from grass-roots community peacebuilding, to influencing international and intra-national negotiations – need to be read as part of Quaker peace testimony alongside the stories of resistance to war or refusal to kill. The recent histories of Quaker peace work in Sri Lanka and Rwanda, or of negotiations at the United Nations for conventions banning child soldiers, or of the development of the Alternatives to Violence programme in and beyond prisons, offer examples of how the sustained decision *against* violence as a means of resolving conflicts gives rise to an equally sustained set of conversations and practices about peaceable alternatives – with practical and tangible effects.[9] These are what I discuss in the next chapter as 'holy experiments', processes that begin from the guidance of the Holy Spirit and from what is already 'known experimentally', but that have unpredictable outcomes and are subject to risk and interruption.

Sinking down to the seed: addressing Quaker quietism

There are many reasons why we might want to move on quickly to the positive side of testimony – peace work rather than nonviolence, truthful speaking rather than the denial of lies. An emphasis

---

9   There is an extensive and growing literature on Quaker peace work, including much that arises directly from the experiences of those involved. For contemporary examples, an impressive range of forms of, and approaches to, Quaker peace work are reflected in recent Swarthmore Lectures – by Sydney D. Bailey (1993), Simon Fisher (2004), Helen Steven (2005) and Rachel Brett (2012). These could be set alongside the *Light that Pushes Me* collection already referred to (2014). The history of Quaker peace work in Sri Lanka has, as far as I know, yet to be written, as has a comprehensive history of the Alternatives to Violence Project. For a recent sympathetic and critical account of Quaker involvement with the United Nations and similar bodies, including a review of the literature, see Jeremy Carrette, 2013, 'The Paradox of Globalization: Quakers, Religious NGOs and the United Nations', in Robert Hefner et al. (eds), *Religions in Movement: The Local and the Global in Contemporary Faith Traditions*, London: Routledge.

on negative testimony carries the risk of a move towards quietism – doing nothing at all, rather than risking doing something wrong. The process of negation could take us to the point where human action and divine action, human speech and divine speech, appeared almost to be opposed or in competition – the safest option, spiritually, being silence and inaction that awaits the word and speech of God. This would be, at least potentially – and often in practice – a radically 'unworldly', inward-turned and apolitical spiritual practice, with little about it bearing the character of dramatic testimony. The interruption of destructive patterns and structures in the world would in practice lead to the establishment of a non-worldly alternative space – which by default allows the rest of the world to carry on more or less undisturbed.

Standard histories of Quakerism have tended to identify a fairly rapid move into quietism after the apocalyptic fervour of the early decades.[10] Robert Barclay's *Apology for the true Christian divinity* (1678), influenced inter alia by Quietists from continental Europe, is regarded as a key textual marker of the shift. Even Quaker writings from the first generation already indicate the strong attractions of a quietist path, and the apparent logic of this development. Consider, for example, the words of Isaac Penington from 1661:

> Give over thine own willing, give over thine own running, give over thine own desiring to know or be anything and sink down to the seed which God sows in the heart, and let that grow in thee and be in thee and breathe in thee and act in thee. (Penington 1662, 43–4; *QF&P* 26.70)

It is easy to see how this can be read as an injunction simply to do nothing, in any sphere of life – to refrain from political action as well as from liturgical form, from theological reflection or from structured spiritual practice (which is, in context, what Penington

---

10 Although the complexities and diversity of the period, and the potential pitfalls of the 'quietist' label, are increasingly recognized – see for an overview Robynne Rogers Healey, 'Quietist Quakerism', in Stephen W. Angell and Pink Dandelion (eds), 2013, *The Oxford Handbook of Quaker Studies*, Oxford: Oxford University Press, pp. 47–62.

was most worried about). It may in fact not be coincidental that Penington's statements on nonviolence were much more conservative, in political terms, than those of many contemporaries and successors; he argued that the 'present estate of things' required the use of the sword, inter alia, for defence against foreign invasions, and indeed that 'a great blessing will attend the sword' when used to that end (see *QF&P* 24.21). Of course, this moderate position on nonviolence is a consistent minority voice in Quaker history, and not always associated with quietist spiritualities.

However, even the words quoted above, not to mention Penington's writings more generally, are more complex in their implications for faithful engagement with 'the world' and its concerns. The 'seed that God sows in the heart', in Penington's writings as in the thought of early Quakers more generally, is Christ – whose universal and transformative work is appropriated in an individual's 'giving over' of will and desire, but is not limited to changes in the individual's spiritual state.[11] There is no necessary contradiction between the mystical emphasis on self-negation and the prophetic emphasis on public (negative) testimony.

Indeed, the image of the 'seed' – which is a very frequent christological image in Quaker writings of the first few generations, now often forgotten – offers another way into thinking about the indefinite but real transformation for which 'negative testimony' seeks to make room. Christ as 'seed' is both a present reality and a future promise. The growth of the seed is as it were 'in character'; its future form is not arbitrarily but integrally related to what is already present in the seed, but its development still has the character of surprise. Moreover, in the reading of Genesis 3.15 that Quakers shared with many of their contemporaries, the curse on the serpent in the Garden of Eden ('I will put enmity between you and the woman, and between your seed and her seed', RSV) connects the 'seed that

---

11 Penington's remarkable extended theology of the 'Seed' is set out in his 'The Seed of God and of his Kingdom', in Isaac Penington, 1681, *Works*, Vol. 4, London: Benjamin Clark. See also Maurice A. Creasey, 1956, 'Early Quaker Christology', PhD thesis, University of Leeds – overview available at https://www.woodbrooke.org.uk/data/files/CPQS/Summaries/Maurice_A_Creasey.pdf.

God sows in the heart' with the decisive conquest of the power of evil, the 'Seed Christ that is over all and doth reign' (Fox 1663; *QF&P* 20.23). Numerous early Quaker writings on the 'seed' drew together the emphasis on inward transformation (the seed sown in the heart), the opposition at the centre of Genesis 3.15 (the 'enmity' between the seed of the woman and the seed of the serpent) and the surprising historical transformations and reversals that might be expected from, as Anne Docwra put it, the 'day of small things' in which the 'least of all seeds' grows and produces fruit.[12]

Elizabeth Bathurst, one of the greatest Quaker theologians of the second generation, makes a similar point in pneumatological terms when she writes of

> the universal principle ... a measure of the quickening [i.e. *life-giving*] spirit, even of that spirit which raised Jesus up from the dead; by the indwelling of which in us, we come to be renewed in the spirit of our minds, and to have our mortal bodies quickened, so as to capacitate us to serve the Lord with our spirits, and with our bodies. (Bathurst 1691, p. 70)

Here attention is drawn to the life-giving and renewing character of the 'universal principle' – and, indirectly, to deep reasons why the 'double negative' cannot be world-denying. The Spirit, as Bathurst writes of it here, is not only the spirit of life, but the spirit of *resurrection*. It is the Spirit 'which raised Jesus up from the dead' – in other words, that 'kills death', overturns the negative, speaks a decisive (and real and embodied and witnessed) 'no' to the powers that crucify Jesus. This, Bathurst claims, is the gift that is offered to all and can be found by all, and by which Quakers' collective life is formed. As the Spirit of resurrection it obviously

---

12 Anne Docwra, 1683, *An epistle of love and good advice to my old friends and fellow-sufferers in the late times*, p. 5. Another particularly frequent early Quaker use of Genesis 3.15 was in defences of women's public preaching. For a discussion of examples from the work of Elizabeth Bathurst, with some discussion of Margaret Fell, see Sarah Apetrei, 2009, 'The Universal Principle of Grace: Feminism and Anti-Calvinism in Two Seventeenth-Century Women Writers', *Gender & History* 21, pp. 130–46.

TESTIMONY

effects the 'quickening' of the body as well as the mind and spirit, and obviously results in service and testimony as well as 'giving over' of self.[13]

More specifically, though, both Penington's words about 'giving over thine own running' and Bathurst's accounts of the presence of the 'quickening spirit' make most sense as an interpretation of Quaker worship. This is the most obvious context in which, in Quaker practice, 'doing nothing' changes things. In the final section of this chapter I look at Quaker worship, based in silence, as a frame for understanding the positive potential of 'testimonies against' – the importance of a sustained, collective practice of 'doing nothing'. Public meetings for worship were in fact described as 'testimony' from early decades – partly because they were (at several points) illegal.

'The Silent Assemblies of God's People': Quaker worship and testimony

In the Introduction I suggested that a foundational Quaker experience – foundational both in the stories Quakers tell about their origins, and in continuing Quaker life and practice – is 'being gathered'. As is well known, Quaker worship is based on silence, and silence appears to have been a significant feature of Quaker worship from the earliest decades. It was associated with the practice of the 'seekers' who had left various existing church communities, but it continued to be central to the practice of those who believed themselves to have 'found' or (perhaps better) to have been found by the Spirit of God.[14] Meetings for worship based in

---

13 For a discussion of Bathurst's theology, and in particular of her account of the indwelling Spirit, see Yasuharu Nakano, 2008, 'Elizabeth Bathurst's Soteriology and a List of Corrections in Several Editions of her Works', *Quaker Studies* 13/1, pp. 89–102.

14 The historical evidence for early Quaker silence in worship is fairly clear; it features both in Quaker writings (albeit mostly dating from the 1660s onwards) and in attacks on Quakers. See for an overview Rosemary Moore, 2000, *The Light in their Consciences, The Early Quakers in Britain 1646–1666*, University Park, PA: Pennsylvania State University Press, pp. 143–4, although Moore suggests, rightly in my judgement, that 'further research is needed' on the historical precedents for the practice of silent worship.

silence continued – and continue – to repeat the movement of being gathered and empowered, the movement from 'doing nothing' to 'something happening'. And, as a result, Quaker worship based on silence has, I want to suggest, profound ethical implications.

For anyone who is not used to Quaker worship, the idea that 'silent' worship might relate to ethics could be counter-intuitive. There is a long and significant tradition of positioning and describing silence in worship as the proper response to the presence of holiness. Thus the well-known hymn, taken from the fourth-century Liturgy of St James where it precedes the consecration of the eucharistic elements:

> Let all mortal flesh keep silence
> and in fear and trembling stand;
> ponder nothing earthly-minded,
> for, with blessing in His hand,
> Christ our God to earth descendeth
> our full homage to demand.[15]

At first reading, this sounds like an injunction to keep silence as a way of separating oneself from 'the world', from whatever is fleshly and earthly – to become timeless and spaceless, taking us straight back to world-denial and quietism. At second reading, however, it becomes clear that the hymn locates silence in reflection on the incarnation – so, in the closest possible *connection* between God and 'mortal flesh', the fullness of divine presence in the 'earthly'. Silence is kept here, I suggest, not because the worshippers are to ignore or abandon the embodied character of the act of worship, nor in order to create a boundary between the holy and the profane, but precisely because the fullness of the presence of God calls forth '*full* homage'. Where to speak or to act would be to identify some particular characteristic or function of the worshippers as that which orients

---

15 Developments in the use of silence in eucharistic liturgies, particularly in the Eastern Church, during this period can, as Harris notes, be directly linked to developments in Christology post-Nicaea (Charles Harris, 1932, 'Liturgical Silence', in W. K. Lowther Clarke (ed.), *Liturgy and Worship*, London: SCM Press, p. 778).

TESTIMONY

them to God, silence recognizes their whole being as God-directed – becoming holy through relation to the holy God. Silence is, then, a mark of 'holiness', holiness not primarily as *separation* but as *wholeness* – or, as Dan Hardy puts it, the capacity to 'maintain its fullness according to its own kind, without . . . collapse into other kinds'.[16] Worship is the placing of whole lives in relation to God.

But what does this placing of 'whole lives' in relation to God mean for ethics? The silence that 'happens' could equally, in almost all situations, be heard as a collection of background noises – inside and outside the space within which the worship is conducted, 'natural' and 'artificial', pleasing and disturbing. When silence is kept, the background noises become, if anything, more apparent (it is a well-known liturgical principle that, as soon as a period of silence is called for, somebody will have a coughing fit). To keep silence, and hence to allow the background noise to become apparent, is not to turn *away from* worship *towards* 'the world', nor to turn *away from* 'the world' *towards* worship; it is to recognize and enact their mutual implication. Keeping silence does not, in practice, shut the world out; it is eminently open to interruption and disruption, to unexpected sound as well as to unexpected speech – and that is part of the point.

Unprogrammed worship, based in silence and open to all manner of interruption, brings people into relation, not only with God and with one another, but with the humanly uncontrollable complexity of the world. There is more *in* creation than any part of creation can name or interpret. Worship forms people in a new way of knowing the world, but part of what is learned is how incomplete their knowledge is – not just of themselves but of God. The silence is, however, more than a mere gesture towards the limits of knowledge – we don't know what is going on. Keeping silence invites an extension of knowledge and concern in the context of infinitely extended divine knowledge and concern. It does this,

---

16 Daniel W. Hardy, 2001, *Finding the Church*, London: SCM Press, p. 9. Hardy, in fact, gives this as the meaning of 'purity' (one of the two key characteristics of 'the holy', the other being 'propriety') – which is even more significant for our purposes, given the associations between silence and 'purification'.

especially, by being a shared and communal silence – that will not allow an individual to retreat from the presence of others into a private space, and that remains grounded in a particular 'here and now'.

What has this to do, specifically, with ethics? Silent worship as such does not automatically translate into some particular action. Silence cannot be taken out of context; it is not, as such, quotable, citable or transferable. It has, as it were, no take-home message. Not only is a time of silence, while it is happening, not experienced as time directed towards the achievement of some predetermined end; but the time of silence viewed as a whole cannot easily be instrumentalized towards some particular ethical or social goal. This in fact tends to make the time of worship more obviously continuous with the time of 'ordinary' life. Worship does not happen in 'time out of time' that can then, in the form of its 'timeless' lessons and truths, become simultaneously present to all times. It happens in real time; whatever it effects, in the people who enact it, is effected without negating their life in ordinary time.

In a certain sense, all that happens in liturgical silence is that time passes. Keeping silence is a 'waste of time', and the particular kind of 'waste of time' that silence is has profound ethical implications. Silent worship is, among other things, practice in the right giving of attention, and the right giving of attention has profound ethical and political implications. After noting that attention – time for the other – 'can only be spent: it cannot be hoarded or saved', Philip Goodchild writes:

> To have to allocate attention is a difficult responsibility to bear. It is much easier to have one's attention attracted, or to be distracted. For attention is rarely given freely; it is subject to all manner of impulses.[17]

If we can read worship in terms of the giving of attention to what *really deserves* that attention, we can give Goodchild's comments on

---

17 Philip Goodchild, 2002, *Capitalism and Religion: The Price of Piety*, London: Routledge, p. 210.

distraction and the subjection of attention to 'impulses' their full weight, without therein leaving the exercise of 'difficult responsibility', the allocation of attention, to rely on a self-founding decision. To create a time of silence is to forgo, for a while, the deliberate attraction of attention in any particular direction; not just to give up a particular well-established solution to existing problems, but to 'give up' the focusing of attention that defines the problem in a certain way.

The trust expressed in the keeping of silence is that worship and the life of faith forms people who give attention freely to what most deserves it – that silent prayer hears, as Tom Heron put it, 'the infant's cry/amidst the cocktail prattle'.[18] Silence kept in communal worship, I have suggested, is not merely 'taking time', but is 'taking time-with'. It is, as such, an education in a mode of relating to 'ethical' questions that directly contradicts many of the ways in which 'ethics' is constructed in public discourse. A conflict, a situation of suffering or a decision about the good presents itself, in silent worship, as something that demands attention even while it is still far from a solution. Worship based on silence forces people to restrain, in the first instance, that form of the desire to solve a problem that arises from the desire to be rid as quickly as possible of something that troubles us. Silences in the context of prayer, particularly, challenge 'ethics' to relate to real problems neither by providing facile solutions nor by ignoring the insoluble.

It is important, however, that something does (sometimes) *change* in unprogrammed worship based on silence. On the most basic level, there is (unplanned) spoken or enacted ministry of various kinds – although this is not necessarily or usually the best measure of the 'effect' or the change brought about. In the well-known passage quoted at the beginning of this section, Robert Barclay describes an experience of 'the evil weakening in me and the good raised up' through time spent in Quaker 'silent

---

18 Tom Heron, 1977, 'Would You Have Ears to Hear?', in *Call it a Day*, St Ives: Ark Press, p. 8. I am grateful to Timothy Peat Ashworth for introducing me to the work of Tom Heron (the father of the artist Patrick Heron, and himself an active Christian pacifist and socialist).

assemblies'. Practical and specific change in collective practice can also be linked fairly directly to Quaker worship; as I have mentioned, and as I discuss further elsewhere in the book, unprogrammed worship beginning from silence is the basis not only of regular 'meetings for worship' but also of decision-making and collective discernment.

Quaker worship, then, as a sustained and shared practice of 'doing nothing' that both forms community and reorients ethical and social life, can be understood both as a source and a grounding of Quaker testimony and an image for how it works. As a long tradition of apophatic theology recognizes, keeping silent before God is not just the same as admitting ignorance about God; and in the same way and for analogous reasons, Quaker testimonies of denial or refusal are not just the same as giving up on the world. Both of them are about breaking away from patterns of thought or behaviour that prevent people from seeing, experiencing or responding to the truth; and both of them embody the trust that 'way will open', that new possibilities for worship, speech or action will emerge.

3

Speaking Truth to Power, and Other Holy Experiments

Life otherwise

> The cross of Christ . . . truly overcomes the world . . . they that bear it, are not so chain'd up, for fear that they should bite, nor locked away, for fear that they should be stole away: no, they receive power from Christ their captain, to resist the evil and do that which is good in the sight of God . . . True godliness don't turn men out of the world but enables them to live better in it and excites their endeavours to mend it. (Penn 1682/1981, pp. 56–7)

We have already seen that Quakers' understanding of testimony is in many ways much broader than that generally taken for granted in most Christian groups. Quaker testimony is, we have seen, not limited to speech. Individual and collective actions are testimony – not as a secondary extension of the idea of testimony, but rather at its core. Moreover, I have suggested that Quaker testimony fits a legal model of testimony much better than a historiographical model. The truth that it attests is in the present and the future as well as, or rather than, in the past; testimony is given not only, as it were, concerning what God has done, but concerning what God is doing and will do.

SPEAKING TRUTH TO POWER

In this chapter, I develop further the idea, introduced in the previous chapter, that Quakers' sustained practices of refusal – negative testimony – give rise to new forms of practice, to 'holy experiments'. Quaker testimony, I have suggested, is not simply world-denial – escaping to a spiritual rather than material life, a life beyond the world. Rather, it is the experiment with a 'life otherwise' within *this* world – the 'here and now' as the place where the presence, guidance and power of God are encountered. In order to explore further the move beyond negation and refusal, I begin from a focus on a characteristic and long-standing Quaker emphasis on 'speaking truth'.

Truth, or integrity, appears on most of the Quaker testimony lists of the twentieth century. It is thus identified as a central term that both characterizes a body of historic Quaker testimony and provides a shared norm or reference point for future action. As we have already seen, Quaker tradition contains from the earliest decades a wealth of theological reflection on truth – often centring on the Johannine affirmation of Christ as Truth. Indeed, in addition to the various uses already discussed, 'truth' has been used as a shorthand for the whole community's commitment and way of life – as in the query put to representatives of each area at national meetings from the 1660s, 'How does Truth prosper among you?'

Besides this general use, however, there is a broad, deep and consistent storied tradition among Quakers of practices of truthfulness, of speaking and communicating truthfully. In this chapter, then, I explore how some specific Quaker traditions of 'speaking truth' relate to negations of the kind I discussed in the previous chapter – practices of 'denying lies'. I begin with a discussion of plainness and plain speech, and use this as a way into thinking about Quaker testimony as experiments in 'life otherwise' – in the terms, rather surprisingly, of Michel Foucault. The discussion of Foucault, whose final lectures consider disruptive practices of truthful speech and witness, leads into a consideration of one of the ideas most widely associated with Quaker activism in the twentieth century – 'speaking truth to power'. By referring back to the original context of this phrase, I show how 'speaking truth to power' makes

TESTIMONY

sense in the context of Quaker thought and practice – and how, why and to what extent Quakers might expect 'speaking truth to power' to be effective, or at least an experiment worth trying.

Plainness and plain speech

'Plainness' as an ideal, and as an organizing principle for various aspects of communal and individual practice, has a long Quaker history. At two ends of the story, Richard Bauman identifies the 'rhetoric of plainness' as central to seventeenth-century Quakerism, and Peter Collins places 'plaining' at the heart of his account of British Quaker identity in the twentieth and twenty-first centuries.[1] Between the periods of these two detailed studies lies a complex story of more or less codified plain speech, plain dress, plainness in architecture and other aspects of design, and the various sustained denials and refusals of 'luxury' now often discussed under the heading of 'simplicity'.[2] Quakers, Collins notes – with very little exaggeration, even given the sweeping nature of the claim – 'have always preferred the plain to the embellished or ornamented' (2009, p. 205). Plainness is an aesthetic principle, reflected widely in Quaker material culture even before and after the era of codified 'plain dress'; and, more importantly for this chapter, it is a principle of speech closely linked to truthfulness.

'Plain speech' in Quaker testimony includes, unsurprisingly, a series of refusals. The best-known example, particularly from the early decades, is the refusal of modes of 'polite' address (both spoken and enacted) that marked out social distinctions and could be used by the speaker to claim or gain social advantage. This included the use of 'thee' and 'thou' as the second-person singular regardless of the rank or status of the addressee, and more widely the avoidance of conventional signs of deference or in-group membership.

---

[1] Richard Bauman, 1983, *Let Your Words Be Few: Symbolism of Speaking and Silence among Seventeenth-Century Quakers*, New York: Cambridge University Press; Peter Collins, 2009, 'The Problem of Quaker Identity', *Quaker Studies* 13/2, pp. 205–19.

[2] 'Simplicity' as negative-and-positive testimony, which relates closely to contemporary Quaker environmental concern, is discussed at more length in Chapter 7.

SPEAKING TRUTH TO POWER

Thomas Ellwood's account of the dramatic effect of this refusal, among his peer group of young upper-class men, is often cited:

> A knot of my old acquaintance . . . all saluted me, after the usual manner, putting off their hats and bowing, and saying, 'your humble servant, Sir', expecting no doubt the same from me. But when they saw me stand still, not moving my cap, nor bowing my knee, in way of congee to them, they were amazed, and looked first one upon another, then upon me, and then one upon another again for a while, without speaking a word. (Ellwood 1714/2011, pp. 24–5; cf. *QF&P* 19.16)

In its context in Ellwood's memoirs, this passage reflects both the enormous importance attached by Quakers to the 'plain and true speech', and the social cost it could entail. Ellwood describes spending the night before this encounter tormented with worry, over 'how I should . . . despatch the business I was sent about' and 'how I should demean myself towards my old acquaintance' with only the 'plain speech' at his disposal.[3] On this particular day, as he describes it, most people he meets – including this group of old friends – respond with surprise and confusion but not with outright or immediate hostility; but he recounts, for example, several later occasions on which his father attacked him violently for refusing to remove his hat or to use formal modes of address. If anything (as he himself saw it) he got off relatively lightly for his refusal of 'hat-honour'; refusal to remove their hats before

---

3 Thomas Ellwood, 1714/2011, *The History of the Life of Thomas Ellwood, Written by Himself*, ed. Rosemary Moore, New Haven, CN: Yale University Press, pp. 23–4. Ellwood is known outside Quaker circles as a pupil and friend of Milton – see Elizabeth T. McLaughlin, 1967, 'Milton and Thomas Ellwood', *Milton Quarterly* 1/2, pp. 17–28 – and among Quakers as the compiler and editor of George Fox's journal as well as the author of an influential spiritual autobiography. The account, in the latter work, of Ellwood's first day of 'plain speech' gives a vivid picture of the everyday small-scale internal and external conflicts occasioned by adherence to these early collective testimonies. Ellwood, who was obviously troubled by conflict (at least in his face-to-face relationships), braves a few meetings in order to carry out some business for his father, and then in the evening (one suspects, exhausted by the succession of difficult situations) slips into a back street to avoid encountering more people whom he would have to greet.

magistrates or other officials was the pretext for the imprisonment of several Quaker men.[4]

Early 'plaining', then, was not simply about removing any and every unnecessary ornament of speech or behaviour, but about directly opposing those 'ornaments' of speech and behaviour that tended, as the Quakers saw it, to accord undue honour to people and detract from the honour due to God – Ellwood described hat-honour as 'a great idol' (1714/2011, p. 38). More widely, Quaker testimony around truthfulness imposed discipline on speech and communication, not just for the sake of sincerity or accuracy but also out of concern for the wider social and spiritual implications of existing regimes of communication, for, as it were, the connection between small-scale untruths and social or spiritual 'big lies'. The point of truthfulness was not only to satisfy one's own conscience and achieve personal integrity by speaking in accordance with one's own beliefs; it was, rather, to bring communicative practices as a whole into correspondence with truth.

A further example of truthfulness as a social rather than (simply) an individual concern is the early insistence by Quaker shopkeepers and merchants on selling goods at fixed prices, as opposed to inviting customers to bargain. This might make most immediate sense as a simple insistence on accuracy of representation – not to claim that a thing is worth more, or less, than one believes or knows it to be worth. In the literature, however, the refusal to haggle is linked to a diagnosis of the social implications of advertising goods at inflated prices – 'deceitful merchants' in cities amass superfluous wealth by cheating 'the simple', children or 'poor country people'.[5] In the literature on fixed prices, commitment to

---

4 Ellwood, *History of the Life*, pp. 37–8. Ironically, Ellwood managed to lose all his hats rather quickly as a result of his insistent refusal to doff them (his father tended to snatch them off his head and throw them away). He caught a severe cold as a result of going around bareheaded in winter (p. 38).

5 See George Fox, 1658, *A Warning to All the Merchants in London, And Such as Buy and Sell*, London. Quakers are generally credited – following Max Weber's work – with inventing the system of fixed prices, although the reasons for its widespread adoption are complex. The social and political dimensions of the Quaker insistence on fixed prices, downplayed by Weber, are highlighted in Stephen A. Kent, 1983, 'The Quaker Ethic and the Fixed Price Policy: Max Weber and Beyond', *Sociological Inquiry* 53/1, pp. 16–32.

'the truth' draws together theological affirmation, a holistic and prophetic mode of biblical interpretation, a reading of the present situation with a particular awareness of injustice and exploitation, and a clear and specific set of injunctions for individual action. Commitment to honest dealing and in particular to fixed prices begins with affirmation of the Light of Christ in all, to be acknowledged and answered in all; the biblical injunction to merchants to 'give just weight and full measure' is mapped on to the call to be faithful to the inward 'measure' of Christ. All of this issues in a specific practice of 'denying lies' (refusing to inflate prices) that also and at the same time gives rise to new shared traditions of action and reflection.

In the story of fixed prices we have a very direct, and rather ambivalent, example of how a sustained practice of refusal – refusing to advertise goods at inflated prices, or to engage in the low-level deceit necessary for successful haggling – could result, over time, in a specific positive change, affecting not only Quakers but the wider context to which their testimony related. Fixed prices eventually emerged as a norm for many forms of trade, and eventually brought considerable economic success – following an initial period of disadvantage – for the Quaker merchants who pioneered the approach. Although this looks at first glance like the classic example of how the Protestant ethic, and the rules that governed the lives of Protestant groups, fuelled the spirit of modern capitalism, it is slightly more complicated than that.

On my reading, the insistence on fixed prices was, among other things, a specific response to a situation of social fragmentation and economic inequality – the situation in which 'poor country people' were vulnerable to exploitation by city merchants, where communities had become sufficiently fragmented for it to be possible to cheat children. The fixed price, as it emerged at least initially, was a reparative and creative social 'emergency measure', as well as a way for Quakers to reconcile their principles with their trade. It was not just an individual discipline, but a social experiment. If my proposals in the previous chapter hold good, the change in business practices and the success of fixed prices was not

TESTIMONY

quite an incidental side effect of Quakers' determination to stick consistently to their principles. Testimony, as I have portrayed it, is future-oriented and open-ended. Consistency in maintaining 'testimonies against' goes alongside actions expressing the hope for positive change.

If this is easy to see in the case of fixed prices – and to see on a rather more dramatic scale in relation to nonviolence and peace work – it is rather harder to see how the disruptive practices of 'plain speech', encountered in Thomas Ellwood's account of his life, could have anything other than a negative and critical effect. In order to be able to understand Ellwood and others like him as part of a wider shared testimony of truthfulness, I need to look more closely at the relationship between 'denying lies' and politically and socially significant truthful speech.

Speaking truth to power (1): with and beyond Michel Foucault

Michel Foucault seems an extremely unlikely ally in the attempt to understand what Quaker testimony is about. In Foucault's best-known discussion of issues relating to Quakers, he is a key critical voice. He reads the Quaker-run Retreat – revolutionary in its day among institutions for the insane – not as a benign advance of humanitarianism, but as a subtle exercise in extending and deepening social coercion and control.[6] More generally, Foucault's emphasis on regimes of truth and knowledge, as produced by and productive of systems of power, suggests a suspicious reading of any and every claim to tell the truth, to do the truth or to act in accordance with truth.[7]

---

6 Michel Foucault, 1961/2001, *Madness and Civilisation: A History of Insanity in the Age of Reason*, trans. Richard Howard, London: Routledge.

7 I am grateful to Jon Mitchell for ongoing discussions of Quakerism and Foucault, particularly in relation to the Retreat. For another use of Foucault to analyse Quaker thought and practice, see Gay Pilgrim, 2008, 'British Quakerism as Heterotopic', in Pink Dandelion and Peter Collins (eds), *The Quaker Condition: The Sociology of a Liberal Religion*, Cambridge: Cambridge Scholars Press, pp. 53–68.

SPEAKING TRUTH TO POWER

However, in Foucault's final lectures (Foucault 1984/2011) he turns directly to questions of truth-telling, and treats it as an ethical and political practice that is inextricable from particular forms of life and modes of self-formation. Looking at the classical world and the world of late antiquity, he tells a story about truthfulness that connects truthful lives with truthful speech – and both of them with counter-cultural practices of 'denying lies'. I want to suggest that his account of the 'life of truth' – particularly as reread through theological eyes by Craig Hovey, among others – provides a useful additional lens through which to read Quakerism and Quaker testimony, both in its origins and in terms of its ongoing significance.[8] At the same time, this process raises critical questions about truth-telling – particularly around the relationship between truthfulness and faith, and between the individual's commitment to a truthful life and the establishment of shared norms and understandings.

In his later lectures, Foucault focuses on the story of an ancient practice – as he puts it, a 'game' – of truth-telling. The practice is denoted by the term *parrhesia*, a term that also resonates in later discussions of Christian theology and testimony. *Parrhesia*, as Foucault describes it, is the risky action of one who calls the governing authority to account – from a position of relative powerlessness, and in a way that transgresses existing 'codes' of speech both in terms of what may be said and in terms of who is expected to speak and be heard. The *parrhesiast* interrupts the ordinary process of politics, the ordinary exercise of power, through a fundamental critique of its operating norms and assumptions. *Parrhesia* is, moreover, understood as action under obligation; the *parrhesiast* speaks out of duty, both duty to the subject matter of his or her speech (the truth that must be told) and duty to self. Ironically and significantly, *parrhesia*

---

8 Craig Hovey, 2011, *Bearing True Witness: Truthfulness in Christian Practice*, Grand Rapids, MI: Eerdmans. I discuss Foucauldian *parrhesia* and 'cynicism' in relation to contemporary questions of truth-telling in Rachel Muers, 2014, 'The Ethics of Stats: Some Contemporary Questions about Telling the Truth', *Journal of Religious Ethics* 42/1, pp. 1–21.

is often translated as 'free speech', even though in its origins it is the speech of someone who is not *supposed* to be free to speak in this way at this time: 'You risk death to tell the truth instead of reposing in the security of a life in which the truth goes unspoken' (Foucault 1983/2001).

A starting-point for exercises of *parrhesia* is the refusal of flattery; *parrhesia* pierces and contradicts flattery. Flattery, in Foucault's analysis, is not just insincere praise, but more broadly the practice of speech in which the speaker tells the powerful audience (the rulers or the mob) exactly what they want to hear – pandering to the popular will or to what the authorities expect. Flattery, as a policy, not only reinforces whatever set of problematic communicative practices already exist, but renders future acts of truth-telling both more improbable and more risky; flattery not only responds to, but also reinforces, the prejudice of the mob or the ruler's sense of self-importance.[9] The *parrhesiast*, the free-speaker or speaker of truth, by contrast, opens up new discursive or communicative space – directly in the political arena, in the pre-Socratic examples that Foucault considers, and subsequently through philosophical formation undertaken for the good of the city. The *parrhesiast* refuses to speak in the expected way, according to the existing structures of power; but instead of simply keeping quiet, he finds (in 'the truth' and in himself) a basis on which to speak and think differently.

Moving through the story of classical and late antique *parrhesia*, Foucault arrives at the figure of the Cynic – who, he argues, rather than being a 'particular, odd and ultimately forgotten figure in ancient philosophy', in fact represents 'an integral part of the history of Western thought' (1984/2011, p. 174). The Cynic as Foucault portrays him is not just someone who speaks 'freely' out of a sense of obligation to the truth and to self, but someone who *lives* freely in accordance with truth – 'life in the scandal of the truth'. He attempts, as nobody else does, to walk the talk,

---

9 Michel Foucault, 1984/2011, *Courage of Truth*, ed. F. Gros, trans G. Burchell, New York: Palgrave Macmillan, pp. 7, 39.

to manifest, embody or dramatize philosophical claims – in the case of the ancient Cynics, for example, beliefs in the 'natural', the 'pure' and the 'unconcealed' life. Cynicism, as Foucault describes it, is 'the form of philosophy which constantly raises the question: what can the form of life be such that it practices truth-telling?' (1984/2011, p. 234).

Crucially, the Cynic – again in Foucault's presentation – does not become radical or scandalous only, or mainly, through saying radical things. The Cynics are not particularly innovative in the philosophical claims they make. They are scandalous because they visibly and publicly collapse the gap between philosophical claim and lived practice. The Cynic cultivates the truthful self by disregarding social expectations (the expectations of 'rhetoric', the rules that preserve social relations) in order to live out his philosophical word. He seeks to bind *himself* to the truth of what he says.

Foucault's vision of the truth-telling life, or rather the account he gives of the Cynic's life as a truth-telling life, is grounded in denial and negation – and it directly links forward, in his speculative trans-historical account of Cynicism, to various forms of early Christian asceticism. The Cynic 'changes the value of the currency', overturns ordinary criteria for value or acceptability (Foucault 1984/2011, pp. 226–8; see the translator's footnote on the issues involved in the French and English rendition of *parakharattein*). The argument, however, is that this changing or devaluing of the social currency comes about not by arguing but by *doing* something differently – living 'an other life'.

Foucault emphasizes the 'innerworldly otherness' of truth – where truth-telling, as paradigmatically in the case of the Cynic's *parrhesia*, is about disturbing an established pattern of discourse and social relations and allowing an other to appear. The move of distancing oneself from particular regimes of speech, and one's own place within them, can be undertaken in the interests of being more fully present *in* a particular place and context. Although Foucault himself would not read this as a 'religious' move, for the Quakers and many others obedience to the call of God meant

TESTIMONY

learning to see the world differently, learning to see things and people as they are.[10]

Parrhesia appears in the New Testament in many forms – as open or public speech, as 'bold' speech, and confidence in God. Foucault himself is most interested in the texts that place *parrhesia* as boldness or confidence – free assurance – both before God and through God, which allows him to set up a contrast between Greek and Christian *parrhesia*. At the same time, as he acknowledges – and as Hovey discusses at length – the New Testament does contain numerous examples of *parrhesia* as public speech. It is hard fully to distance this, the free speech of the apostles in the public square and especially in situations of trial or controversy, from the 'free confidence' they claim before God.

Free confidence and unimpeded communion through God and with God – the 'mystic's' experience, and the experience claimed by early Quakers – is only in tension with public and prophetic 'free speech' and truthful living, if you start with the assumption that 'true godliness' has nothing to do with this world or its history. However, as I have been discussing, Quakers' understanding of divine truth – as it is encountered and lived in history – is inseparable from the call to truthful and self-involving testimony.[11]

---

10 It is fairly well established, and not very surprising, that Foucault misses a lot in his reading of Christianity. Christianity, for Foucault, departed from classical *askesis* when it linked asceticism to faith in the one God, to a truth that lies beyond the world. Christian asceticism as he reads it is not just a matter of living life in this world 'otherwise', but of living the life of 'another world'. But, as Jeremy Carette and others have argued, the sharp contrast drawn here between Cynical and Christian *askesis* is not particularly well founded nor particularly stable in terms of the complex history of Christian spiritual practice. It assumes a separation between God and the self, or between attention to God and attention to the self, that does not always apply – and, I would add, certainly does not apply to Quakers. See Jeremy Carette and James Bernauer, 2004, 'Beyond Theology and Sexuality: Foucault, the Self and the Que(e)rying of Monotheistic Truth', in Jeremy Carette and James Bernauer (eds), *Michel Foucault and Theology: The Politics of Religious Experience*, Aldershot: Ashgate, pp. 217–32.

11 For a discussion of the importance of *parrhesia* in seventeenth-century England – as a rhetorical figure for bold speech, and as a characteristic particularly associated with the Marian martyrs – see David Colclough, 2005, *Freedom of Speech in Early Stuart England*, Cambridge: Cambridge University Press, especially pp. 77–119.

SPEAKING TRUTH TO POWER

In many ways, early Quakers bear a disturbing similarity to Foucault's Cynics.[12] Consider again Thomas Ellwood's encounter with his old friends. Ellwood rather directly 'changes the value' of the social currency – the currency of hat-honour and of formal expressions of greeting. He does so not by arguing against them, but by operating according to different rules. He describes what he is doing both as a refusal – 'making no congee' – and as the consistent and principled espousal of an alternative approach to social relations, summed up in the idea of 'plain and true speech'. As he implicitly admits elsewhere in his writings, the arguments for refusing hat-honour and formal courtesy – for example, that expressions of submission and subordination are due only to God, that formal requirements for expressing respect can obscure a lack of true respect, that it is simply inaccurate to call himself anybody's 'servant' – can appear both uncontroversial and trivial. They are the sorts of claims about which his friends, or he himself in earlier years, might have said 'of course, we all believe that'. The oddity of the Quaker Thomas Ellwood, then, is not the beliefs but the decision to practise them – in a particularly consistent and contrary way that defaces the social currency and causes a breakdown in ordinary processes of exchange.

Ellwood, however, takes up his stance as part of a collective and (already) recognizable identity; when he refuses to take off his hat, his friends hail him as 'a Quaker', and when Ellwood accepts this identification he is, at least in retrospect, clear that he has through his actions located himself with a 'despised people'. He has not just indicated that he agrees in principle with Quaker beliefs; he has made himself part of a community. This decisively affects the significance of his action – for him, for his interlocutors and for

---

12 There are some intriguing precedents to this link between Quakers and Cynics. In Thomas Brown's bitterly satirical 'Letters from the Dead to the Living' (1760, *Works of Mr Thomas Brown, serious and comical*, Vol. 2, London: Henderson, pp. 7–8), Diogenes the Cynic is imagined in the land of the dead alongside the 'modern cynicks' Fox and Naylor [*sic*]; all three have been completely transformed and have 'set up for fops'. Much more positively, though still in satirical vein, Thomas Carlyle (1836, *Sartor Resartus*), in the voice of the narrator Teufelsdröckh, praises George Fox as 'greater than Diogenes' (pp. 167–9) – on the basis of Fox's famous home-made leather breeches.

later readers. The refusal to exchange the ordinary social currency was linked to the formation of a new social group – within which, communication that used the 'plain and true speech' was a matter of course, and new forms of organization and patterns of authority were being developed. Ellwood was not just part of a rebellion against 'the way things were'; he was engaged in a sustained experiment in doing things differently.

This does not mean that his Quaker formation was strong enough to make his testimony against acknowledgement of social rank easy or automatic. He was not acting from inside a particularly well-developed and confident counter-culture. There was, at this point, not much safe social or ecclesial space into which he or other Quakers could retreat in order to work out a plan of action – and not much interest in forming or defending such safe space. As I noted in the previous chapter, the core community-forming activity, the meeting for worship, was often held in public even in the face of occasional legal sanctions or officially sanctioned disruption. Quaker experiments in 'life otherwise' – and the intense disagreements among Quakers themselves that arose in the course of these experiments – were frequently conducted in public; but they were not conducted by lone heroes striking out solitary paths.[13] When Thomas Carlyle expressed his admiration for George Fox (in an earlier text connecting Quakers and Cynics), he was attracted to the strange 'life otherwise', the desire to act and live truthfully regardless of the social consequences, set out by one individual. But alongside the many stories of extreme, aggressive, costly or puzzling individual 'testimony against' the present order – besides Fox's own – the story of early and subsequent Quakerism needs to be told as a story of 'being gathered', receiving and forming a common life that sustained, formed and made sense of testimony. This is important if only to do justice to what the Quakers themselves said about what was happening.

---

13 Ellwood was himself in due course a major voice in intra-Quaker as well as external controversies.

SPEAKING TRUTH TO POWER

Speaking truth to power (2): experimenting and wasting time

Quakers and others are often, in my experience, rather disappointed when they learn that one of their favourite Quaker phrases – and one of the phrases most quoted outside Quakerism – has a very short pedigree. 'Speak Truth to Power' is the main title of a pamphlet published by the American Friends Service Committee in 1955.[14] It is now particularly closely associated with Bayard Rustin, one of the authors of the pamphlet and a leader in the civil rights movement, who used it in letters and speeches in the course of his many campaigns.[15] Although the authors of the pamphlet tie it quite specifically to 'a charge given to Eighteenth Century Friends' and then in the final section implicitly to the seventeenth century, it appears nowhere before 1955.

However, 'speaking truth to power' has been taken up subsequently, both as a good summary of a characteristically Quaker approach and as a description of Quaker activism at various specific points.[16] Noam Chomsky – himself at one point associated strongly with 'speaking truth to power' because of his classic articulation of the public truth-telling role of the intellectual – could say in 2000, 'My Quaker friends and colleagues in disrupting illegitimate authority adopt the slogan: "Speak truth to power"', and goes on to explain why he disagreed with this 'Quaker' position.[17] The phrase has found other homes well beyond Quaker contexts in the late twentieth century, being taken

---

14 American Friends Service Committee (AFSC), 1955/2012, *Speak Truth to Power: A Quaker Search for an Alternative to Violence – A Study of International Conflict*, Philadelphia, PA: American Friends Service Committee.

15 I deliberately highlight Rustin here among the authors, because he was one of those who used the phrase 'speaking truth to power' elsewhere, but also because his name was omitted from the original published list of authors – chiefly at his own request, and because as an openly gay man recently convicted on a 'morals charge' he did not wish to attract adverse publicity to the document or to AFSC. Restoring his name to the list in later editions of *Speak Truth to Power* not only enabled his work to be recognized, but also drew attention to the many levels of his struggle to 'speak truth'.

16 See, for example, the discussion of 'speaking truth to power' in Nancy Black Sagafi-nejad, 2011, *Friends at the Bar: A Quaker View of Law, Conflict Resolution, and Legal Reform*, Albany, NY: SUNY Press, p. 69.

17 Noam Chomsky, 2000, *Chomsky on Miseducation*, ed. Donaldo Macedo, New York: Rowman and Littlefield. See also Noam Chomsky, 1969, *American Power and the New Mandarins*, New York: Random House.

TESTIMONY

up for example by Edward Said in his Reith Lectures; but for many it still carries strong associations with Quaker activism.

Why should this be so? I want to understand 'speaking truth to power' by looking again at the characteristics I highlighted of *parrhesia* as Foucault describes it – truthful speech that evades or challenges a particular structure of power, that refuses to say what is expected and instead says what needs to be said. This will prove to be easier once we examine the pamphlet itself in more detail, and the theological claims that underlie it.

It is easy, in fact, to be misled by the simple slogan into too limited an understanding of what Bayard Rustin and his colleagues are talking about. The refusal to alter or moderate one's speech for the status of the person addressed – which we saw above in Ellwood's refusal of hat-honour – feeds into a long and well-remembered tradition of Quaker appeals and approaches to the 'powerful', particularly in circumstances where they had no pre-established right of access or structures that assured them a hearing. Famous, for example, are Mary Fisher's journey to preach to the Sultan of Turkey, or Joseph Sturge's delegation to Tsar Nicholas II in an attempt to prevent the Crimean War. Direct attempts to appeal to those who hold power – by whatever direct or indirect means become available – continue to form a staple of Quaker activism.[18]

---

18 An incidental tribute to the effectiveness of this approach – in drawing attention to Quakers and their concerns, if perhaps not in actually changing anyone's mind – appeared in an aside in the UK Parliament Home Affairs Select Committee's hearings on changes to marriage legislation:

Q 267 Tim Loughton (East Worthing and Shoreham) (Con): Can I just explore the Quaker position a bit, Mr Bartlet? I am not as familiar with it as perhaps I should be, particularly as I have a group of Quaker constituents who are persistent in writing to me on a regular basis about all manner of things . . .

. . . What is your relationship with, and what is the Quaker view of – in my experience of dealing with the Quakers, it is slightly different from that of other religions – the Government, the role of Government, and how beholden you are to Government?

Michael Bartlet (Quaker Parliamentary Liaison Officer): Thank you. That is a very good question. Since the time of the Commonwealth, Quakers have always had a relationship with Government that has not been entirely easy . . . (UK Parliament, 2013, *Proceedings of the Public Committee hearings on the Marriage (Same-Sex Couples) Bill*, Thursday 14 February).

SPEAKING TRUTH TO POWER

The obvious criticism – which was certainly made of Joseph Sturge and his colleagues – of this strand of 'speaking truth to power' is that it has more to do with clearing one's conscience than with genuinely responsible action. There is a fine line between actions like theirs and futile hand-wringing, by people who hold their principles dear, who find it relatively easy to advocate these principles to everyone, and who deceive themselves into believing that 'power' can be brought round to their point of view simply by rational argument. This is why Chomsky argues that speaking truth to power is 'not a particularly honourable vocation', because those in power generally already know the 'truth' – about the unjust or destructive effects of their actions – and have decided to carry on regardless:

> The audience is entirely wrong, and the effort hardly more than a form of self-indulgence. It is a waste of time and a pointless pursuit to speak truth to Henry Kissinger, or the CEO of General Motors, or others who exercise power in coercive institutions – truths that they already know well enough, for the most part. (Chomsky 2000, p. 21)

One response to this criticism, bearing the previous chapter's discussion in mind, would be to question whether effectiveness is the only criterion by which a 'vocation' (such as speaking truth to power) can be judged. To follow the guidance of the Holy Spirit – whether to 'utterly deny' established methods for gaining and keeping power, or to engage in largely silent unprogrammed worship as a precondition for doing anything at all – is, on the face of it, to commit oneself to wasting a lot of time. At least, it wastes time to the same extent that the woman who anoints Jesus' feet wastes ointment and money.

Another response, however, which engages more with the substance of the critique, would be to give a fuller account of the set of practices that constitute and sustain 'speaking truth to power' – and hence help to demonstrate, again along the lines of the previous chapter, that there is an 'effective' testimony here as well as, or rather than, a self-indulgent affirmation of unshakeable principles. Both the account I have sketched of *parrhesia* and the history of Quaker testimony help to show how this fuller account emerges from the original pamphlet *Speak Truth to Power*. The core claim of the pamphlet, speaking to the context of the Cold War, is that 'the urgent need is not to preach religious truth, but to show how it is possible and why it is reasonable to give practical expression to it' (p. iv). Adherence, at least on some level, to certain 'religious truths' – as, for example, that 'love endures and overcomes, that hatred destroys' – is assumed. The audience are mostly – to switch back to the terms of seventeenth-century Quakers – *professors* of Christian faith. The point of the document is not to repeat back to the audience the truth that they already 'profess', or even a truth that they have already heard and might or might not accept. The point is to draw attention to the gap between profession and current practice, *and*, crucially, to propose practical experiments, to be undertaken individually and collectively.

Moreover, the intended audience is not only 'those who hold high places in our national life' but also 'the American people who are the final reservoir of power in this country'. Although the pamphlet frequently appeals to the democratic ideal and to democratic processes, this shift of focus away from those who 'hold high places' has deeper implications for the relationship between truth and power. The aim is to confront and transform how power is understood. The nation as a whole is called to repentance as turning about, *teshuvah*.

The authors of *Speak Truth to Power*, having decided not to 'preach religious truth' or to restate a pacifist position, call for 'thought and experimentation that begin with the unconditional rejection of organized mass violence'. Throughout the document, the call to an 'ultimate and fundamental break with violence' (p. 53) that will 'liberate' individuals and states to act responsibly resonates alongside the careful and surprisingly frequent affirmation that this is not primarily a debate about pacifism, Christian or otherwise. The key is *nonviolence* as the basis of a process of social change, rather than pacifism as a principled position that might (depending on the circumstances) never make much difference to what a person actually did. Perhaps surprisingly, nonviolence – a 'negative testimony', a refusal – is shown to be more practical than pacifism; the decision for nonviolence, on the individual, social or national scale, demands that one finds alternatives. It is not just low pragmatism – the desire to keep as many people as possible on their side and engaged with their arguments – that leads these American Quakers repeatedly to state that they are not asking everyone to become pacifists, or that they expect their call to find resonances well beyond pacifist circles. They are, in fact, aligning themselves with the tradition of testimony that goes back at least as far as the Declaration to Charles II. 'As to [their] own particulars' they renounce violence, acting on their discernment of the guidance of the Holy Spirit and thus of the truth at the heart of every historical story and situation. What matters fundamentally is not that others make similar statements of renunciation 'in principle', but that others are 'liberated' to follow the same guidance, to engage in the same exploration, to 'learn peace by practicing peace' (p. 54).

Bayard Rustin's central involvement in the production of the document draws attention to the public, political and confrontational nonviolence of the civil rights movement as a possible example of the kind of 'experiment' for which the document calls. Speaking truth to power, as it appears in this document and in the context of the work undertaken by Rustin and others who put it together, is 'speaking truth' in a way that engages and transforms structures of power. Nonviolence – including the central importance of community, attention to the seeds of violence and conflict in everyday life, and the 'voluntary acceptance of suffering' (p. 42) – appears in the document as a coherent 'philosophy' grounded on Christian faith and tested to some extent in previous and present generations; but it also appears as a risky and open-ended experiment, of which none of the results are guaranteed. It is 'no calculated risk . . . [but] an uncalculated risk in living by the claims of the Kingdom' (p. 69). This in turn – the uncertainty of the approaches being advocated, by contrast with the security supposedly offered by military superiority – points towards a radically different understanding of 'power'. Nonviolence is, as presented, a powerful practice; but its 'power' encompasses a willingness to fail and a readiness to suffer. The 'free speech' of people who speak truth to power is not backed by force.

This emerging alternative account of power also helps to explain the binary oppositions evident in this and in so many other Quaker polemical writings. There is language that resonates with the Johannine oppositions of light and darkness, truth and lies. But, as by now we might expect, there is also a concerted effort to break down the oppositions (for example, between civilized and barbaric peoples, or between the free and the unfree nations) that organize and justify an existing regime of power. By advocating experiments in practical nonviolence, rather than bringing in another pair of opposites – we the pacifists, over against them the militarists – the authors introduce an opposition or a choice that potentially affects every person and every situation – the choice to rely on force or to risk an alternative. Once again, what is portrayed is not a battle between two equivalent forces, but the 'battle' between a destructive pattern of continued and repeated fights to the death, on the one hand, and the promised and revealed fullness of creaturely flourishing, on the other.

Speak Truth to Power drew on a long history of Quaker 'experiments' in nonviolence, concluding with William Penn's famous 'holy experiment' at the founding of Pennsylvania. The brief history of that experiment given by Rustin and his fellow authors (p. 44) focuses on the decision by Penn and his companions to agree terms with the original inhabitants of the land before, rather than after, the settlement, and to go and live unarmed throughout the earliest years of the colony. There is realism about the limited effects of this policy, the strains under which it was placed by later developments, and the equivocal (at best) outcomes for 'the American Indian'.

There is even more realism when the authors acknowledge elsewhere the repeated failures of Quaker collective discernment, the long time it took Quakers to become fully engaged in anti-slavery causes, the numerous less than glorious counter-examples to every example of 'speaking truth to power'. In the context of a text that is not intended to be an apology for Quakerism, nor for Christian pacifism, this realism tends in fact to strengthen the case. Obviously *parrhesia*, either as free assurance or as free speech, does not rely on appearing to be perfect or appearing to be right. Even more importantly in this context, highlighting the ambivalent results and the wrong turnings in the history of Quaker 'experiments' makes it even clearer that this is about the risky following of leadings rather than about the implementation of a settled policy – and certainly not about ending up on the right side of an argument or even the right side of the history books.

The authors of *Speak Truth to Power*, like numerous Quaker predecessors, are not indifferent to the effects or to the success of their work. 'We do not fear death, but we want to live, and we want our children to live', they write (p. 70). They express deep anxieties about the likely effects of present policies, and the urgency of their appeal is linked to a detailed reading of the signs of the times that maps prophetic language and categories on to the present. But they do not rest the truth of their claims either on the capacity of anyone to follow the experiment of nonviolence faithfully or on a future positive change that this experiment might bring about.

'Answering that of God in every one': how speaking truth is effective

There still seems to be a gap, however, between this kind of persuasive 'speaking truth to power' and the confrontational 'testimonies against' discussed in this and in previous chapters. What are we really saying about the effectiveness of testimony – an effectiveness that is real and specific and makes sense, but is also unpredictable and beyond the control of those who give it? We can make better sense of this unpredictable effectiveness, I think, if we hold together the communicative and the practical aspects of testimony. Testimony is life, but it is life that speaks; it is speech, but it is speech that 'lives' in a particular context. It is *truthful* action, not just 'correct' action. And speech, communicative action, is 'effective' most obviously when it is heard, recognized and acted upon. For testimony to be 'effective', it needs to find a hearer; it needs to be persuasive; it needs to call forth a response that is a genuine interpretation of this testimony, making sense of it. And the interpretation of testimony will, like the testimony itself, be contingent, located, embodied and enacted; it will also be a kind of truthful action.

Now, as I have suggested, Quaker tradition has a specific set of resources, and a specific set of underlying assumptions, for thinking about how testimony is heard and responded to. The core commitment to the universal Light of Christ and to the power of the Holy Spirit to 'lead into all truth' appears as an explicit theme only tangentially in *Speak Truth to Power*, but taken as an underlying assumption it deepens our reading of the document and of Quaker testimony still further. I have already suggested that beliefs concerning the 'Light that enlightens everyone' gave impetus to Quaker preaching and to making 'lives speak' in every possible situation. Everyone without exception had the divinely given capacity to respond to the truth when they heard or saw it, to recognize and turn away from death-dealing patterns of life, and to find and follow their 'Guide'. The general appeal – 'speaking truth to power' by calling on everyone to refuse or deny lies, speaking to a wide and general audience of the effective power of 'redemptive love' – works, not only because of a general prior knowledge the audience has of Christianity, but because each member of the audience can receive, attend to and be changed by the gracious presence of divine truth.

We can approach this question of testimony's communicative effectiveness through the idea of 'answering that of God in every one', taken from a particularly well-known letter of George Fox:

> Be patterns, be examples in all countries, places, islands, nations, wherever you come, that your carriage and life may preach among all sorts of people, and to them; then you will come to walk cheerfully over the world, answering that of God in every one. (Fox 1694/1952, p. 263; *QF&P* 19.32)

SPEAKING TRUTH TO POWER

Testimony, this passage suggests, becomes effective in 'answering that of God in every one'. 'Speaking truth to power' in Quaker tradition works not just because the speaker has free confidence before God, but because truthful speech 'answers', corresponds to, the hearer's own God-given capacity for discernment and transformation. So it makes sense, finds a hearing, changes things – because what looks like a risky and isolated initiative turns out to be an *answer*, a fitting response, to what is already going on. God is already at work 'in all places, peoples, islands, nations'. Testimony does not initiate or provoke the movement of God to humanity nor the drawing of humanity back towards God; it 'answers' that movement, responds to it fittingly, enters into relationship with it. But – and this is the rather counter-intuitive dimension of Quaker testimony – exactly what testimony 'answers' and exactly what it means to 'answer' is only discovered by making the experiment.[19]

Again it is important to balance this experience and promise of 'answering that of God in every one' with the recognition that testimony matters even if nothing comes back – even if it apparently meets with no success, as if there is nothing there to 'answer'. Testimony is first and foremost an 'answer' to the guidance or promptings of God for oneself – in Luke Cock's words, following 'each of you ... your own Guide' (Cock 1721/1842, p. 279; see *QF&P* 20.22).[20] Repentance, turning around, refusing to continue along the same course, is the first way in which testimony 'answers'

---

[19] Jeffrey Dudiak, Corey Beals and others have identified possible connections here (and indeed elsewhere in Quaker ethics) with the thought of Emmanuel Levinas. See the essays in *Quaker Religious Thought* 114 and 115. I suggested in response to their work that 'testimony' might be a fruitful area for further reflection on the relationship between Levinas and Quaker theological ethics: Rachel Muers, 2010, 'Levinas, Quakers and the (in)visibility of God: Responses to Jeffrey Dudiak and Corey Beals', *Quaker Religious Thought* 114, article 6. The response from Jeffrey Dudiak, 2010, 'Response to Muers and Wood', *Quaker Religious Thought* 115, article 5, adds the important corrective that Quaker thought does not *begin* with ethics.

[20] The sermon by Luke Cock from which this quotation is taken – recorded in several slightly different forms – gives a striking account of how corporately maintained testimony shaped an individual's life over time; Cock's attention to his own 'Guide' (which certainly appears as a 'light that pushes me') causes him over several years to 'speak the truth from [my] heart', to 'bear my testimony in using the plain language', to 'bear my testimony against tithes', and to 'bear testimony to the Hand that had done all this'.

the movement of God to humanity and the drawing of humanity back towards God. And this 'answer', this faithful response, does not depend on anything beyond individual calling and convincement. So, Thomas Ellwood's decision not to raise his hat – to go back to the early, odd and everyday example with which this chapter began – was not based on any assumptions about the response he would find or the effects he would have.

On the other hand, his actions did 'answer' something in his contemporaries. His actions were on some level intelligible – not just marking him out as a Quaker, but communicating something about Quaker experience and principles, and as such they were recognizably challenging in specific ways, and not merely odd. (Ellwood's father, for instance, 'read' them quite accurately as a direct challenge to paternal/patriarchal authority.) And in at least some cases, even of early Quaker testimony and even among those who would not or could not join the movement, the response to enacted testimony such as Ellwood's was not violent rejection, but active consideration or co-operation.

It is important, also – and in keeping with a broader sweep of Quaker writing about testimony – that the reference is to 'answering' that of God *in every one*. The work of God in the world 'already there' was encountered through people. 'Answering that of God in every one' might look like being understood, being accepted, being read rightly, being interpreted or taken up in a way that is effective. And this in turn suggests that the effectiveness of testimony as communication – the fact that it is understood, taken up, made meaningful, imitated, re-narrated, argued about – is itself part of the work of the Holy Spirit 'guiding into all truth'.

On this account, testimony is 'true' not just as a set of brute facts – this is the way the world is going, whether anyone likes it or not – but as fullness of meaning; and the work of God in the world is not just 'changing things' but making sense, revealing the full glory of God in the full flourishing of created and redeemed life. The leading edge of salvation history – as I described the location of testimony in an earlier chapter – does not advance by just 'making things happen' but by 'answering', by being understood and by calling forth response. Testimony enters into the movement of 'answering', free response to the non-coercive call of God; and in itself it 'answers' or reflects something of the pattern of divine communication, something of the pattern of revelation in Christ. As I have presented it, testimony is nonviolent self-involving communication that 'wins' by persuasion, that is, by offering itself to be interpreted and misinterpreted. It is in 'the spirit of Christ' not only by leading people to imitate Christ but by being caught up in a Christ-shaped movement of communication and interpretation – the Spirit guiding into all truth.

James Nayler's last words, following the (apparent) disastrous failure of his own lived testimony, capture from his experience some of the implications of living and testifying in this Christ-shaped movement of communication:

> There is a spirit which I feel that delights to do no evil, nor to revenge any wrong, but delights to endure all things, in hope to enjoy its own in the end . . . Its crown is meekness, its life is everlasting love unfeigned; it takes its kingdom with entreaty and not with contention, and keeps it by lowliness of mind . . . I found it alone, being forsaken. I have fellowship therein with them who lived in dens and desolate places of the earth, who through death obtained this resurrection and eternal holy life. (Nayler 1660/1716; *QF&P* 19.12)

The 'spirit' Nayler finds is recognizably Christ-shaped – and also recognizably the spirit in which *he* finds he is able to act and live, 'in fellowship' with past and present sufferers and saints. Taking a kingdom 'with entreaty but not with contention' recalls again how testimony is offered to interpretation and becomes effective through interpretation. Without 'contention' or superior force, all that is available is 'entreaty' and the precarious trust that this action or speech 'answers' something in another person. The 'entreaty' of testimony is not necessarily (just) a polite request – but it might be the kind of 'entreaty' that ends many of the Quaker polemical texts (including Nayler's), or the kind of direct appeal to readers that occasionally breaks through 'Speak Truth to Power' – or the unspoken entreaty of Thomas Ellwood to his erstwhile friends to consider what he is doing.

In fact, the 'here and now' of testimony – the immediacy of its appeal, the focus of attention on what needs to be said and done in the present moment – means that it *has* to rely on others for its interpretation and reception. Ellwood, Nayler and Fisher do what they are given to do in the present moment; they have no 'space' in which to plan or predict its effects, and they do not really understand what it means. The paradigm case, familiar to many with experience of Quaker worship, is spoken ministry in a context of unprogrammed silent worship.

All of this suggests – finally – that the unspoken third term in 'speaking truth to power' is love. The connection of truth and love prevents testimony from being simply a waste of time, a self-indulgent adherence to principle, or an exercise in being awkward for the sake of it. 'Truth' given its full weight and scope in Quaker tradition – the truth of the world created and loved by God, the presence of Christ to and for all, the guiding and gathering activity of the Holy Spirit – is inseparable from love. 'Speaking truth to power' does not end in a stand-off because 'speaking truth' challenges and transforms the terms on which power is held. The priority given to action, in Quaker understandings of testimony, also puts the emphasis on the form and manner of communication. We might say that there simply is no 'speaking truth', no genuine testimony, if it is incompatible with love. This will be a principle worth bearing in mind in the consideration of the 'case studies' that follow in the next few chapters.

4

'Swear not at all': *Oaths, Nonviolence and Conscience*

Conscientious cranks

The initial focus of this chapter is an extended case study of a specific Quaker 'negative testimony' that relates closely to speaking truth – the refusal to swear oaths, particularly religious oaths. I move to this case study at this stage, in part, because it offers a particularly clear illustration of many of the claims I have already made about testimony. It is a sustained, storied and community-defining tradition of practice; it makes sense, at least in its earliest forms, in the context of a 'here and now' prophetic and christocentric reading of biblical texts; it is primarily negative, and oppositional or conflictual in character, although it relates closely to a range of positive moves for individual and social change; and it is related, albeit in ways that are not immediately obvious, to nonviolence and to the responsibility to 'answer' God in everyone.

Besides illustrating several of the suggestions that I have already made about testimony, the case of the refusal of oaths points us back to the deep historical connections between Quakers, on the one hand, and Anabaptist – and here also Baptist – traditions. Engaging with some Anabaptist and Baptist writings on oaths – both historical and contemporary – allows us to see more clearly both the 'family resemblances' and the subtle differences of emphasis. A key difference of emphasis is around the use and understanding

TESTIMONY

of 'conscience' – a pivotal term in many early modern writings on oaths.[1] Towards the end of this chapter, then, I consider the relationship between objections to oaths and 'conscientious objection', as it is now understood. I suggest that reading 'conscientious objection' within the history of Quaker testimony provides an important theological, and indeed political, perspective that is often neglected in contemporary debates about conscientious objection – by putting the 'cranks', as they have recently been described, back into the communities of practice and reflection that sustain their individual protests.[2]

Quakers and oaths: an overview

[They] gave me the book to swear on, and the book saith, Swear not at all: But I told them, if they could prove that after Christ Jesus and his apostles had forbidden men to swear, they had allowed it, I would swear. Thus I said, and my allegiance lies in truth and faithfulness, not in swearing, and so should all your allegiance lie, if you did well. I do not deny swearing on some account, and own it upon others, but I deny it, because Christ and the apostle have said, I should not swear at all. (Fox 1694/1952, p. 485; see *QF&P* 19.37)

Taking oaths implies a double standard of truth; in choosing to affirm instead, be aware of the claim to integrity you are making. (*QF&P* 1.02.37)

The refusal to swear oaths could well be the most consistent feature of Quaker testimony – apart, that is, from the holding of public meetings for worship. It looks likely that Quakers consistently and

---

[1] In my work on Quakers and oaths I have been much helped by discussions with Mel Prideaux and Frank Cranmer, and by Steve Holmes and other participants in a research seminar at the University of St Andrews.

[2] For the media debate following the description of conscientious objectors as 'cranks' in a high-profile television documentary, see Charlotte Meredith, 2014, 'Jeremy Paxman Brands Conscientious Objectors of WW1 "Cranks"', *Huffington Post*, 2 February, http://www.huffingtonpost.co.uk/2014/02/04/jeremy-paxman-britains-great-war-cranks_n_4721895.html.

'SWEAR NOT AT ALL'

collectively refused to swear oaths before they consistently and collectively refused to fight. A declaration of a 'testimony against swearing' by 'those whom the world calls Quakers' was published in 1654[3] – some years before the Declaration to Charles II – and there are numerous accounts of the practice and consequences of refusing oaths from the earliest decades of Quakerism.[4] The 'testimony against oaths' appears, sometimes but not always in those words, in all the books of extracts and books of discipline published by Yearly Meeting in Britain over the years; and the 1994 *Quaker Faith and Practice* assumes, with rather little discussion (see above), that Quakers will normally refuse to take an oath in a court of law or any other context in which it might be required.

Today, in Britain or elsewhere, with the swearing of formal oaths a relatively rare occurrence and with alternatives readily available, this looks like a quaint and unimportant oddity. Historically, however, the refusal to swear oaths was a Quaker testimony that carried significant cost. It was, for example, the focus of the state persecution specifically directed against Quakers in the so-called Quaker Act of 1662 – properly the 'Act for Preventing the Mischeifs [*sic*] and Dangers that may arise by certain Persons called Quakers and others refusing to take lawfull Oaths'.[5] Even before and outwith the Quaker Act, Quakers' refusal to swear oaths was frequently used against them in legal settings, and was often at least the pretext for imprisonment and other punishments.

In Britain, the refusal to swear oaths, either in public and state contexts or in making private arrangements, continued to place Quakers at numerous legal and social disadvantages – over and above those experienced in England by all non-Anglicans – until

---

3 Anonymous (sometimes attributed to George Fox), 1654, *The Glorie of the Lord Arising, Shaking Terribly the Earth, and Overturning All . . . Also a Testimony from the Lord against Swearing, with a Word to the Heads of the Nation, and the Judges of Life and Death, by those whom the world calls Quakers*, London: Giles Calvert.

4 See for a range of examples Richard Bauman, 1983, *Let Your Words Be Few: Symbolism of Speaking and Silence among Seventeenth-Century Quakers*, New York: Cambridge University Press.

5 'An Act for Preventing the Mischeifs [sic] and Dangers that may arise by certaine Persons called Quakers and others refusing to take lawfull Oaths', 1662. *Statutes of the Realm: volume 5: 1628–80*, pp. 350–1.

the second half of the nineteenth century. Various public offices, including that of Member of Parliament, were closed to those who would not swear (what would now be called) an oath of office; and it could be difficult either for Quakers, or indeed for anyone who relied on Quakers' evidence, to secure legal redress for wrongs done to them.[6] The use of oaths to seal business and other transactions was also sufficiently common, at least in the early eighteenth century, that the refusal of oaths could significantly restrict Quakers' capacity to engage in trade. The acceptance of oaths as a basic and necessary component of social relations, in the context from which Quakers originated, is demonstrated by what happened when the Quaker leaders of Pennsylvania banned the imposition of oaths; the non-Quaker inhabitants were so disturbed by this removal of the ordinary safeguards of justice and public order that they petitioned the King to reverse the prohibition.[7]

The Quaker Act and the publication of the 1654 'testimony against all swearing' reflect the fact that the refusal to swear oaths was, from an early stage, collectively owned by Quakers as a community-defining practice, and generally recognized from the outside as something characteristic of Quakers. In this it was rather like the plain speech discussed in the previous chapter – but even more easily identifiable and nameable as a 'Quaker' characteristic, because it involved non-cooperation with a specific official demand. In the succession of legal measures from 1696 until the mid-nineteenth century, which opened up the option of affirming rather than swearing an oath, exemptions were in the first instance specifically limited to Quakers (and to one or two other groups); the refusal of oaths was associated so strongly with identifiable religious affiliation that no broader provision was deemed necessary or indeed advisable.[8]

---

6 For an insight into this, see Edwina Newman, 2007, 'Children of Light and Sons of Darkness: Quakers, Oaths and the Old Bailey Proceedings in the Eighteenth Century', *Quaker Studies* 12/1, pp. 73–88.

7 Andrew R. Murphy, 2003, *Conscience and Community: Revisiting Toleration in Early Modern England and America*, University Park, PA: Penn State University Press, p. 203.

8 Moravians and Separatists, who also refused oaths on religious principle, were likewise granted specific exemption.

'SWEAR NOT AT ALL'

The refusal to swear oaths was also, from an early stage, a matter in relation to which community oversight was exercised and collective discernment sought in order to resolve hard cases – even though at first sight it might seem a relatively straightforward pattern of conduct to implement, with few grey areas. A particularly conspicuous hard case arose in 1699, a mere ten years after freedom of worship was granted to Quakers and other Nonconformists. John Archdale became the first Quaker to be elected as a Member of Parliament. A contemporary (non-Quaker) observer records what happened next:

> The Quakers of this town held a general meeting, at which William Penn was president, and they considered whether Mr Archdale could in conscience take the oaths, in order to sit in the House of Commons as a Member, and after several debates, they resolved that he could not.[9]

Archdale, following this decision by the local meeting, requested permission of the Speaker and Parliament to replace the oath with a solemn affirmation – an option that had recently been opened up to Quakers involved in civil legal cases. He was refused permission to affirm, and left without taking up his seat. Archdale's apparent willingness to seek and accept a collective decision about how to take forward the testimony against oaths, in this unprecedented situation, reflects the seriousness with which the issue was taken.[10] It was a matter of collective and community-defining testimony.

---

9 Sir William Cook to Thornhagh Gurdon, 12 Jan. 1698[–9], Suffolk Record Office (Ipswich), Gurdon manuscripts 142; cited by Eveline Cruikshanks and Stuart Handley, 2002, 'John Archdale', in D. Hayton, E. Cruikshanks and S. Handley (eds), *The History of Parliament: The House of Commons 1690–1715*, Martlesham: Boydell and Brewer, http://www.historyofparliamentonline.org/volume/1690-1715/member/archdale-john-1642-1717.

10 It was more than 130 years before Joseph Pease became the first Quaker MP to take his seat. The concessions agreed for Pease and other Quaker MPs – and subsequently, in 1858 after far more discussion and far more delay, for Lord Rothschild as a Jewish MP-elect – were referred to frequently in subsequent debates about the admission of the self-declared atheist Charles Bradlaugh to Parliament, and in due course the opening to all MPs-elect of the choice to affirm loyalty rather than to swear a religious oath.

TESTIMONY

A larger-scale example of collective deliberation on a hard case, in relation to the swearing of oaths, is the very extended national debate among Quakers over the proposed form of the 'solemn affirmation' that was introduced to meet their concerns – a debate that even William Braithwaite, the famous historian of Quakerism, described after many pages of detail as a 'tedious tale'.[11] I will say something more about the content of this discussion later, but for the moment we should simply note that it was judged to be important enough to occupy the time and energy of Quakers nationally for many years.

Thinking through the refusal of oaths

How ought the persistent refusal of oaths by Quakers to be understood and assessed? Why did this particular issue matter so much?

I am not going to try to systematize or harmonize all the reasons why Quakers refused and continue to refuse oaths. Even if it were possible to give a single coherent account of the theological arguments used by all the early Quakers to explain their refusal to take oaths, and to relate this in some positive way to what subsequent generations of Quakers have said, this would not mean that all the other different ways in which Quakers have talked about or explained the practice were 'wrong'. Testimonies, as I am presenting them here, are sustained traditions of practice that make sense in many different ways. They generate creative rereadings and reinterpretations in theology, in political and ethical debate, and in further action; they 'answer' many different contexts, in thought as well as in individual and social life.

This is particularly clear in relation to oaths, right from the beginning. It can be bewildering to see how many arguments are used even in the early Quaker literature on oaths. At least some commentators assume without discussion that Quakers refused to swear oaths just because they took Matthew 5.33–37 and James

---

11 W. C. Braithwaite, 1921/1961, *The Second Period of Quakerism*, 2nd edn, Cambridge: Cambridge University Press, pp. 182–204, here p. 204.

5.12, maximally interpreted, as instructions to be obeyed in all circumstances: 'Do not swear at all.' This is partly true, and can be backed up from Quaker writings (not least from the quotation from Fox's journal, above). But it is equally true that Quakers refused oaths because they thought that oaths were empty religious ceremonies – obsolete liturgical forms – dispensed with in the new age inaugurated by Christ. It is also true that they refused oaths because they were committed to truthfulness in all circumstances, without double standards or special considerations of time and place – on similar lines to the practice of 'plain speech', discussed in the previous chapter, that refused double standards of courtesy or respect. It is also true that early Quakers deplored the illogicality of oaths, which place barriers in front of the conscientious person but can do nothing about those who are prepared to 'swear and lie'.

In fact, the earliest Quaker literature on oaths is like a snowball, gathering more and more layers of reflection and argument – and culminating in the enormous compendium *A Treatise of Oaths* presented to the King and Parliament by William Penn (and others) in 1675, and giving every reason that can possibly be thought of for refusing to swear an oath.[12]

To complicate matters further, Quaker texts on oaths, at least in the early years, tend to be aimed at specific non-Quaker audiences or sets of arguments. They are either polemics or apologetics, rather than internal 'teaching' texts. They result from the desire to explain the refusal of oaths to a non-Quaker audience, in order to challenge and perhaps mitigate the harsh response of that audience to Quakers' practice. Penn's enormous treatise on oaths was composed mainly to persuade the King and Parliament to accommodate the 'tender consciences' of Quakers and others who refused to swear oaths. Penn and his co-authors introduce the pamphlet as 'containing several weighty reasons why the people called Quakers refuse to swear' – but there is a question

---

12   William Penn and Richard Richardson, 1675, *A Treatise of Oaths, containing several weighty reasons why the people call'd Quakers refuse to swear*, London.

about how and where the reasons carry 'weight'. Many of them work better as external justification – why it might be all right to refuse oaths – than as credible accounts of why anyone would actually decide to refuse an oath in the first place. So, to give the most obvious example – quotations from classical authors might, perhaps, help to persuade classically educated outsiders that the Quakers' position had some rational justification (although at times the honest reader has to admit that Penn seems to be more interested in showing off his own erudition than in making the case stronger). But the views of classical authors would not be recognized by Quakers, before or since, as explaining why they, the Quakers, adopted that position, and stuck to it in the face of considerable pressure to change.

So, if we started out with the assumption that a move like the refusal of oaths is the result of putting a belief, or set of beliefs, into practice, Quaker texts on oaths would present us with a puzzle. These texts seem to assume the fact – already, apparently, obvious to the authors of the 1654 *Testimony against all Swearing* – that certain people (including, but not limited to, Quakers) simply 'could not swear'. That fact is (it seems) not to be argued with; the only question is what to do with it and how to make sense of it, how to respond to it in thought or in practice. The (negative) practice comes first; the theological or anthropological or ethical explanation comes later. As we saw in earlier chapters, the sustained tradition of practice generates interpretations from those who own it and live it, as they reason about it in different contexts and with different interlocutors. In the refusal of oaths, as in other instances of testimony, beliefs are not mainly put into practice; a consistent practice is 'put into' successive formulations of belief. What is more, the formulations and explanations often seem to be created in response to, or for the benefit of, specific audiences.

This does not mean, however, that there is no point in looking at Quaker discussions of oaths. The 'snowball' of talk about oaths may not have a solid core – a single consistent key reason that supports all the others – but it does, I want to suggest, have an initial 'push' that gives it its continued direction. We can see this in Penn's treatise, but more clearly and starkly in the early accounts of the courtroom dramas in which Quakers refused oaths – such as the one quoted at the start of this chapter.[13]

My suggestion is that, in the courtroom dramas and in the early tracts on oaths, the refusal of oaths arises from the experience of a dramatic transformation, reconciliation and repair – not just or even not mainly of an individual person, but of a divided world and of a divided linguistic community. The point at which the oath is demanded – paradigmatically, for early Quakers, the courtroom – is a point of confrontation between the newly inbreaking truth of reconciliation and new life in Christ, and the 'old' order of falsehood. For the Quaker participants the courtroom drama around oath-taking is located, to use my earlier terminology, at the leading edge of salvation history.

But why are oaths, in particular, the site and occasion of the courtroom drama that turns into a social and cosmic drama? Oaths are supposed to guard against lying and to secure peace. But from the perspective from which the early Quakers speak and write, failure to speak the truth, failure to bear truthful witness, or failure to speak in a way that secures peace – the failures against which oaths are supposed to guard – are only possible in a world at enmity with God. Oaths are a symptom – perhaps the core symptom – of a problem, masquerading as the cure for the problem.

Several early written testimonies against oaths make them a central symbol of the confrontation between falsehood and truth, between the way the world has gone and the way God calls the world to be. The world in which oaths are sworn is, in these texts, the world not only of falsehood but of 'strife'. Thus, for example, Gervase Benson, in the prologue to an account of the particular 'oppressions' suffered by Quakers for refusing to swear oaths, writes: '[H]e that receiveth the Son's testimony is come out of all oaths, and strife the occasion of them, to the yea and nay in all his communications' (Benson 1656). This makes a particular kind of sense in the seventeenth-century context, in the aftermath of a succession

---

13 The idea of the Quaker 'courtroom drama' is from Bauman.

TESTIMONY

of state-imposed oaths used to suppress religious and political dissent and secure military support; but it makes a wider theological sense in the confrontation between truth and truth's enemies in which the Quakers understood themselves to be caught up.[14]

The early Quaker texts on oaths speak from a perspective of reconciliation with God, unity with the Son, life under the lordship of Christ – where there is no need for swearing oaths, because there is no possibility of lying and no possibility of disputes about the truth. Swearing an oath appears from this perspective not as the norm but as an utterly unintelligible departure from the norm of Christ. This is why there are people who 'cannot swear' – in the same way as the authors of the 1662 declaration say that they 'cannot learn war'. Undivided truth and undivided words are the starting point; swearing an oath is 'drawing into unrighteousness'.[15]

Now, this account is in rather strong contrast to the 'default position' for those who want to find theological reasons for Quakers' refusal of oaths. Historians of oath-taking and oath-refusal have tended to seize on Quakers' (and, for that matter, Anabaptists') references to Matthew 5.33–37 and assumed that what was at stake for them was the perceived requirement to take this particular command of Jesus literally. The person who refuses oaths is portrayed as a theologically unsophisticated biblical literalist who chooses to make a particularly big point about a particularly small issue – on which, for anyone in the business of trading proof-texts, there is in fact plenty to be said on both sides. Of course, these New Testament texts are prominent in the relevant pamphlets; the Matthew text appears to have been cited frequently in the courtroom, and it is disputed and discussed widely in the polemical and apologetic literature. Evangelically inclined Friends of the nineteenth century, for example, were particularly keen to repeat and expand those justifications of the 'testimony . . . against the

---

14 Further evidence of this view of oaths is in Samuel Fisher, 1661, *One Antidote More Against That Provoking Sin of Swearing*, London: Robert Wilson. Fisher presents 'swearing' as a key manifestation of the 'seed of evildoers'.

15 *The Glorie of the Lord Arising*, 1654.

'SWEAR NOT AT ALL'

burthen and imposition of oaths' that referred directly to scriptural prohibitions.[16]

The suggestion that they were 'just doing what the Bible says' does not, however, really do justice to what is going on, at least for the early Quakers. The formative christological 'argument' against swearing oaths, found in numerous texts, is thus based not simply on the command of Christ in Matthew 5, but more fundamentally on the recognition of Christ as himself the truth, the ultimately true and reliable witness. Theologically speaking, the Johannine writings and the Epistle to the Hebrews are more basic to the refusal of oaths than the obvious proof-texts. Reading Hebrews 6.16 – 'an oath given as confirmation puts an end to all dispute' – in the context of Hebrews 7.20–22 in which Jesus' priesthood is 'confirmed with an oath', some early Quaker texts name Christ himself as the Oath of God, the oath to end oaths, the present and living guarantor of the reign of divine truth. The reported saying of Christ, 'Swear not at all', is thus not primarily a command, but primarily a proclamation – indeed, a self-proclamation. 'Swear not at all' makes sense because the one who utters it is the one who fulfils it, and the one in and through whom God fulfils it; Jesus Christ brings an end to the swearing of oaths. This complex connection between Christology and the refusal to swear oaths is expressed by Ellis Hooks, in another example of Quaker writing saturated with unmarked scriptural quotations and allusions:

> And Christ the Oath of God ends all oaths that tyed up to God . . . which Christ destroyes the Devil, the author of Stryfe, who [*sc. Christ*] is the Rest himself, and is the Way, the Truth and the Life that brings up to God, and is God's Covenant, in whom Man hath peace with God, that destroyes that which led out from God and Christ; He it is that saith, Swear not at all. (Hooks 1661, p. 5)

---

16 London Yearly Meeting, 1861, *Extracts from the Minutes and Epistles of the Yearly Meeting*, London: Friends' Book Depository, p. 127.

TESTIMONY

The Quakers' naming of Christ as the Oath of God – although nowhere near as prominent in their Christology as the images of light and seed – is striking and points again to the scope of the claim that underlies the refusal of oaths. Christ as the Oath of God is the definitive self-declaration and self-commitment of God, who 'puts an end' to the dispute between God and humanity that is also the source of disputes among people. The use of the Hebrews text in this connection is all the more noteworthy because 'an oath given as confirmation puts an end to all dispute' was rather often used, particularly in the early modern commentaries, as an argument *in favour* of oaths as a provisional or interim measure – a counterweight to, rather than an intensification of, the Matthew 5 text forbidding oaths.[17] This is a further reminder, if one were needed, that specific biblical texts are less significant in the underlying structure of the Quaker testimony against oaths than is a comprehensive 'take' on the world, rooted in individual and collective experience of convincement and transformation.

It is also worth noting that calling Christ the 'Oath of God' carried, in the seventeenth-century context, a contextually specific political weight, comparable to how the affirmation of Christ as Lord functions in contexts and situations in which political 'lordship' is in dispute. At the time of the Quaker courtroom dramas, for over a century the oath had been a key tool for constructing state authority, for forming a commonwealth, or subsequently for securing loyalty in political associations. The wider literature on oaths from the preceding decades reveals a complex set of negotiations about what counts as breaking or keeping an oath, how one oath supplants another, under what circumstances an oath of

---

17 As far as I have been able to ascertain, this Quaker interpretation has few precedents or parallels. There is a possible hint towards it in John Chrysostom's commentary on Hebrews, in which he translates the word 'guaranteed' in Hebrews 6.17 as 'mediated' and refers straight away to Christ as mediator (Chrysostom, Homily 11 on Hebrews, commentary on 6.17). Jonathan Griffiths has also recently argued on textual grounds that Christ in Hebrews is the 'word of the oath' (Jonathan Griffiths, 2009, 'Christ as the personal "word of the oath" in Hebrews 6:13—7:28', paper presented at British New Testament Society seminar on the Catholic Epistles, University of Aberdeen).

allegiance may be broken, and so forth.[18] England from the time of the Henrician Reformation made very extensive use of state oaths as a means of constructing – as William Cavanaugh puts it – a 'confessionalized state', a state whose power was closely associated with religious conformity. The Quaker proclamation of Christ as the 'Oath of God', in this context, was a political statement that claimed to subvert the terms of politics altogether, to debase the political currency – not only to opt out of the system, but to see it overturned.

All of this shows, in turn, that the Quaker refusal to swear oaths was experienced and interpreted as the direct and inescapable consequence of a changed situation, the situation in which the 'Oath of God' had put an end to oaths. It was not, in other words, a matter of choice; it was, given the dramatic and transformative work of God in their lives, the only possible way to act. Arguments and threats were equally powerless to change Quakers' course of action, because they were equally powerless to affect the truth that that action reflected and in which that action participated.

The biblical settlement from which Quaker testimony arose yielded a way of recognizing and speaking about persistent opposition to the truth given in Christ – and about the deep-seated illogicality, and ultimate unsustainability, of this opposition. Oaths – who should take them or be forced to take them, whether they can be broken or suspended and under what circumstances – were a 'known problem' in seventeenth-century England. The Quakers addressed this 'known problem', like somewhat later the problem of military power, by assuming it was a false problem – taking themselves out of the whole system that generated it.

However, as we have seen, this did not exactly prevent Quakers from listening to what their opponents were saying. There is an enormous volume of controversial literature on oaths, from the

---

18 For an overview of this, see David Jones, 1999, *Conscience and Allegiance in Seventeenth-Century England; The Political Significance of Oaths and Engagements*, Rochester: University of Rochester Press. For the argument that the rejection of oaths was a form of popular rebellion, see Christopher Hill, 1964, *Society and Puritanism in Pre-Revolutionary England*, New York: Schocken.

TESTIMONY

seventeenth century onwards – with Quakers and their opponents swapping point-for-point dissections and refutations of arguments, even when the points at issue would be in themselves insufficient to decide the main question. This testimony – like the 'peace testimony' – was, and remains, something that could be reasoned about, argued for and made publicly intelligible; which is not, of course, the same as saying that everyone could be persuaded to agree with it.

Again, it is possible on the basis of the earlier discussion to see why this should be so. The truth of Christ, as Quakers describe it, is, ultimately, the truth of and for the world – not unintelligible but maximally intelligible. It makes *more* sense than anything else, and it makes a kind of sense that could not have been predicted in advance. This does not mean that it is congruent with nature, or with natural reason as presently accessible; both experientially and scripturally it is clear to the Quaker authors that most people, most states and most available legal frameworks do not understand or accommodate what they are saying.

Richard Bauman's analysis of the 'drama' of the courtroom scenes in which Quakers were called upon to swear oaths discovers a set of common 'symbolic oppositions' in the Quakers' rhetoric and actions, in which the Quakers as true witnesses are ranged against those who collude with or submit to 'worldly power'. The point was, as Bauman goes on to demonstrate, not that Quakers were opposed to a *particular* worldly power (the king to whom they were being asked to swear allegiance), but that they were setting themselves against the power *structure* that relied on, and was reflected in, oaths – and, more generally, against whatever power structure or pattern of life would suppress divine truth.[19]

The fact that Quakers were not opposing 'the king' *for the sake of an alternative ruler* could be, and was, used from the earliest decades to argue for toleration. Quakers could not be accused of giving allegiance to *any* 'worldly' power, established or revolutionary; they could in good conscience affirm (but not swear) that

---

19 Bauman, 1983, *Let Your Words Be Few*, pp. 108–9.

they had no intention of conspiring to overthrow the monarch. Bauman suggests that the struggle for toleration, and its aftermath, turned the refusal of oaths into an anti-political stance and forced Quakers to withdraw from public life: 'the Quakers purchased their religious freedom at the sacrifice of engagement in worldly politics' and developed 'a social policy founded on quietism' (Bauman 1983, p. 118). As I mentioned earlier, this previously common narrative of Quaker 'quietism' has been challenged in at least some recent studies of Quaker history. Certainly, even if we just stick with the story of oaths, the story of John Archdale (the Quaker MP-elect who refused the oath – and made the public request to affirm) does not look like a story of putting religious freedom before engagement in politics. It looks more like an attempt to push the limits of toleration in order to play an active role in public life – and Archdale's subsequent career, as Governor of North Carolina, suggests that he was happier to seek alternative outlets for his political energy than to rest content with his 'religious freedom'.

This issue of the relationship – or lack of it – to state authorities, reflected in the refusal of oaths, brings us close again to the links between the refusal of oaths and the refusal of violence, and also to the related but distinct patterns of reasoning in Anabaptist and Quaker testimony against oaths. I have suggested that in the seventeenth-century context at least there is a strong connection between the refusal to swear an oath of allegiance to anyone, and the refusal to take up arms on behalf of anyone. Contemporary theologians commenting on the refusal of oaths in Anabaptist and Quaker traditions have found continuing – not just historical – relevance in this connection. Hovey, for example, writing in a collection of essays on Anabaptist theological ethics, provides a persuasive analysis of the relationship between oaths and state power. He concludes that the oath 'betray[s] a reliance on the power of magistrates – and ultimately the sword – at the expense of the power of a truthfully spoken "yes" and "no"'.[20] Here, Hovey

---

20 Craig Hovey, 2010, 'Narrative Proclamation and Gospel Truthfulness: Why Christian Proclamation Needs Speakers', in Chris K. Huebner and Tripp York (eds), *The Gift of Difference: Radical Orthodoxy, Radical Reformation*, Winnipeg, MB: CMU Press, pp. 87–103.

connects the refusal to swear an oath – particularly, here, a state oath – with the refusal to be complicit in the violent enforcement of an official version of the truth. Unarmed truth in the mouth of (here) the Anabaptist martyr is placed over against the state power that can afford to ignore truth because it wields the sword; and the continuing contemporary relevance.

The early Quaker texts on oaths, as we have seen, likewise identify close connections between oaths and violence. This is hardly surprising, given the political volatility of their times and of the preceding century. Successive governments had sought to secure their hold over the population by a combination of military might and the enforcement of oaths. From this perspective, however, and in contrast to Hovey's suggestion, it does not really matter whether the oath that is refused relies on 'the power . . . of the sword' to enforce it. The point is more that the very need for an oath – the mistrust and the fear of falsehood that calls for the oath – is part and parcel of the 'strife' to which Christ puts an end, and the refusal of the oath is *as such* a refusal to be part of the 'strife'.

It is, in fact, not particularly helpful to concentrate on the violent power behind the imposition of an oath, and to suggest that this is the heart of the matter. Religious oaths are in fact not generally backed up by 'the sword' in the hand of the ruler who imposes them, because they do not need to be. Their power lies in their invocation of the fear of divine judgement – which is why, for example, John Locke viewed the atheist who feared no divine judgement as a particular threat to a state that relied on people keeping their oaths.[21] In the logic of the religious oath – as used at least since the Tudor period in England – the ruler, or the magistrate, cannot compel loyalty, fidelity or truthfulness by physical force; so he or she uses the religious oath to

---

21 John Locke, 1689/2003, 'A Letter Concerning Toleration', in Ian Shapiro (ed.), *Two Treatises of Government and a Letter Concerning Toleration*, New Haven, KT: Yale University Press, pp. 211–55.

'SWEAR NOT AT ALL'

enlist the fearful conscience of the subject to compel loyalty and truthfulness.[22]

To refuse to take or administer oaths, in this context, might be read as the refusal to use the threat of divine judgement for a specific political end. It does not imply lack of belief in divine judgement per se (Quakers were perfectly prepared to acknowledge such belief through most of their history); but it does imply a scepticism about how that judgement maps on to the judgements of monarchs and governments, and a specific objection to instrumentalizing the threat of divine judgement for one's own or another's ends. The discussions among Quakers of the text of 'the Affirmation' – as in the 'tedious tale' recounted by W. C. Braithwaite – included an extensive negotiation to expunge any reference to God's judgement from the words spoken by the person affirming. The fact that such a reference was inserted in the first place reveals how significant this belief was thought to be for the maintenance of civic order; the fact that the Quakers objected to it suggests that the 'testimony against swearing' was linked at this stage to a suspicion of state-imposed religion in all its forms.[23]

---

22 The connection between the swearing of an oath and belief in divine judgement and punishment, specifically, was a common staple of debates about the use of oaths in the eighteenth and nineteenth centuries. The question of whether a child could give evidence under oath, for example, might be decided by whether he or she showed an understanding of, and belief in, the last judgement. See the famous, but still probably historical, exchange between Mr Justice Maule and a child witness:

> Judge: And if you do always tell the truth where will you go when you die?
> Girl: Up to heaven sir.
> Judge: And what will become of you if you tell lies?
> Girl: I shall go down to the naughty place, sir.
> Judge: Are you quite sure of that?
> Girl: Yes, sir.
> Judge: Let her be sworn, it is quite clear that she knows more than I do!

John Spencer and Rhona Flin, 1993, *The Evidence of Children: The Law and the Psychology*, London: Blackstone, p. 51.

23 Braithwaite, 1921/1961, *Second Period*, pp. 182–204. Under pressure, and after a very extended consideration, the Quakers did compromise on the inclusion of a reference to God in the wording of the affirmation – 'lest we be deemed atheistical'.

TESTIMONY

This, however, takes us directly to the issue of religious freedom and conscientious objection, the ways in which Quakers were spared the obligation to conform.

Conscientious objection: testimony and permitted dissent

As we have already seen, the first generations of Quakers were already assuming it as common knowledge that certain groups of religious believers – themselves and the Anabaptists – could not swear an oath 'for conscience's sake', and were asking for legal or official allowance to be made for the 'tender consciences' of these groups. So the subsequent history of Quaker refusals of oaths, in Britain at least, is also a history of the complex modern relationships between the state and groups of religious believers who refuse, 'for conscience's sake', to comply with what is expected of all citizens or subjects. The idea of conscientious objection is now strongly associated with refusal of military service; but the first *conscientious objection* recognized as such by the law – in 1838 – was the objection to swearing oaths.[24]

In keeping with my approach throughout this book, in this chapter I have looked at the Quaker refusal of oaths not as a general rule of right conduct but rather as a practice at the 'leading edge' of salvation history – a dramatic enactment of the confrontation between truth and falsehood. This means, however, that I cannot ignore the wider social and political consequences of the refusal of oaths. The Quaker testimony discussed in this chapter is not an armchair debate; it started as some rather obstinate and public antisocial behaviour, which met with official responses. After the establishment of toleration, the shape of these official responses was largely determined by a long, complex – and theologically charged – debate about how to maintain public order in the face of conscientious objection.

---

24 For a full discussion of the legal history of the idea of conscientious objection, see Constance Braithwaite, 1995, *Conscientious Objection To Compulsions Under the Law*, York: Ebor Press. On oaths, see in particular Ch. 1; and on the first use of 'conscientious objection', see p. 26.

'SWEAR NOT AT ALL'

The appeal to freedom of conscience was one among many important contexts for the debate over oaths. The oath in early modern England was important as a technology of conscience – a means of securing loyalty through something other than brute force. Alongside the affirmation of Christ as the Oath of God we find, in the Quaker refusals of oaths, many statements more obviously and closely related to a theological emphasis on the free and uncoerced conscience under the lordship and direction of Christ. Alongside the 'here and now' language in texts like Ellis Hooks', which gives social and even cosmic significance to the refusal of oaths, there is other language that is more individualized, more focused on the individual's free and conscientious obedience to Christ that could not be abrogated by obedience to a monarch. Margaret Fell, for example, when brought to trial on the basis of her refusal to take the oath of allegiance (although the main point at issue appears to have been the meetings held in her house), repeatedly asserted the primacy of her allegiance to Christ over her allegiance to the king, stated that she was on trial 'for conscience's sake', and finally declared:

> I never took an oath in my life; I have spent my days thus far, and never took an oath; I owe allegiance to the king, as he is king of England; but Christ Jesus is king of my conscience. (*A Complete Collection of State Trials*, Vol. 6, 1816, p. 634)

Here, Fell comes closer to Baptist and Anabaptist arguments against oaths, which centred on the free and uncoerced conscience of the believer recognizing the lordship of Christ. Roger Williams' rejection of religious oaths in Rhode Island was based not primarily on the scriptural prohibition of oaths, but rather on the iniquity of forcing anyone to confess particular religious beliefs or perform particular acts of worship – in violation of the freedom of each person's conscience before, and for, Christ.[25]

---

25 For a discussion of Williams' reasoning on oaths, and how it fitted into his wider understanding of religious freedom, see Stephen R. Holmes, 2012, *Baptist Theology*, London: T&T Clark International, pp. 125–6.

TESTIMONY

However, Fell, and others who rested their appeals against the imposition of oaths on the appeal to Christ's unassailable sovereignty in the individual conscience, also drew on the broader social and theological critique of oaths outlined above. The conscientious refusal of oaths was inseparable from the wider claim that oaths were a direct denial of the lordship of Christ – not only over the individual's conscience, but also over the wider society and polity. In Fell's trial, when she was asked if she would (at least) hear the oath read, she responded in prophetic-polemical terms: 'I do not care if I never hear an oath read, for the land mourns because of oaths' (*A Complete Collection of State Trials*, Vol. 6, p. 634). Her use of Jeremiah 23.10 ('because of swearing the land mourns') 'scales up' the courtroom drama, from a struggle over one woman's allegiances to Christ and the king to a struggle over the good of 'the land'. But the connection between the two levels is not just that Fell is doing what she thinks is best for society, or resisting a practice that she knows to be socially injurious. If we take her seriously when she says 'Christ Jesus is king of my conscience', she is not grounding her action in a specific social or political analysis; *but*, because the same Christ Jesus who is 'king of [her] conscience' is also the 'light that enlightens' all, and the truth being revealed in the world, the refusal of the oath makes sense beyond the sphere of her individual decision.

It is important in this, also, not to ignore the middle of the scale – between one woman making a public declaration of allegiance, and the vision of a cursed and mourning land, lies a specific community. Interwoven with the issue of the oath, at Fell's trial, is the keeping of meetings for worship in her house. She was on trial not as one person who happens to refuse an oath of allegiance, but as the person who enables gatherings of Quakers – and this, alongside her known previous connections to anti-Royalist individuals and groups, was what made the trial politically significant. In refusing either to swear the oath or to stop holding the meetings, Fell defends a shared religious practice, rather than (only) an individual freedom of conscientious belief.

Looking at it another way, in the context of the years of experience that Fell had by this time acquired as an organizer, advocate, mentor and adviser of fellow Quakers, the individual stand she makes in the courtroom drama is supported and made possible by the 'keeping of meetings'. From the court's point of view she stands as a representative and ringleader of Quakers; from her point of view, she stands with the community whose collective testimony is at stake – and whose shared discernment, formed in the context of worship and common practice, informs her own claims about the meaning of Christ's lordship over her conscience.

Now, I want to suggest that Fell's stance as 'conscientious objector' to the oath offers an important perspective on conscientious objection – one that is liable to be lost if conscientious objection is analysed only from the point of view of the modern state. It is easy for the person who objects, on grounds of 'conscience', to some requirement placed on him or her by the state, to look either like an isolated 'crank' – as the deliberately provocative commentator recently described the conscientious objectors of the First World War – or like a heroic defender of the indissoluble freedom of the individual. In the history of conscientious objection, however, there is a curious middle space to which I have already alluded. Initially, not only in Britain but also in the USA and elsewhere, the right to conscientious objection (to the oath, or to military service) was tied to membership of a particular religious community.

At least some recent histories regard this 'communal' objection, understandably enough, as an unsatisfactory intermediate stage on the way to a satisfactory account of conscientious objection. Moskos and Chambers depict different stages in the legal recognition of objection (in this case, principally to military service): from, first, an assumption not only that all conscientious objection is religious but also that it is tied specifically to membership of a recognized peace church; to, second, a continuing assumption that it is religious but with a focus on individual conviction rather than group identity; to, third, a willingness by the state to recognize reasons of conscience not articulated in religious terms.[26]

---

26 Charles C. Moskos and John Whiteclay Chambers II, 1993, 'The Secularisation of Conscience', in Moskos and Chambers (eds), *The New Conscientious Objection: From Sacred to Secular Resistance*, Oxford: Oxford University Press, pp. 3–21.

TESTIMONY

As I have suggested, Quakers' emphasis on the enlightening and saving presence of Christ to each person gives rise to the possibility of setting the individual, obedient to Christ, over against any and every collective attempt to compel or sway obedience. But, as I suggested in my discussion of Margaret Fell's trial and indeed of John Archdale's political career, in Quaker testimony the individual conscience is located within a reflecting and worshipping community, a context of shared testimony and mutual responsibility.

In fact, several of the early Quaker texts on the relationship between conscience and the state deal with the conscientious obligation to meet together for worship – coming into direct conflict with the laws against public meetings. The conscience governed and guided by the Light of Christ, and caught up in the movement of the Spirit, draws people to public worship. This becomes particularly clear, for example, in George Whitehead's *Conscientious Cause of the Sufferers Called Quakers*. Whitehead argues that obedience to 'conscience' requires, for Quakers, not merely the worship of God but the public worship of God:

> Some charge it on us as obstinacy or wilfulness for meeting in any considerable or great numbers publicly, and thereupon conclude that our suffering is not upon a conscientious account . . . to which I answer, that it is singly in tenderness, conscientiousness and obedience unto the living God, in the leading of his eternal Spirit, for the glory and advancement of his Name and Truth . . . the Gospel [is] not to be bound, but as it was manifest in the universal love of God, which is of a general extent to all . . . all ought to be left free to have the benefit of it. (Whitehead 1664, p. 2)

What does it mean, in the history of conscientious objection, when Quakers – or any other group – are given 'special treatment'? What is going on when a state permits citizens to refuse some action that is taken to be to the survival of the state *and* ties that permission to membership of a particular religious community? One way to read it is as a step on the way to the de-politicization of religion (and particularly of Quakerism) – turning religious identity into something that cannot be reasoned with or about in public, something that is non-negotiable but relatively easy to work around because always a minority interest. And one might see that either as progress – towards a fully 'secular' public sphere and full religious freedom – or as regress, making religion politically and socially irrelevant, and setting up a political space in which all we have in the end is the individual 'crank' over against the might of the state.

But what happens if we place at the centre of the drama of conscientious objection the conscience formed by a vision of historical and social transformation – in which the 'end of oaths' or the 'end of war' is arriving not just for one person in his or her individual conscience but within history? This kind of conscientious objection actively seeks social and political expression, and seeks to become public – certainly through dramas of refusal and negation, but also through arguments and persuasion (like Penn's tracts on oaths), seeking to 'answer that of God' in a wider context. It also arises from shared deliberations within a particular community. Looking at conscientious objection in the 'peace churches' if we attend to the internal and external relations of those peace churches – if we take them seriously as social and political presences – helps us to see how conscientious objection can be an expression not just of individual freedom but of the prospect of social and political transformation. 'Toleration' – and the recognition of potentially disruptive and 'cranky' religious communities that reason with one another – can be not just a way of containing a problem but a way of maintaining openness to future change.

One important corollary of this, of course, is that the dissenting or objecting communities itself – the Quaker community – is not internally monolithic. On the question of resistance to war, for example, recent research has uncovered the extent to which Quakers were divided on the question of participation in the 1914–18 war. Quakers variously made 'conscientious' decisions to enlist, to accept alternative service, or to refuse all participation –

TESTIMONY

in some cases under sentence of death.[27] One young man from a Quaker family could write to his father in 1914 (in a letter quoted in a British Quaker event to commemorate the centenary of the outbreak of war):

> The Friends have stood for Peace for centuries – but now it is a question of extirpating the greatest enemy to world peace that the world has ever seen . . . Where does the Quaker idea fit in here? Surely it fits in like this, as I believe many Friends have said: 'This is a question for every man's individual conscience.' Well, since my conscience lets me go, don't you think it is my duty to go? (Letter from Andrew Stewart Fox to his father, 1914)[28]

Arguably, Andrew Fox's letter reflects one pole only of the interplay in Quaker thinking between individual conscience and shared discernment. However, even among those Quakers who saw the need for collective deliberation there was genuine uncertainty and difference of view over the shape of the appropriate Quaker response – for example, over the appropriateness or otherwise of supporting battlefield medical units.[29] The distinctive form of twentieth-century Quaker peace testimony – including the reaffirmation of a clear position of nonviolence even or especially in the context of national mobilization, as well as a renewed emphasis on positive peace work and war relief – emerged gradually from these deliberations.

So, while it would be convenient for many purposes, both for Quaker self-description and so that non-Quaker authorities know where they stand, to be able to make claims about what all Quakers must or should do, the history of Quaker testimony does not quite

---

27 See on this Thomas C. Kennedy, 2001, *British Quakerism 1860–1920: The Transformation of a Religious Community*, Oxford: Oxford University Press; Brian D. Phillips, 1989, 'Friendly Patriots: British Quakerism and the Imperial Nation 1890–1910', unpublished thesis, University of Cambridge.

28 Thanks to Miranda Girdlestone for help with this quotation.

29 I am grateful to Janet Scott, Gavin Burnell, Susan Robson, Jane Dawson, and many others involved in British Quaker commemorations of the centenary of the First World War, for conversations on this subject.

allow it. There is a history of shared discipline and collective discernment – and there is the recognition that the conscience cannot be forced, that even within a community the Spirit wins its kingdom 'by entreaty', and that testimony has to be worked out in particular cases that cannot be fully predicted or understood in advance.

So what does this internal difference and debate mean for shared Quaker testimony? Quakers have had good reason in the past for wanting to present a 'united front' on many key community-defining issues. We might perhaps suspect that the price of a clear and visible collective testimony on ethical and social issues will always be that internal dissent is – as it were – kept relatively quiet. The practice of 'disownment' of Quakers who in some way endangered the public witness of the group, or acted against agreed or established Quaker practice, is far rarer now than it was in previous generations but plays a significant part in the Quaker story. Quaker writings on decision-making processes differentiate rather clearly between consensus and the agreed 'sense of the meeting' – where the latter might require someone who was not personally in agreement to accept that the group *as a whole* is led to act in a certain way. One of the challenges for anyone trying to write about Quakers collectively – and especially taking account of Quaker history – is to be faithful both to the real diversity of Quaker thought and practice, and to their commitment to shared processes and shared discipline. In the next chapter, I look at this issue more closely in relation to the complex history of Quaker 'martyrs', returning eventually to the case of James Nayler.

5

Religious Freedom and Solidarity: Quaker Martyrs and their Communities

Quakers and religious freedom

In this chapter, I take up the interconnected questions of freedom – especially 'religious freedom' – the relationship between individual and shared witness, and the ways in which Quaker approaches to theology and ethics can handle internal difference and conflict.

As I have already suggested, Quakers hold in common with several 'gathered church' traditions a strong historic emphasis on religious freedom. They have advocated both the freedom of religious communities to gather for worship and to organize themselves without state interference, and the freedom of individuals to follow and act on the leadings of God as conscientiously discerned. The emphasis on freedom, while it has deep theological roots, itself arises (for Quakers as for many other groups) as 'testimony against' state prescriptions of, and restrictions on, forms of worship. As we have seen, when the holding of public meetings for worship was specifically prohibited for several years in the 1660s, even attending Quaker worship was a form of 'testimony against' the establishment of religion. The period of persecution in the early years of the Restoration – as Quakerism passed from the first to the second generation – left a deep mark on Quaker self-understanding, practice and theology in many ways, but one of the most obvious was a tradition of commitment to freedom of religious thought and practice.

RELIGIOUS FREEDOM AND SOLIDARITY

Now, both in the contemporary context and throughout the modern period, religious freedom is a highly contested and controversial notion. For a start, the emphasis on religious freedom among Quakers should not be confused with a claim that all forms of religious practice are in some way equally valid and deserve celebration and recognition. Whatever their present liberal and/or pluralistic credentials, Quakers were not always advocates of anything resembling pluralism. The ferocity of their early attacks on the established church (which had remained 'established' in many respects even under the Commonwealth) was matched by their harsh critique in print and in person of various independent and dissenting congregations – and by a consistent anti-Catholicism, sustained long after Quakers became a tolerated group, and only less noticeable because it was shared by most of their main interlocutors in seventeenth- and eighteenth-century England. The rhetorical use of 'the Jews' to represent obsolete and repressive religious dispensations was likewise common in Quaker texts, and likewise part of a shared vocabulary of polemic.

Thus, the Quaker claim that the Light of Christ enlightened 'every man that cometh into the world' did not imply that the Light of Christ informed the religious practice of 'every man', but rather that all were given the capacity to know and follow the truth. If anything, the Light would bring people *away* from any and every 'form' of religion; the 'freedom' it granted was the starting point for the critique of religion, not for the affirmation of existing religious forms. As I have suggested, one strand of the Quaker resistance to religious oaths was their resistance to the imposition of forms of worship – both in principle and, more fundamentally, because this form of worship was one against which the rightly guided conscience, 'Christ Jesus [as] king of [the] conscience', would raise insuperable objections.

The approach to religious freedom generated by belief in the 'light in all' is exemplified in the writings of James Nayler – to whose life and work I return in this chapter. In answer to a question from the anti-Quaker polemicist Richard Baxter – 'Is not he a pagan and no Christian that thinks that the light which is in all the Indians, Americans, and other pagans on earth, is sufficient without Scripture?' – Nayler accepts and owns Baxter's interpretation of the Quaker understanding of the 'light in all', but turns the accusation of 'pagan' worship back upon the accuser:

> [I]f the Indians and pagans own that law written in their heart, and come to receive power to bring forth the fruits of it, which thou dost not, I shall say of you both as Paul did of the Jews (Rom. 2:12–13, &c.): not the hearers of the law are just before God, but the doers of the law shall be justified. But art not thou a pagan, if not worse, who would conclude all in condemnation, but who comes to hear you hirelings, and your expositions of the Scriptures? (Nayler, 1656, pp. 193–4)

The point is primarily a negative one, simultaneously theological and political – a critique of the supposed attempt, by Baxter and others, both to restrict the scope of God's salvific action and to justify the imposition of a particular form of religious practice. Nayler says nothing to praise the religion of the 'Indians and pagans'; the underlying assumption seems to be that if they 'own that law written in their heart' they will change their practices of worship and prayer. The core claim is that all are included in the comprehensive movement of saving revelation that comes from God – that all can know, follow and live in the truth. This does not necessarily make Quakers pluralists, or even universalists, and it does not automatically ground a belief in the *value* of each human being. Various different theological anthropologies and theologies of religion are compatible with belief in the 'Light that enlightens everyone'. I have suggested that its main outworking in practice is a focus on freedom of religion and of conscience – and also on public testimony, appealing to the God-given capacity of all to recognize and turn to the truth, seeking to 'answer' that of God in everyone.

This negative account of religious freedom – the freedom to critique or refuse forms of worship – does not quite tell the whole story. As we saw in the account of Margaret Fell's trial, the question of the oath was interwoven with the question of freedom of

RELIGIOUS FREEDOM AND SOLIDARITY

worship. Fell and her fellow Quakers, understanding themselves as a people gathered in some sense 'out of nothing' and not only out of existing church communities, sought freedom to keep their meetings. They sought the positive freedom to continue with the 'holy experiments' into which people found themselves led individually and collectively. As George Whitehead wrote, 'tenderness, conscientiousness and obedience to the living God' called them into public meetings for worship. An order – a pattern of community life – emerged and was to be maintained.

We do need, however, to acknowledge the prominence, over several decades, of Quaker 'testimony against' restrictions on religious freedom. Quakers testified, both in word and in action, against set forms of worship (both as prescribed by the state and as determined by a church hierarchy), against tithes (as forms of taxation that supported both the church and the landowners), and against the compulsory observance of festivals and the 'religious' naming of days. As with various other early Quaker 'testimonies against', these critiques and refusals of religious practice became in subsequent centuries marks of Quaker peculiarity, rather than regular challenges to majority practice. Quakers were content to record the date of a document as 'tenth day of the second month' and to hold their meetings for worship on a First Day, without demanding or expecting that others would change their practice. Studies of the long and tangled history of the refusal of tithes do reveal considerable ongoing hardships suffered by Quakers who refused to pay (what was by the late seventeenth and early eighteenth century) essentially a local tax. They also, however, reveal a wide range of attitudes by non-Quakers to the scruples of Quakers – from the angry determination to pursue ruinous fines through the courts, to a surprisingly high level of amused tolerance for the oddities of a group by then considered harmless.[1]

---

[1] The parliamentary record of the debates over the Quakers' Tithe Bill gives some insight into how Quakers and their peculiarities were regarded, a generation after toleration – *An Account of the Proceedings and Debates on the Tithe Bill*, 1737, London: J. Roberts. The proponent of the Bill (designed to allow Quakers to pay tithes as a local tax without thereby recognizing the authority of the established church) praises Quakers as 'a most useful and a most innocent part' of society, and accepts the sincerity of the 'scruple of conscience' that forbids payment of tithes while refusing to say that that scruple has 'any tolerable foundation' (pp. 30, 35).

TESTIMONY

In a contemporary context, it is hard to imagine many of the early Quakers' negative religious 'testimonies' as anything other than harmless eccentricities – 'pecularities' in a derogatory sense, marking Quakers as very 'peculiar' people. But this automatic reaction shows, among other things, the extent to which 'religion' has come to be regarded as politically and socially insignificant. Religious freedom is the freedom to be peculiar, provided one does not impose one's peculiarities on others. But this is not where Quakers' testimony was originally located; Quakers' peculiarity was not 'for the sake of being different', and was not intended to produce religious indifference or an uncritical affirmation of any or all religious forms. It was a direct attack on (what they perceived as) prevailing socially sanctioned idolatries – practices that systematically misdirect worship, that place something other than the true God at the centre of attention and devotion. In fact, as I shall discuss in Chapter 7, a better equivalent of Quaker negative religious testimonies in the contemporary North and West might be 'testimonies against' the core practices of consumerism, and the systemic and profoundly destructive misdirections of worship that they embody and entrench. The new Quaker 'religious freedom' might consist, for example, in rejecting the status, honour and value accorded to the global brand – and thus being 'free' to act and think in ways that might serve rather than prevent the full flourishing of created life.

For the rest of this chapter, however, I want to consider the history of Quaker testimony for religious freedom in the light of its implications for another key issue – the relationship between on the one hand the individual, acting according to conscience and following his or her 'own Guide', and on the other hand the religious community and the wider social context. I begin by looking at the celebrated Quaker martyr Mary Dyer – and I then reread her story and its reception through the more complex story of James Nayler.

The statue and the flag: Mary Dyer and her testimony

Mary Dyer, Quaker. Witness for Religious Freedom. Hanged on Boston Common 1660. 'My life not availeth me in comparison to the liberty of the truth.' (Inscription on the statue of Mary Dyer on Boston Common)

She did hang as a flag for others to take example by. (Attributed to a member of the Boston General Court in a Quaker account of Dyer's execution: Besse 1753, pp. 206–7; see *QF&P* 19.18)

Mary Dyer was executed in 1660, following repeated defiance of Massachusetts' anti-Quaker laws. Her status within the Quaker movement itself is represented by the ironic re-quotation of the comment by one of her executioners that she was a 'flag for others to take example by'. Her wider recognition and appropriation is seen hinted at in the plaque on the statue of Dyer on Boston Common, honouring her as a 'witness for religious freedom' and quoting her affirmation of 'the liberty of the truth'.[2]

The statue itself – created in 1959 by the Quaker sculptor Sylvia Shaw Judson – shows Dyer not preaching but sitting in what is recognizably the silent waiting of Quaker worship. Dyer confronts the public space and draws attention not with her actions or visible status but with her unmoved presence. She does not even look the passer-by in the eye; both her gaze and her pose suggest an entirely unselfconscious calm, a simplicity or singleness of focus that has no visible object. The statue is set on a high pedestal that might easily serve as a throne, but this figure of Dyer could be sitting anywhere. She does not claim the space, she simply happens to be found there. It is a remarkably effective sculpture of silence. It works in part because of the contrast between Dyer's stillness and a complex, noisy and conflicted public space.

The statue's inscription, taken as an interpretation of Dyer and her life, raises rather sharp questions about this manifestation of Quaker testimony, which I consider further below. The statue itself, though, presents a particularly clear and persuasive image of the

---

2 On Mary Dyer and Quaker 'hagiography', see David L. Johns, 2013, *Quakering Theology: Essays on Worship, Tradition and Christian Faith*, Aldershot: Ashgate, Ch. 4.

TESTIMONY

relationship between Quaker worship, Quaker testimony as I have described it here, and the figure of the martyr.

Martyrdom as the limit-case of testimony – the limit-case of identifying oneself with the truth of God, putting oneself wholly at the disposal of the truth of God – is a well-established space of theological reflection, no less in the contemporary context than in the seventeenth century. One intriguing strand of contemporary work on martyrdom focuses on the relationship between the martyr and the church community that remembers him or her. William Cavanaugh, for example, drawing on the stories of Christian resistance to political repression in South America, emphasizes the contrast between the martyr's nonviolence and the violence of the surrounding context – and then draws out the implications of this nonviolence for the subsequent history of the martyr. The martyr can do nothing, at any point, to secure or control the interpretation of her testimony. She gives herself over entirely to the truth she proclaims and lives – which means that she gives herself over entirely to be heard and interpreted by others. She puts herself and her testimony in the hands of the community that comes after her, remembers her or reads her. The martyr – as Craig Hovey, Michael Budde and others also suggest – is in a way the limit-case of the risks of testimony. This is not just for the apparently obvious reason (that is, that she risks being killed) but because she risks being forgotten, misrepresented – or found to have been wrong.[3]

The risk taken by Mary Dyer in this respect is described ironically in the reported comment of the witness to her execution – that she 'did hang as a flag for others to take example by'. What he meant, of course, was that she would warn others from taking a similar course. What subsequent Quaker 'hagiographers' have

---

3 William Cavanaugh, 1998, *Torture and Eucharist*, Oxford: Blackwell; Craig Hovey, 2008, *To Share in the Body: A Theology of Martyrdom for Today's Church*, Grand Rapids, MI: Brazos; Michael Budde, 2011, *The Borders of Baptism: Identities, Allegiances and the Church*, Eugene, OR: Cascade, Ch. 10. See also Michael Budde and Karen Scott (eds), 2011, *Witness of the Body: The Past, Present and Future of Christian Martyrdom*, Grand Rapids, MI: Eerdmans.

meant, in quoting the same expression, was that Dyer was to be admired and in some respect emulated. She has been read and reread in numerous ways – including, but not limited to, a 'witness for religious freedom' as on her statue. She 'hangs as a flag', allowing herself to be pulled into and to remain in public attention – and because very few of her writings survive, she is interpreted and responded to through her actions and her body, with little opportunity to 'script' anyone's responses to her death.

This necessary vulnerability of the martyr to reading and misreading, as I have already suggested, is a feature of all testimony. It is how we can think about testimony as effective – not because it imposes a clear plan or shape on the future, but because it 'answers' and is answered in the ongoing work of the Holy Spirit in history. The Mary Dyer story and statue are especially significant for Quaker thought about testimony because they bring home its particular, local and embodied character – which applies even more when testimony is primarily thought of in terms of action.

Dyer, as portrayed by Judson, will not let us escape the 'here and now' – this woman sitting here, a specific body and set of actions, which repeatedly provoke new thought and interpretation but cannot be *replaced* by an interpretation. She does not tell you, as the observer, exactly what she means; she makes you think. For those who do not see the statue itself, the disturbing details of her story have a similar effect of bringing one up short and making one think. She is led out to be executed, watches her male companions die, is reprieved at the last minute on the appeal of her son. Her husband, not a Quaker, has also written a pleading letter that attempts to cast doubt on her conviction and that adds in details of her prison conditions: she was 'being wett to the skin . . . thrust into a room whereon was nothing to sitt or lye down upon but dust' (W. Dyer 1659/1902). The accounts of her trial and death are detailed and arresting; she is, as David Johns suggests, the ideal candidate for Quaker hagiography.

The danger, however, is that Dyer – as martyr, statue or 'flag' – will be placed out of reach; not that she will become superhuman

TESTIMONY

or impossible to emulate, but that she or any other martyr will be seen only as something strange, out of the ordinary, even shocking or monstrous.[4] But Dyer does not obviously need to be set apart from others – in her life, in her death or in the way she is interpreted. The statue – at least from where I stood, looking at it on Boston Common some years ago – sends out two messages. The pedestal says 'Stop and look at this remarkable woman'; but Dyer's pose, at least to anyone who has spent time in Quaker meetings, says 'Sit down and join her', or 'Where are the others?' As depicted, she is in a meeting for worship. What she is doing makes sense if she has a community around her, not looking at her but waiting with her. And this, as we shall see, is true of her life as much as of her statue.

First, however, we need to look again at the question of 'religious freedom' – for which Dyer is said to be a witness. What, exactly, is meant by interpreting Dyer's testimony in terms of religious freedom? If it is the sovereign right and capacity of the individual to determine the content of her beliefs for herself, in accordance with her idiosyncratic canons of judgement – the right to be as peculiar as one wants in religious matters – it is of relatively little theological interest, and not something for which anyone should need to die.

A contemporary observer who starts from the assumption that all claims to truth in religion are equally false – *or* equally valid – would see both Dyer and her accusers as fundamentally misguided. They were wrong to ban Quakers from Massachusetts, but she was wrong to think she had any need or calling to preach in Massachusetts. The significant difference between the two parties, on this account, was that the Boston authorities chose, and were able, violently to enact their misguided belief in the superiority of their own religious judgement. When Dyer's husband appealed

---

4 On her prior, pre-Quaker, history as a Boston 'monster' – having given birth to an anencephalic daughter characterized as a 'monstrous' child, and subsequently having been expelled with her friend Anne Hutchinson from the church and the colony – see Anne G. Myles, 2001, 'From Monster to Martyr: Re-presenting Mary Dyer', *Early American Literature* 36/1, pp. 1–30.

RELIGIOUS FREEDOM AND SOLIDARITY

for her life, one of his key claims was that she was only following her 'light' as the Boston magistrates were following theirs – both misguided in terms of religious judgement, but they much more misguided because of the cruelty that resulted:

> Have you a law that says the light in M. Dyer is not M. Dyer's rule, if you have for that or any the fornamed a law, she may be made a transgressor . . . ye have no rule of God's word in the Bible to make a law titled Quakers nor have you any order from the Supreme State of England to make such lawes. Therefore, it must be your light within you is your rule and you walk by. (W. Dyer 1659/1902)

This kind of approach to the religious conflicts of the seventeenth century (and earlier and later) has, as Leo Damrosch notes, tended implicitly to shape historians' interpretations of the James Nayler incident, three years previously. Nayler is read as a harmless madman, his accusers as equally mad – because of their religious motivations – but considerably more dangerous.

Now, far as this is from how any of Dyer's (or indeed Nayler's) contemporaries saw the situation, it cannot in fact be dismissed as a complete misinterpretation of Dyer's testimony, even on her own terms. She can be read as a sign against the violent suppression of dissent, a 'witness for religious freedom' in bearing testimony against the laws that condemned her and members of her community. Nonviolence as active (and suffering) opposition to violence might be central to the meaning of martyrdom. Testimony against the 'bloody law' of Boston was clearly integral to Dyer's intention and to the intentions of the other Quaker martyrs of Boston. William Robinson and Marmaduke Stevenson, executed in 1659, wrote of their intention to 'try [the] bloody law unto death' (Bishop 1661, p. 97). The 'testimony' of these Quakers is not just the content of their preaching but the simple fact of their resistant and nonviolent presence.

One way of reading and repeating the testimony of Dyer, then, is as a testimony against manifestations of the 'persecuting spirit'

TESTIMONY

in religious and political life – against the demand for order at the expense of patience and charity, and against the fearful protection of group privilege. Again, this makes sense in Dyer's context. Histories of martyrdom, and wranglings over the status and continuing significance of particular groups of martyrs, was a familiar part of the post-Reformation religious landscape. Quakers (and others) were asked how they could reject doctrines and forms of church order that had been upheld by the martyrs – from the early Christian martyrs to the Marian martyrs in England.

A standard approach to identifying 'true martyrs' in the post-Reformation era was given by the dictum 'not the punishment but the cause makes the martyr'; in other words, a person became a martyr not by dying bravely 'for her faith' but by dying for the *true* faith. This was, as Brad Gregory notes, an approach with a long and distinguished history, and it made sense in a context in which there was persecution on many sides and for many causes.[5] Another response to the question of 'whose martyrdom counts', however, was to locate the theologically determining difference between martyrs and persecutors, not in their variously correct or incorrect doctrine but in the very fact that one group acted as persecutors and the other group suffered persecution. Debates over whose side of a doctrinal question was closer to the beliefs and principles of 'the martyrs' was short-circuited by introducing an alternative question – which side was *acting* like the martyrs and in keeping with the spirit of Christ, and which like their persecutors?

The Anabaptist Balthasar Hübmaier took this approach already in the short sixteenth-century treatise 'On Heretics and Those Who Burn Them', arguing that 'Christ did not come to butcher, destroy and burn, but in order that those who live should live more abundantly', and that those who condemn heretics to death are 'the greatest heretics of all... against the doctrine and example of Christ' (Hübmaier 1524/1905, p. 86). James Nayler responded

---

[5] Brad S. Gregory, 'Persecution or Prosecution, Martyrs or False Martyrs?', in Budde and Scott (eds), *Witness of the Body*, pp. 107–24.

RELIGIOUS FREEDOM AND SOLIDARITY

in this vein to Richard Baxter's challenge concerning the early Christian (and, later in this debate, the Marian) martyrs:

> Qu. 4. [Baxter, posed in an earlier pamphlet] Were not these faithful servants of God that suffered martyrdom under heathen and Arian persecutors, just such ministers as these men vilify? or wherein was the difference, and do not these wretches justify their murders?
>
> *Ans.* I say no, nor like them, no more than the sufferer is like the persecutor, and therein was the difference and is the difference: they suffered in obedience to that measure of light in their times, and we suffer in obedience to the light of Christ in these times; they suffered by the chief priests in their times, who had got power from the magistrate; and we suffer by the chief priests who have got power from the magistrate; and it is not the name of pope, bishop, or priest, that makes just such, or not such, but the practice wherein they are found; and such are the servants of God who are found in the work of God, and such are the servants of the devil who are found persecutors then and now justifying their murders, who then acted such. (Nayler 1656, pp. 39–40)

Nayler suggests that any religious leaders who 'got power from the magistrate' and are 'persecutors' are the direct equivalents of those who opposed the earliest Christians – whatever their identified doctrinal or ecclesial allegiance ('the name of pope, bishop or priest'). Once again, the 'here and now' and the 'there and then' are brought together not only by the presence of the same 'light of Christ', but also by the dynamic around the 'light of Christ' – of violent suppression met with resistant suffering. For Nayler the 'difference that makes a difference' theologically, both then and now, is not a difference of belief or ecclesial organization, but the difference between persecution and 'suffer[ing] in obedience'. The continuity between the testimony of the 'servants of God' now and that of the servants of God in the early days of Christianity lies partly in the way they live and act – their 'being found in the work of God' – but more broadly in their role in the historical drama of revelation and reconciliation.

Looking at earlier comments about Quaker activism, though, it is also important to note that this approach to martyrdom does not reduce Christian identity to a certain kind of 'work', nor theology to ethics and politics. To be 'found in the work of God' is, in the wider context of Nayler's work and of Quaker thought of this period, to be led by and conformed to the wider – and dramatically transformative – 'work' of God in the world. 'Practice' defines not the servants of God but their persecutors; the servants of God are recognized first, as Nayler sees it, not by what they do but by what and how they suffer. It is remarkably easy, in fact, to trace the line from these polemical works written before Nayler's downfall to his final affirmation of the 'spirit that delights to do no evil, nor to avenge any wrong', who is 'found' in situations where no world-transforming action is possible.

Important as this aspect of Quaker readings of religious conflict is, however, it seems not to do full justice to Mary Dyer and her testimony – or, not to provoke the most creative and faithful interpretations of who she is and what she does. After all, even if the precise content or shape of the martyr's testimony – exactly what she says or does – is less significant than the fact that she endures persecution for it, she still says and does *something* in particular, and the content and shape of her testimony matters a great deal to *her*. When Dyer and her companions declared their aim of entering Massachusetts to test 'Boston's bloody laws', the core of the mission was not simply resistance to a persecuting religious establishment, but the ongoing and life-determining authoritative claim of God. They become witnesses 'for religious freedom', not by directly arguing against the Massachusetts laws but by undertaking a specific mission and activity – acting, as they understood it, under divine guidance and direction.

For Dyer in particular, an important component of this mission was solidarity with her fellow Quakers. The 'liberty of the truth' of which she speaks is not just her own freedom to believe (which was not really in question), or even her own freedom to proclaim truth publicly, but the liberation of those suffering under the 'bloody laws'. The quotation on the statue is in fact an edited extract from the second letter she wrote from prison to the magistrates of Boston, following her last-minute reprieve from execution on her penultimate visit to the city: 'My life is not accepted, neither availeth me, in Comparison of the Lives and Liberty of the Truth and Servants of the Living God, for which in the Bowels of Love and Meekness I sought you' (M. Dyer et al. 1659/1841, p. 14).

In an earlier letter from prison, Dyer uses her gender and her class location – as a woman of wealth and position, as well as of noted beauty – to shape her appeal to the Boston magistrates on behalf of her fellow Quakers. She casts herself as Esther appealing to Ahasuerus, calling for the compassionate repeal of a law that condemns to death the people 'prized' by her; relocating herself again in the biblical narrative, she emphasizes the choice she has made 'rather to suffer with the people of God, than to enjoy the pleasures of Egypt' (M. Dyer et al. 1659/1841, p. 10). She consciously places her own life – and her specific social and intellectual resources – in the service of the 'people of God'.

As at Margaret Fell's trial, discussed in the previous chapter, what is at stake in Dyer's ministry is not simply the freedom of individual conscience, but the well-being of a community and the continuation of a shared 'experiment' in truthful living, that lies behind and makes sense of anything the individual does by way of conscientious resistance. Her life story can, in fact, be read as a series of acts of loving accompaniment, through others' suffering and at the cost of her own comfort. Before she joins the Quakers, she chooses to accompany her friend and mentor Anne Hutchinson into disgrace and expulsion in the antinomian controversy; her arrest in Boston is occasioned by her visiting fellow Quakers in prison. She only becomes a 'lone heroine' by accident, and against her will; she expects and wants to die alongside her travelling companions.

More than this, however – and to place Dyer's testimony in its proper scale and scope – her compassionate solidarity and pleading for justice was, in her understanding, also an attempt to answer the

TESTIMONY

presence and work of God in the people she addresses. She appeals, in her letter, to 'the faithful and true Witness of God, which is One in all Consciences, before whom we must all appear', calling individuals to a process of inward examination and repentance; and she also appeals to (what would appear from context to be) the social basis and direction of future transformation, the 'Seed here among you, for whom we have suffered all this while, and yet suffer' (M. Dyer et al. 1659/1841, p. 10).[6]

Dyer probably does not expect her mission to succeed in winning the liberty of her companions or in facing down the laws. At least on the evidence of her letter, however, she does expect her testimony to make sense, to 'answer' the self-revelation of God that is 'one in all' and already present, if hidden and ignored, in the people and the society she addresses. She cannot negotiate or compromise with 'Boston's bloody laws' themselves, but she has good reason to try to communicate with the people who make and enforce the laws – not because they are good, reasonable or nice people but because they are, individually and collectively, already within the scope of God's presence and work; testimony can 'answer that of God' in them. Moreover, there is no need to separate out the emotional and not obviously theological appeals that she makes, for compassion and fellow-feeling for people who are suffering, from her appeal to 'the faithful and true Witness of God . . . in all Consciences'. The 'true witness of God' in *her* conscience and that of her companions is how they see what is going on and respond with compassion and solidarity; obedience to God is inseparable from reading the world truthfully and responding to its calls and needs.

As a 'witness for religious freedom', then, Mary Dyer does not only stand for the right of individuals to think or believe what they like – and still less does she stand for the idea that all religious

---

6 Dyer's multiple uses of 'seed' language in this short letter further demonstrates the versatility and scope of the term, and its capacity to cross the boundaries that Quaker testimony tended to cross. 'Seed' for Dyer refers variously to the Quaker community itself; to the power by which that community and others are shaped and sustained, and which meets with opposition; to the loving presence of God to and for all, without exception; and to the active presence of God (even) in the life and history of a persecuting society.

views are equally good or deserving of respect. She can be read as a witness for the wider 'liberty of the truth', which entails a truthful and compassionate response to the needs of others, and the gathering of new and renewed communities.

Perhaps the best way to take up and read Mary Dyer's 'witness for religious freedom' is from the position the Sylvia Shaw Judson statue seems to invite – sitting beside her. What this might mean, looking back at my earlier accounts of meetings for worship based on silence, is, first, that both the deep pain and the personal complexities of her story could be held and attended to over time without needing an instant response. In the context of a meeting for worship that seeks guidance and tries to develop shared testimony, there would also be an attempt to hear Mary Dyer – not just to replicate what she says, but to work out what the next steps might be. We might probably want to spend more time than some of the early hagiographies do with the ethical ambiguities of her decision – choosing her Quaker communities over her responsibilities to her own children, putting at risk the life that had been saved at considerable cost to others. But sitting with Mary Dyer does not mean looking up to her, or 'supporting' all her actions – it means being prepared to be gathered into a community with her, and guided forward. It quite possibly means being prepared to ask oneself what and where are the present 'bloody laws' that cause suffering to the children of God in the interests of maintaining an existing order, and whether and how we are called to confront them.

Sitting with Mary Dyer might be uncomfortable because of the challenge that she presents to those of us who do not engage in costly acts of solidarity. She is the kind of martyr whose testimony, in the words of Julia Esquivel quoted by Emmanuel Katongole, keeps us from sleeping – even in a mostly silent meeting for worship.[7] Sitting with James Nayler, however, poses in some ways an even more difficult challenge. Nayler also, as we have seen, deliberately – or at least willingly – places himself on a collision

---

7 Emmanuel M. Katongole, 'Threatened with Resurrection: Martyrdom and Reconciliation in the World Church,' in Budde and Scott (eds), *Witness of the Body*, pp. 190–203; quoting Julia Esquivel, 1982, *Threatened with Resurrection*, Elgin, IL: The Brethren Press, pp. 59–61.

TESTIMONY

course with a governing power that is willing to use extreme measures against religious opponents and their (politically as well as religiously disruptive) activities. He also does so in the company of others – Martha Simmonds and her friends, Robert Rich who writes an account of the trial – even though he is finally portrayed as an isolated figure who serves as a representative figurehead. His final sense of 'being forsaken' is accompanied by an experience of 'fellowship' with all who suffer as he does.

So why might it be difficult to sit with James Nayler? Successive generations of Quakers found it relatively hard to sit with him, because his testimony appeared to damage or collide with theirs, to break the outward and inward unity of the Quaker movement, and to set itself at odds with the development of an 'ordered' people (to use terminology that appears in the historical chapters of *Quaker Faith and Practice*, and will be discussed further in my next chapter). Nayler – with his history of bitter conflicts with Fox and Fell among others, in which the continuing Quaker leaders do not come off particularly well – represents the brokenness of the Quaker community itself. His relative isolation in his trial, conviction and punishment point us back to the extreme vulnerability of the martyr – he risks not only suffering and dying, but being misunderstood, rejected or found to have been wrong. The 'appeal for interpretation' that he represents has not been fully met – possibly because Quakers still do not quite know what to make of him.

The encouraging fact, though, is that subsequent Quaker communities have continued to tell Nayler's story, in part because of the specific theological gifts his writings represent, but also as a story about the genuinely ambiguous and risky character of historical testimony. In exposing the willingness of the Quaker movement to abandon one of its own, the Nayler story reveals how the line of confrontation between truth and lies, which is also the line of confrontation between 'heretics and those who burn them', runs through any given community and any given person. In something of a similar vein, when the pacifist theologian James McClendon reads and reflects on the story of Dietrich Bonhoeffer – killed for his part in the plot to assassinate Hitler – McClendon notes the difficulties that Bonhoeffer's story poses for a Christian pacifist position and concludes that the temptation to pass judgement (either way) on Bonhoeffer himself is one that should be resisted. The critical questions, McClendon says, need to turn back on to the church and the society around Bonhoeffer, and on to contemporary churches and societies – and in the end on to oneself.

It is hard to read about Nayler without taking sides – but it is also hard not to feel uncomfortable about taking sides, because of the sense that everyone (including those who put Nayler on trial, and certainly including Cromwell as the head of state trying to handle the political ramifications of the trial) is trapped in, and by, a situation with no obvious way out. The tragedy does not easily resolve itself into a happy ending, even with hindsight. What Nayler's own writings, read in the context of his life, suggest is that the defence of an order of things – even a 'gospel order', a shared order emerging as the precarious result of a community's holy experiment – is always going to carry with it the risk of the abuse of power, and eventually to being 'found persecutors' rather than 'found in the work of God'. Nayler (again the man and his work, as we have seen it) has a specific and disturbing way of speaking truth to and about power. He puts the question sharply as to whether and where the victims of a system are being blamed for its abuses – like the martyrs blamed for their obstinacy, or the persecuted heretics for their bad doctrine.[8] He pushes the responsibility back on to those who hold the power (military, political, social or financial) to use it in

---

8 I have noted a tendency towards victim-blaming in some recent histories of religious conflict – not to mention in the labelling of the First World War conscientious objectors as 'cranks', discussed in the previous chapter. Ephraim Radner's magisterial *A Brutal Unity*, which discusses church divisions through inter alia the so-called European 'wars of religion' contains an extended discussion of conscience and the need to 'sacrifice' the individual conscience – for example, the promotion of an individual's religious convictions – for the sake of social peace and order. (Ephraim Radner, 2012, *A Brutal Unity: The Spiritual Politics of the Christian Church*, Waco, TX: Baylor University Press, especially Chapter 7 'Conscience and its Limits'.) This makes some ethical and theological sense if everyone has a weapon and is equally prepared to use it (and therefore needs to negotiate terms on which to lay it down); but it does not make very much ethical or theological sense to blame nonviolent Anabaptists like Balthasar Hübmaier for failing to 'sacrifice their consciences' – presumably, in order to save someone else the trouble of burning them at the stake.

ways that do not create victims – or at the very least, not to blame the victims they create. These are crucial questions for the majority of Quakers in the contemporary North and West. Nayler's testimony can challenge them to recognize and take responsibility for the power they have, to understand and confront the 'seeds of war' in the way that power is exercised – and, prompted also by Mary Dyer's work, to redirect it towards compassionate solidarity.

Looking further afield: risk, solidarity and religious freedom

Quakers in the contemporary North and West might be helped further, in their readings of Dyer and Nayler and other contested 'heroes' of the seventeenth century, by paying more attention to the experiences of Quakers in areas of contemporary religious conflict and in contexts in which compassionate solidarity can prove to be an extremely costly form of witness. I have already alluded to the lived and written testimony of members of the Quaker Peace Network Africa, arising from a wide range of recent and ongoing conflict situations. The experience of Abdul Kamara, the founder of the West African Quaker peace network, draws attention to the historically ambiguous and risky character of testimony, to the central importance of compassionate solidarity, and to the danger of isolation and failure. Kamara's movement towards reconciliation work in Sierra Leone began, as he recalled it, when he refused – on the spur of the moment – to take part in the revenge killing of a member of an armed group who had tortured him and raped his sister. His later work entailed close involvement with ex-combatants, including the groups who had been responsible for the attacks on his family.

> My mother was very very disappointed in me, seeing me doing this reintegration. She said, 'What are you doing? These are the people who tortured you. These are the people who raped your sister ... What are you doing? You are a disgrace.' I found myself not knowing what to do, whether to continue with my conviction to build peace, or to do what my mother said. Thank God I did

what my conviction asked me to do. (Abdul Kamara in Britain Yearly Meeting 2014, p. 34)

Kamara, like many of his fellow peacebuilders, follows his guide ('my conviction') in the face of strong and well-grounded countervailing ethical arguments – and, in the context he describes, with few reliable precedents and no guarantee of success. He makes this move, furthermore, from a position of extreme vulnerability that places him in solidarity with other victims of violence. Further reflection on his story might ask about the communal support that was – or was not – offered to Kamara in his decision-making processes and afterwards, and at the implications of claiming or enacting solidarity with those conducting this kind of extraordinarily risky experiment in 'answering that of God'.

One further area for reflection and action – which might emerge from the imagined meeting for worship with Dyer and Nayler among others – is the implications for interreligious dialogue and ways of attending to religious difference, among Quakers themselves and more widely.[9] At the start of this chapter, I suggested that the Quaker testimony on 'religious freedom' did not amount to an affirmation of any and all religious views as good or valid. But trust in the universal Light did and does, as we have already begun to see, provide an impulse to dialogue – not with the aim or expectation of reaching agreement on doctrine, but with the aim and expectation that truthful speech and action would 'answer' something already at work in the life of the other person. There is no programme, and no definite end point for this kind of dialogue; it is undertaken experimentally and – as some of the Quaker testimony we have already considered suggests – not without risk.

At least some of the recent theological literature on interreligious dialogue presents it as 'experimental' in at least some part of the Quaker sense – irreducibly local and particular, open to change

---

9 For a discussion of Quaker texts in relation to a specific form of interreligious encounter (scriptural reasoning), see Rachel Muers, 2012, 'Why Inter-faith Reading Makes Christian Sense II: The Tent and the Net', in Mike Higton and Rachel Muers, *The Text in Play: Experiments in Reading Scripture*, Eugene, OR: Wipf and Stock/Cascade, pp. 141–56.

TESTIMONY

but without a definite programme of development. At least some of the non-theological literature, meanwhile, draws attention to the wider social and political context of interreligious dialogue – and the dangers of being co-opted into a politically convenient account of what 'religion' is or should be. In this context, Quakers can offer a history of commitment to non-coercive witness to the 'universal love of God, which is of a general extent to all' (as George Whitehead put it). They can also offer some experience of living with 'experimental' ways, in complex and conflictual religious situations, of knowing and following God – and some rather persistent critiques of any attempt to make religion fit into a politically convenient box, particularly if that move will create more outsiders and eventually more victims.

6

Being Witnesses: Marriage, Sexuality and Tradition

Gospel order

I have mentioned briefly in previous chapters the idea of 'gospel order'. This is a complex term in Quaker thought, associated strongly with the 'order' of local and regional decision-making meetings (separately for men and women) established in the early decades, but with a far wider theological and practical scope. 'Gospel order' is, in broad terms, the social and communal order that emerges from the sustained experience of 'being gathered', the sustained practice of testimony, and the shared exercise of unprogrammed silent worship at the heart of all of this. It is both the positive provisional 'finding' of the Quaker experiment – at least as it relates to internal community organization and relationships – and the conditions within which that experiment goes on. As with many key Quaker terms – including 'testimony' itself – gospel order is understood as both something found and something done. The surprising 'finding' – surprising every time, although not in general – is that the Spirit of God is 'not a Spirit of disorder but of peace', and that what follows the testimonies of refusal is not chaos or random innovation but a definite shape of life. 'Gospel order', set alongside the idea of testimony, suggests, in fact, a Quaker approach to tradition – capturing the emphasis on the continuing guidance of the Spirit and on future-oriented discernment, but also the experience that a life thus guided is brought into 'the glorious order of the gospel' (Fox 1694/1952, p. 525; see *QF&P* 19.49).

TESTIMONY

In this chapter, I look at an area of Quaker thought and practice that relates closely to 'gospel order' and is currently a source of considerable internal and external controversy – as it was, for somewhat different reasons, in the early decades of Quakerism. Quaker practice in relation to marriage, and Quaker theological reflection around marriage, provides what might look like a strong counter-example to the picture I have painted so far, of 'testimonies against' and of conflictual and transformative encounters with the cultural context. On the one hand, the celebration of marriage is clearly not just or mainly a testimony 'against' something; and on the other hand, liberal Quakers in the contemporary West, in recent decisions to recognize and celebrate marriages of same-sex couples, stand accused (including by some Quakers) of a betrayal of their tradition and a capitulation to prevailing cultural norms.[1]

I address this challenge, in what follows, first by looking more closely at what it means to call marriage 'Quaker testimony', and how this might fit into the account of testimony I have already given; and then by examining recent developments in Quaker thinking about marriage and sexuality in the light of the key terms and ideas discussed in this book. It should be said from the start, first, that I do want to argue that the recognition and celebration of marriages between same-sex couples is an intelligible and faithful development of Quaker testimony; and, second, that I cannot possibly on my own terms argue that it is the *only* intelligible and faithful development of Quaker testimony on this matter. At the time of writing, questions of sexuality and marriage divide global Quakerism, and Quakerism within some countries (most notably the USA), to the point where peaceable dialogue and shared discernment processes

---

1 In preparing this chapter I have drawn on work I was asked to do, in the aftermath of changes in British Quaker marriage practice and subsequently of British marriage legislation, both for the AHRC/ESRC Religion and Society network and for Britain Yearly Meeting, in particular the Committee for Christian and Interfaith Relations. I am grateful to Simon Reader, Linda Woodhead, Marigold Bentley, and others involved, for requests that made me think. I also acknowledge helpful conversations with Frank Cranmer about the 2013 marriage legislation; and with Susannah Cornwall, John Bradbury, and others involved in an ongoing project on the theology of marriage, about many related issues.

scarcely seem possible.[2] Quakers are probably, if anything, some way behind other worldwide church families and groupings in working through differences on matters of sexuality – partly because there are relatively few structural imperatives to do so.[3]

There is, as far as I can see, relatively little point in attempting to identify agreement or common practice, among Quakers globally, on sexuality per se.[4] There is more point in uncovering some of the broader continuities, with the wide sweep of Quaker practice and thought, that enable specific developments – here, the recognition of same-sex marriage – to be recognized as ways forward. In keeping with my emphasis on the embodied and historically located character of testimony – its 'experimental' character, in my terms – much of this chapter focuses on the experiences of Quakers in Britain (mostly, to be accurate, in England), in their encounters with a specific and changing set of social and legal structures.

Looking back: Quaker marriage as 'testimony against'

In 1663 Charles and Mary Appleby, a Quaker couple from Liskeard, Cornwall, were summoned and questioned by the mayor and

---

2 In 2008, Britain Yearly Meeting reconsidered the policy of publishing all epistles from other Yearly Meetings worldwide, with a view to 'care for gay and lesbian Friends who share an equal place in our Yearly Meeting' – the presenting issue being strongly anti-homosexual language and sentiments in the epistles from certain Yearly Meetings in East Africa. The decision, in the event, was to make all epistles available in print form 'so that we can face our differences in truth and love' – but not to publish them through the Britain Yearly Meeting website (Minute 35 of Britain Yearly Meeting 2008). For an example from a different part of the Quaker geographical and theological spectrum, 2013 saw a split within Indiana Yearly Meeting over questions of authority and structure precipitated by differences of practice in relation to welcoming same-sex couples into Quaker meetings. (For an account that also gives a 'strong reading' of how the issues relate to Quaker history and tradition, see the interview with Thomas Hamm, a member of the newly formed Indiana grouping – New Association of Friends – in *Friends Journal* 2013, http://www.friendsjournal.org/thomas-hamm-on-division-in-indiana/.)

3 For an account of some recent discussions within global networks of yearly meetings (such as Friends United Meeting) and within the Friends World Conference, see Petra L. Doan and Elizabeth P. Kampenhausen, 'Quakers and Sexuality', in Stephen W. Angell and Pink Dandelion (eds), 2013, *The Oxford Handbook of Quaker Studies*, Oxford: Oxford University Press, pp. 445–58.

4 I am not convinced, for example, by the suggestion of Doan and Kampenhausen that 'helpsmeet relationships' are or should be 'at the foundation' of all Quaker views of marriage and sexuality ('Quakers and Sexuality', p. 457).

TESTIMONY

eventually imprisoned in Launceston gaol. Charles Appleby had in the meantime spent several weeks in 'a nasty prison called the dark house'. Their misdemeanour, according to the fellow Quaker who recorded the incident, was that 'they would not be married according to the laws of this Kingdom'. Their simple marriage ceremony had taken place – as is recorded of another couple at around the same time – in 'the assembly of many Friends met together to wait upon the Lord'. Like several other Quaker couples arrested and imprisoned on similar grounds – mostly, as it would appear, by zealous local magistrates rather than in a campaign of organized persecution – the Applebys were eventually released without charge, and presumably resumed their married life.[5]

The Applebys had at least some reason, even without appeals to distinctive Quaker theology and practice, to claim that their marriage was valid. They had, after all, expressed mutual consent and exchanged vows before a group of witnesses, albeit not before any state authority, ecclesial or civil. In claiming that this was sufficient for marriage, they were not being particularly radical or innovative. They were harking back to pre-modern marriage practice, picking up the Reformation's resistance to the recognition of marriage as a sacrament, and drawing on a long-established principle of marriage by expressed mutual consent, which continued (for example) to hold good in Scotland long after a succession of changes in England had brought marriage under extensive state regulation.

In fact, in the confused overlay of marriage laws in Restoration England – a 1653 provision for 'civil' marriage, before a justice of the peace, had lapsed in 1660 – the Applebys would probably have had many non-Quaker neighbours who had not been married before a priest, or who understood the basic principle that expressed and witnessed mutual consent made a marriage valid.[6]

---

5 *Record of the Sufferings of Quakers in Cornwall 1655–1686*, 1686/1928, ed. Norman Penney (Friends Historical Society), London: Friends Book Centre, p. 52.

6 Christopher Durston, 1989, *The Family in the English Revolution*, Oxford: Blackwell. The requirement for marriage to be witnessed and confirmed by a Justice of the Peace was introduced in the 1653 *Act touching Marriages and the Registring thereof; and also touching Births and Burials*.

BEING WITNESSES

But, as their arrest suggests, by not engaging with state authorities they had placed their relationship in a legal and social grey area – and, in a pattern that Quakers were to maintain, setting themselves notably apart from majority practice, even more so than other Nonconformist groups that celebrated marriages outwith the established church.[7] When, much later through the Hardwicke Act, English marriage was brought under a single framework of regulation and reporting, Quakers and Jews were the two groups for whom special provision was made to exempt them from the obligation to be married in the Church of England.[8]

---

7 N. H. Keeble, 2002, *Cultural Identity of Women in the Seventeenth Century,* London: Routledge, p. 117, states simply that between 1660 and 1753 'the marriages of Quakers and others separated or excluded from the Church of England were quite legal'. But the Quaker literature suggests a rather more precarious situation. In any case, many of those 'separated or excluded from the Church of England' had less objection to, and less community pressure against, marriage 'before the priest', and hence had more options than did Quakers for regularizing their situation. Rebecca Probert, 2009, *Marriage Law and Practice in the Long Eighteenth Century: A Reassessment,* Cambridge: Cambridge University Press, p.154, asserts much more plausibly that the evidence concerning social and legal recognition of Quaker marriage in the late 1600s and early 1700s is 'fragmented and contradictory'.

8 Clause XVIII of the *Act for the better preventing of clandestine marriage* (1753 – known as Hardwicke's Act) states that 'nothing contained in this Act shall extend... to any Marriage among the people called Quakers, or amongst the Persons professing the Jewish religion' – providing that both parties to the marriage were members of the relevant religious community. By comparison with other groups affected (other Nonconformists, and Roman Catholics) Quakers appear to have mounted a very effective campaign for exemption from the provisions of the Act; but this does not explain why, as a small group, they gained a hearing. One frequently cited reason is that Quaker record-keeping was sufficiently reliable to be an acceptable substitute for the parish marriage register. Certainly Quakers had insisted from early on that all members made their commitment public, and in connection with this had made a point of keeping records (of births and deaths as well as marriages) and being prepared to show them to the authorities. It also seems plausible that the precedent of making an exception for Quakers in the matter of oaths and affirmation made it more likely that they would be given concessions as an identifiable 'peculiar people' in subsequent legislation. And of course one obvious thing that Quakers and Jews have in common is not (usually) being baptized – which would have raised problems for a priest required to marry them according to the rites of the Church of England. Just to make things more complicated, the 1753 Act does not actually say explicitly that Quaker or Jewish marriages are legally valid; as far as I have been able to ascertain, that was not put into the statute book until 1949. Anyone who has made it to the end of this note and still feels the need to know more about Hardwicke's Act and the resulting tangles in English marriage law (tangles that became all too apparent in the course of consultations on same-sex marriage legislation in the twenty-first century) is recommended to consult R. B. Outhwaite, 1995, *Clandestine Marriage in England, 1500–1850,* London: Hambledon; on Quakers, see pp. 85–6.

TESTIMONY

Why would Quakers have wanted to do marriage so differently? It was not obvious, in the early Quakers' context, that marriage needed to be held within the context of a meeting for worship, brought directly into the sphere of the church community. While the Reformation had – as a broad generalization – accorded greater value to the married state (as opposed to being celibate), it had also tended to secularize the marriage ceremony itself. At least some of what early Quakers wrote about marriage, and many of the features of how they celebrated marriage, demonstrated that they shared – and, unsurprisingly, carried to extremes – the Puritan wish to purge marriage ceremonies and practices of 'superstitious' accretions, dispensing with the accumulation of (as they saw it) 'empty forms'.

If this were all that they had been doing, Quakers would have been unlikely to attract special attention. However, it is fairly clear even from the brief accounts of the 'sufferings' of married Quakers – and even more so from the more extensive Quaker and anti-Quaker writings on marriage – first, that their marriages were recognizably very unusual, and second, that what made them unusual was linked to their solemnization in meetings for worship. Quakers seem to have thought that they were *changing* marriage, not just performing a minimal version of whatever existed already. The frequently quoted passage from a (relatively late) letter of George Fox – 'We marry none, it is the Lord's work, and we are but witnesses' – gestures towards the scope of their claim.[9]

Put briefly, placing the marriage ceremony in a meeting for worship, and calling it 'the Lord's work', allowed it to be acknowledged as a sign of gathering – of the inbreaking and transformative reign of God, the restoration of right relationships between God and humanity and among human beings. Marriage contributed – in some way, which I will discuss below – to this renewed pattern of community. Moreover, the 'witnesses' to this work saw it through, in the face both of problematic existing structures of marriage and

---

[9] George Fox, 1698, *A Collection of Many Select and Christian Epistles*, London: Sowle, Epistle 264.

of the widespread supposition that anything different from the present norm of marriage was disordered and destructive.

So, as we might expect, part of what shapes Quaker marriage is a tradition of 'denying lies'. Part of this was the refusal of 'forms', to which I have already referred; but another part of it is reflected in the wider context of the quotation from Fox, and in the social situation to which it refers. The letter from which the quotation is taken – a relatively late Epistle, written after the major persecutions of Quakers – focuses mainly, not on a positive account of what marriage is, but a critique of existing practices of marriage. The occasion for the critique is the fact that some of those identified as Quakers – like other Nonconformists – were choosing to 'marry before the priest'. The target of the letter, then, is those who are 'pretended . . . Friends' but who do not behave accordingly. Before jumping to the conclusion that this is simply a matter of reinforcing the boundaries of an exclusive community identity, it is worth paying some attention to Fox's argument against marrying before the priest.

> And all those pretended Friend or Friends, who have gone to the priests to marry them, or have been drawn by their relations so to do, in pretence of having their estates secured for their heirs, these have gone out from the light of Christ in themselves . . . and both priests and the world say that they are hypocrites, and that they come to them only to save their estates . . . and they talk of the living God, but it is seen the world is their god, and the priest must do their work to preserve their estate. (Fox 1698, Epistle 264)

The first problem with 'marrying before the priest' – that is, in this context, marrying in a way that secures universal public and legal recognition – is that it is done in order to 'save their estates', that is, to ensure that children are recognized as legitimate inheritors of family wealth. There is an attempt to dislodge marriage from its place in a system of economic and social recognition, or, more precisely, from its function in securing and perpetuating economic and social privilege. Quakers are supposed to want marriage without the respectability. Part of the reason given for this is historic. The text in question contains numerous references to 'ancient testimony' and 'the witness of the martyrs'; the present refusal to accept 'respectable' marriage is grounded in the sufferings of those who previously refused it.

This last, in itself, is not a particularly persuasive argument; just because others have suffered for doing something in the past does not make it right, now or even then. Appealing to past sufferings may be a useful way to keep the community in line and to form a stronger sense of oppositional identity ('we are the people whom the world oppresses because of what we do'), but in itself it bears relatively little theological weight. The deeper plausibility of the argument about the 'witness of the martyrs', however, rests on the claim that those who marry before the priest 'distrust the living God about outward things'. Marriage-without-respectability – marriage not recognized, or only marginally recognized, by a wider society – represents a considerable social and economic risk, mitigated chiefly – in the period when Quaker marriages were not universally recognized – by the ad hoc support of the community.

In Fox's reading of biblical texts on marriage, he focuses on texts that appear to show marriages solemnized through a simple declaration of intention – in the presence of witnesses (an example being Boaz and Ruth), or originally with only God as a witness (Adam and Eve). Marriages thus conducted, and those who contract them, are described as holy; and their holiness is related closely to their simplicity of form. The wedding at Cana is mentioned, apparently to bring the 'witnessing' of marriage into Jesus' ministry.

More widely, marriage is understood here as part of the good order of the world, its orderliness compared to the promiscuity of the fallen state; as Eugene Rogers and others have argued, in which marriage can be seen as a 'negative' ascetic discipline aimed at the re-forming of sexual desire – with the open-ended, affirmative and transformative character of ascetic discipline clearly in view.[10] This,

---

10 Eugene F. Rogers, 1999, *Sexuality and the Christian Body: Their Way into the Triune God*, Oxford: Blackwell; see especially Ch. 3.

however, might be agreed on by those who sought to 'marry before the priest'; the Quakers' opponents could join the Quakers in condemning the sexual libertinism associated with certain other radical groups. The distinctive feature of seventeenth-century Quaker marriage practice was that it affirmed order and discipline while deliberately shunning respectability.

Marriage, in Fox's letter and comparable texts, and practised in the community that they address, is detached from specific existing institutions and related to a vision of life 'before the Fall'. It is important to note, however, that this does not mean a privatization of marriage. In fact, and in the seventeenth-century context, to call marriage 'the Lord's work' and to link talk of marriage to the pre-Fall condition is to make it dramatically transformative of social and political reality. For this community to be 'witnesses of the Lord's work', like the community present at a marriage, is not, as it were, to rubber-stamp a private transaction between two individuals. Rather, it is to be caught up in the movement of testimony that I have described in previous chapters.

One – perhaps inevitable – consequence of this decision to 'do marriage differently' was the relatively strict enforcement by the Quaker community (and particularly by the women's meetings) of the 'order' that it claimed for its distinctive practice of marriage. Barry Levy has argued that for Quakers in the Americas, marginalized in public life and with minimal liturgy, the family became the focus of intense interest as the place in which the holy life was learned and performed – the place in which the Quakers' alternative community took shape.[11]

The other side of this phenomenon, however, is that Quakers *were* seen to be practising a genuine 'alternative' – and not, as we have seen, one that was particularly respectable or honourable. Even after the official and semi-official persecution of Quakers ended, however, suspicion attached to Quaker marriage, and is reflected in ongoing themes of anti-Quaker writings. For the

---

11 Barry Levy, 1988, *Quakers and the American Family*, Oxford: Oxford University Press.

TESTIMONY

oddity of Quaker marriage was not only in the ceremony or lack of it, or in its institutional location. The authority accorded to Quaker women, individually as ministers and collectively as the 'women's meeting' – with particular responsibility for approving marriages – was equally or more disturbing to existing sex/gender codes. The visible spiritual authority of Quaker women lent itself to the public ridicule of Quaker husbands; the henpecked Quaker husband – and/or his domineering Quaker wife – was a staple of popular satire. So was the Quaker whose 'spiritual' and egalitarian understanding of marriage was a front for adultery or sexual licence.[12]

The point here is not simply that Quakers were targets for sexually based comedy and satire – this was also true of Puritans, and later of Methodists and of several other groups whose claims to holiness opened them immediately to accusations of hypocrisy. The point, rather, is that Quaker marriage – and not just the Quaker marriage ceremony – was a sustained challenge to an existing social and sexual order, which entailed various costly refusals and provoked conflict. Quakers took for granted that the present 'order' of things, as enforced by the governing authorities, was in fact to a greater or lesser extent *dis*ordered, systematically blind or antagonistic to divine truth. The persecution of those who 'could not submit to the world's way' in the matter of marriage ceremonies was simply one among many instances of this. So Quakers' enacted resistance to existing norms of marriage was not a generalized rebellion against the institution of marriage, however much it looked that way to the mayor of Launceston. Still less was it a rebellion against all ordering in sexual relationships. It was a specific attempt at the *right ordering* of marriage – seeking to

---

12 On this see Levy, *Quakers and the American Family*, pp. 82–4; Mark Knights, 2011, *The Devil in Disguise: Deception, Delusion and Fanaticism in the Early English Enlightenment*, Oxford: Oxford University Press, Ch. 3. A further intriguing example of the comic use of the public image of Quaker hypocrisy, particularly in relation to sexuality, is Charles Shadwell's play *The Fair Quaker of Deal* (1720), in which the heroine is eventually convinced to return to the established church by a demonstration of how easy it is for a prostitute to 'pass' as a Quaker.

follow the guidance of God in setting marriage into order, within the wider context of God's transforming and reconciling work.

Now, Quakers' commitment to discerning and following the movements of the Holy Spirit in history – particularly in the history on the underside of power, the history of Charles Appleby's 'dark house' rather than Charles Stuart's restored kingdom – also meant acknowledging that 'right ordering' was a future-oriented and dynamic process that did not follow an existing blueprint. The directions of God's ordering activity – towards peace and mutual love, towards free and joyful worship, towards self-giving life together as 'helps-meet in the image of God' – could and should be learned from scripture and from past experience, but none of that could substitute for the present task of attention to the guidance of the Holy Spirit.

Twentieth- and twenty-first-century changes

In 2009, Britain Yearly Meeting in York recorded the decision

> to treat same sex committed relationships in the same way as opposite sex marriages, reaffirming our central insight that marriage is the Lord's work and we are but witnesses. The question of legal recognition by the state is secondary . . . [S]ame sex marriages [will] be prepared, celebrated, witnessed, recorded and reported to the state, as opposite sex marriages are. (Britain Yearly Meeting 2009, minute 25)[13]

At the time in Britain, as the minute suggests, to treat same-sex couples in *exactly* the same way as opposite-sex couples, with regard to marriage, was not fully possible within the law. Quaker weddings were already legally recognized as marriage ceremonies;

---

13 This decision came later – in some cases by a considerable margin – than decisions by various North American yearly meetings to support legal recognition for same-sex marriage (North Pacific Yearly Meeting in 1997, see http://npym.org/docs/minutes/minute1997_marriage.pdf; Canadian Yearly Meeting in 2003), and narrowly preceded a similar decision by Australia Yearly Meeting in 2010.

it was the stated aim of the 2009 Yearly Meeting to work towards this legal recognition for same-sex couples married in Quaker meetings. More to the point, it was the Meeting's stated understanding that, in any case and whatever the law might say, such couples *were* married. The paraphrase of the quotation from Fox ('marriage is the Lord's work and we are but witnesses') and the choice of verbs relating to marriage ('prepared, celebrated, witnessed, recorded and reported' – as opposed, for example, to 'performed') emphasizes this affirmation.

The historical and theological trails that led to decisions by Quaker bodies to recognize and celebrate same-sex marriage are numerous. Same-sex marriage is most often described, within and outside Quakerism, as an issue of *equality* – one preferred term by campaigners being 'marriage equality'. However, as the Britain Yearly Meeting minute suggests and as I have outlined above, there are also important links to the history and theology of Quaker marriage – in which the celebration of marriage becomes itself a form of testimony, a practice of seeing and affirming the truth. In fact, I would suggest that the question of 'equality' is secondary, both in the history and in the theology of the Quaker affirmation of same-sex marriage, to the question of truth.

In its context in the 2009 minute, the quotation points to the crucial role, in Yearly Meeting's decision, of attending to the experience of same-sex (as well as opposite-sex) couples.[14] The decision to recognize the relationships of these couples as marriages was framed, in this minute and in the Meeting's deliberations, as an acknowledgement of what was already the case, rather than as an innovation. Against the criticisms at the time and since, that celebrating same-sex marriage was an unjustifiable and highly risky social 'experiment', the Yearly Meeting affirmed that it was 'experimental' – grounded in experience. The implicit response

---

14 It is perhaps noteworthy that 'listening' to the experiences of gay and lesbian people has frequently been mentioned in statements by the churches as an essential step towards resolving disputes over issues of sexuality. See for example resolution 1.10 of the Lambeth Conference 1998, part c: 'We commit ourselves to listen to the experience of homosexual persons.'

to oft-cited fears about what *might* happen if same-sex couples were to get married was 'we already have some idea, because it already happens'. While the decision was recognized as the beginning of a process – of negotiation over the legal situation, and also of communicating and reflecting on the implications of the new situation – it was also located within a longer and ongoing process of seeking to act and speak faithfully in relation to marriage and sexuality.

Failing to recognize the marriages of same-sex couples would, from the perspective of the 2009 Yearly Meeting, have been untruthful. More precisely, it would have been a failure properly to conform one's words and actions to 'the Lord's work'. On the one hand, the suggestion that 'we marry none' disclaims control over marriage – and hence, again implicitly, rebuts the suggestion that this is an attempt to *redefine* marriage or to promote a particular self-interested agenda. On the other hand, however, the reference to being 'witnesses' to 'the Lord's work', in the context of the longer history of Quaker testimony, is a commitment to action. In practice, in this particular example, the implied commitment to action has been borne out both in the celebration of marriages of same-sex couples and in public campaigns for changes in the law.

It was impossible to deny, however, that the recognition and affirmation of the mutual commitment of same-sex couples – starting some time before 2009 – was itself a relatively new development in Quaker thought and practice. It arose in a specific social context and in the wake of social change. In order to understand how this development can itself be seen as part of a longer story of Quaker testimony, we need to look rather more closely at the document that is often cited as its starting point.

Towards a Quaker View of Sex, published in 1963, is widely regarded – not only by Quakers in Britain – as a small landmark in the recent history of attitudes to sexuality. It gains this status not mainly for its conclusions – which were certainly controversial at the time, but not novel – but rather for the fact that it was published by a national Christian body. Although not an agreed statement by Quakers in Britain, it gave an unprecedented level of 'official' Christian approval to the acceptance of homosexual relationships – at a time when sexual acts between men were still illegal in Britain, and in the context of widespread public debate leading up to the partial decriminalization of male homosexuality. The most widely quoted conclusion of the committee of authors is the proposal that the moral character of a sexual act, and the 'nature and quality' of a sexual relationship, are not determined by its physical form (Heron et al. 1963). The authors seek to locate and evaluate the moral character of a sexual act in the larger context of the lives and relationships of which it is part; they direct critiques at the functionalization of relationships and the trivialization of sexuality, at exploitation in sexual relationships, and, crucially as we shall see, at social and sexual 'hypocrisy'.

Nowadays, *Towards a Quaker View of Sex* is probably more talked about than read. As David Blamires notes in his recent history of British Quaker attitudes to homosexuality, the considerable controversy at the time of the report's initial publication mainly related to its refusal unequivocally to condemn extra-marital (heterosexual) sex. It fitted into a narrative of anxiety about sexual 'permissiveness' in the early 1960s, and gained most of its public shock value – including its shock value within the Society of Friends – from its apparent affirmation of a younger generation's break with 'traditional' sexual mores. Many of the criticisms of *Towards a Quaker View of Sex* related to its perceived affirmation of sexual libertinism, and/or the apparent application – because of the rather vague criteria proposed for evaluating sexual relationships – of something like Fletcher's situation ethics to matters of sexuality.[15] Paul Ramsey argued that the report failed to 'take sexual responsibility seriously enough' by failing to acknowledge the importance of *rules* for Christian ethics – rules that in themselves 'embody . . . responsibility'.[16]

---

15 This is the assumption made by Robin Gill, 2006, *A Textbook of Christian Ethics*, 3rd edn, London: T&T Clark, p. 429. See also David Hilliard, 1997, 'The Religious Crisis of the 1960s: The Experience of the Australian Churches', *Journal of Religious History* 22/1, pp. 209–27.

16 Paul Ramsey, 1967, *Deeds and Rules in Christian Ethics*, New York: Scribner, p. 6.

BEING WITNESSES

The inclusion of excerpts from *Towards a Quaker View of Sex* in still-current textbooks on Christian ethics ensures that it does not drop entirely out of view, but it is rarely read or evaluated as a piece of specifically *Quaker* ethical thought.[17] One of the consequences of this is that it tends to be read for its conclusions, which on their own do look like rather vague statements of principle, a bit like the Quaker 'list testimonies' if you read them on their own without their shared and storied context. If we attend to the context, the occasion and the intended function of the document – the *act* of Quaker testimony that it was in its time – it makes a different kind of sense.

In their own words, the authors of *Towards a Quaker View of Sex* regarded themselves as acting *under concern*. They were responding as they saw it to a 'gift from God, a leading of his Spirit which may not be denied' (p. 3). They were, as the list of names, jobs and qualifications inside the front cover suggests, a mixed group.[18] Many of them were academics, but they were not mainly writing the piece as an academic exercise; they did not undertake original research for the essay, and most of its claims (especially its theological claims) had already appeared elsewhere. Quaker academics wanted to write this book principally as a response to the pastoral needs of their students; from a sense of the insufficiency both of their own existing resources and of their generation's existing resources to answer the questions that were put to them (Heron et al. 1963, p. 5).[19]

There would, of course, have been the option of reaffirming the status quo. Writing the essay and publishing the essay was,

---

17 Gill, *A Textbook of Christian Ethics*, extract 27, pp. 388–93.

18 The attention drawn to their qualifications – and also to the status of several of them as elders of Britain Yearly Meeting, and hence to the (constrained and time-limited) authority they carried in their worshipping communities – is one of the many features of the document that reads oddly to contemporary Quaker eyes. There is a possible comparison with the omission of Bayard Rustin's name from the list of authors of *Speak Truth to Power* – with a view to shaping how the document was read and to ensuring a hearing.

19 I also recall hearing this account of the book's genesis from one of the authors, Anna M. Bidder, in the early 1990s at one of the last discussion evenings she held for Quaker students in Cambridge; she had by then been hosting, and listening to, groups of students for over 40 years.

according to the Introduction, mainly about breaking a public silence about sexuality and sexual ethics. It was a challenge to social hypocrisy and insincerity (p. 5), and to the dangers and inequities sustained by an existing code of respectability. The authors perceived a gulf between publicly available guidance and reflection, and ordinary lived experience as they heard it voiced particularly by younger Quakers. There was a pastoral and practical need for new writing about 'sexual problems and morals' – not in the first place to change sexual behaviour, but simply to make it possible to talk about what was going on. The core point was – to borrow the title of a later work by the Quaker Women's Group – to bring the invisible into the light; and to name and reject some of the ways in which marriage (in a particular context and framed in particular ways) had become a social idol.

Towards a Quaker View of Sex is a document grounded in experience, responding to a 'leading' characterized by compassionate solidarity, and produced in an extended (and, by all accounts, extremely challenging) shared process as a result of which the authors could jointly affirm its contents. Many criticisms can be made of its specific contents. It often reads as oddly outdated in some of its conventionally 'experimental' claims – particularly when the authors talk about what 'science' has established in relation to human sexuality and gender. It would scarcely be taken now as a 'simple fact' that each personality contains a 'balance of the male and the female' and that this is demonstrated by a man who shows 'feminine tenderness and care' – less still, that this alleged fact has any relevance to questions about male or female homosexuality (pp. 32–3). At points like this, the essay draws attention to the risks of any attempt to bring together theology, ethics and science; the scientific 'discipline' moves on, and any theological or ethical conclusions that were tied too closely to scientific claims lose a significant part of their support. The same could be said, of course, of many other attempts to put forward scientific evidence concerning what is or is not 'natural' in human sexuality – on either side of contemporary marriage debates.

In context – this needs to be emphasized again – the authors of *Towards a Quaker View of Sex* were not trying to use their scientific knowledge as the basis for a new set of social rules; they were trying to challenge a rather powerful set of existing assumptions about what was and was not natural, healthy or a recognizable part of human experience. Specifically, these assumptions wielded power over the lives and bodies, in particular, of gay men, whose sexual activity was not only 'extra-marital' and publicly disapproved of, but illegal and publicly unspeakable. The criticisms of the 'liberal' aspects of *Towards a Quaker View of Sex* rather rarely address the sharp end of its 'liberalism' – the critique of anti-homosexual legislation and of publicly sanctioned homophobia. The question of one critic, as to whether what is proposed in *Towards a Quaker View of Sex* is 'an ethics only for the strong, intelligent and middle-class', rather misses the point. What the document does for the privileged (the 'strong') among its authors and readers is ask them to recognize the suffering caused by the system from which they benefit – benefit, that is, in so far as their relationships and their sexuality are socially 'respectable' and protected by law.

Towards a Quaker View of Sex, then, 'speaks truth to power' in a way that recalls both the document of that name – a critical intervention on a public issue intended both to draw attention to existing wrongs and to call for new ways forward – and, more obviously perhaps, recalls Mary Dyer, in following a leading grounded in compassionate perception of truth. The vagueness of its conclusions is a problem only if we suppose that the intention was to provide a comprehensive sexual ethic. However, even the vague concepts – particularly, as we might expect, the negative ones – become rather less vague when thought about in relation to actual situations. Challenging 'exploitation' in sexual relationships and in matters relating to sexuality, for example, caught and still catches a wider range of sexual and social wrongs (the one not easily separable from the other) than does insistence on heterosexual marriage.

Taken seriously – and a step or two further than the authors of *Towards a Quaker View of Sex* would have done – the focus on 'exploitation' suggests that any way of ordering sexuality and sexual relationships needs to be examined critically for the 'seeds' of violence, for the voices it excludes or for the victims it creates. *Towards a Quaker View of Sex* invites, although it does not fully conduct, an analysis of social attitudes to sexuality that goes beyond a focus on individual freedom and its limits. As an aside, it seems to me that in the early twenty-first century – from the position, once again, of an academic with pastoral concerns for students – the critical reordering most urgently needed in sexual attitudes is rather directly concerned with exploitation, the exploitation of women that results from a very persistent sexual double standard (still working within the assumption of normative heterosexuality), from a resurgent misogyny, and from a conflicting set of social pressures relating to body image and embodiment. The continuing work of Quaker feminist theologians and feminist campaigners might well be brought to bear on the next few steps 'towards' a Quaker view of sex. This last point, however, brings me back to the question of 'gospel order'.

Conclusion: towards what view of sex?

I have presented *Towards a Quaker View of Sex*, particularly in relation to homosexuality, as a critical intervention, a piece of negative testimony aimed at denying the lies being told about and around sexuality. What, though – its critics implicitly asked – did this mean for the future; what kind of 'order' could emerge, and what could be said about that 'order' theologically? The suggestion that an appeal to love does not promote any kind of social order is understandable if what is meant by 'love' is romantic attraction. But this does not seem to be what the authors of *Towards a Quaker View of Sex* are talking about; and even if it is what they are talking about, it is not necessarily what Quakers are talking about when they refer to being guided by love or 'attend[ing] to what love requires' (*QF&P* 1.02.28). The more obvious reference is to the guidance of the Spirit of God that gathers and forms communities, transforms individual lives and social contexts – and establishes, to refer again to the text frequently used by early Quakers in discussions of marriage and of church governance, not disorder but peace.

BEING WITNESSES

From this point of view, the story from *Towards a Quaker View of Sex* to the 2009 Yearly Meeting decision – and beyond – is not just a story of progress towards greater acceptance, among Quakers, of individual gay and lesbian people and of same-sex relationships (although it is also that).[20] It is also a story of Quaker communities working out what love requires, and what kind of order can take shape, once the reality of same-sex sexual desire and of faithful committed relationships between same-sex couples is recognized. Working this out does not mean denying the manifold realities of social and sexual *dis*order. Recognizing and celebrating same-sex marriage was not, in fact, an obvious step. Another possible and logical step – from the critique of homophobia – would have been to reject the institution of marriage altogether. It was not even obvious or certain in 2009 – after a very long period of intensive preliminary work and consultation – that the decision would go as it did.[21]

So what did the affirmation of same-sex marriage mean? To a critic, the claim that a currently unrecognized form of marriage is 'the Lord's work' might simply sound disingenuous – the excuse used by any fanatical sect for going its own way and following its own notions, in disregard for tradition, public authority or the common good. It might also sound like a privatization and abstraction of marriage, making it a curiously disembodied transaction between the couple and God – with minimal importance for, or effect on, society. How can marriage be a publicly recognized reality and a public good, and at the same time be just 'the Lord's work'?

Let us begin with the positive claim. I have already suggested, at least implicitly, that marriage – as an embodied social and political practice, sustained intergenerationally – has some of the characteristics of testimony. Marriage is 'the Lord's work' of which

---

[20] See for the full story – as both a history and a memoir – David Blamires, 2012, *Pushing at the Frontiers of Change: A Memoir of Quaker Involvement with Homosexuality*, London: Quaker Books.

[21] Anecdotally, the clarity of the decision came as a surprise to at least some of those most involved in preparing and organizing the business of the Yearly Meeting.

people are 'witnesses'; the same could be said about peacemaking. It is one of the activities, one of the patterns of life, in which people are caught up in the movement of divine truth. God's work and human 'witnessing' are not separate moments; the work of God occurs as the witness is caught up in God's work.

It does, as I have already mentioned and as numerous recent works suggest, make at least some sense to talk about marriage as 'negative testimony' – at least as ascetic practice. Lifelong sexual fidelity is, after all, a sustained 'refusal' of sorts that defines a space within which genuine flourishing emerges. More basically than this, marriage commits people to a sustained and graced 'loss of control'– over one's self-image, identity, body. Christian theological *opposition* to calls for same-sex marriage could, of course, begin from the claim that marriage is one among many forms of ascetic practice, in relation to sexuality, to which Christians are called. But it is also possible to construct a theological account of marriage that includes same-sex union and still has a central place for the ascetic. Eugene Rogers' work, to which I have already referred, is among the best recent examples of this.

It does not seem at all right, however, to talk about marriage in negative terms, even briefly. Looking at marriage is looking at a 'glorious order', at surprising gifts of flourishing and abundant life, at a small and local and historically contingent lived sign of the inbreaking reign of God. It is one of the places where being truthful 'witnesses of the Lord's work' entails not just recognition but celebration. William Penn's letter to his wife Gulielma (née Springett) before his departure for America, after ten years of marriage, catches something of the enduring surprise of marriage, as a real gift of God that resists 'spiritualization':

> My dear Wife, Remember thou was the love of my youth, and much the joy of my life – the most beloved as well as the most worthy of all my earthly comforts; and the reason of that love was more thy inward than thy outward excellencies, which yet are many. God knows and thou knowest I can say it was a match of His making; and God's image in us both was the first things,

and the most amiable and engaging ornament in our eyes. (Penn 1682/1867)[22]

Deciding to 'recognize and celebrate' the marriages of same-sex couples set up, briefly, for Quakers in Britain a situation in which a form of worship to which they understood themselves called – in conscience, like the seventeenth-century Quakers insisting on holding public meetings – was not legal. Part of the concern behind seeking a change in the law was, then, a concern for religious freedom – not freedom in principle to do whatever this religious community might happen to choose, but freedom to follow a path already cleared, or to live out a specific vocation.

Like early Quaker marriage practices, the 2009 decision immediately opened Quakers up to charges of sexual libertinism, of abandoning all sexual and familial order (as well as abandoning Christianity), and of seeking to destroy basic social institutions. Often these charges – whether they are made against Quakers or against other religious and secular proponents of same-sex marriage – seem to be based on the false assumption that any break with a given order is a fall into disorder. Attention to dissenting marriage practices might encourage readers to look instead at the manifold disorders in the historical institution and practice of marriage – including the various 'dark houses' to which transgressors of sexual and gender codes have been confined – and ask how the celebration of same-sex marriages can be a matter of hope.

---

22 For more on the lives and subsequent 'myths' of William Penn's wives – Gulielma, who died in 1694, and Hannah Penn née Callowhill – see Alison Duncan Hirsch, 1994, 'A Tale of Two Wives: Mythmaking and the Lives of Gulielma and Hannah Penn', *Pennsylvania History* 61/4, pp. 429–56.

7

Sustainability and Simplicity

The Kabarak call

One of the major areas of development for Quaker thought and practice over recent years has been in environmental ethics and environmental activism. Discussions over whether sustainability, stewardship, 'earth care' or something similar should be recognized as 'a Quaker testimony' (added to the standard lists) have not always been conclusive, but there is no question that environmental concern is now part of Quaker testimony more broadly. Concern for the environment is collectively owned, not only in Britain and North America but worldwide; it is a 'settled result' of Quaker discernment and decision-making; it helps to form Quaker responses to national and local issues, and it makes a material difference to how Quaker meetings and organizations work.

In 2012 the sixth World Conference of Friends in Kabarak, Kenya, focused on the interconnected issues of peace and ecojustice. The resulting 'Kabarak Call' – appealing to scripture, to Quaker theology and tradition and to contemporary social and environmental analysis – is striking in the clarity and urgency with which it draws together the voices of Quaker communities divided on many other issues:

> Earthcare unites traditional Quaker testimonies: peace, equality, simplicity, love, integrity and justice . . . climatic chaos is now worsening . . . driven by our dominant economic systems, by greed not need, by worship of the market, by Mammon and Caesar. Is this how Jesus showed us to live? . . . We are called

to do justice to all and to walk humbly with our God . . . We are called to be patterns and examples in a 21st century campaign for peace and eco-justice, as difficult and decisive as the 18th and 19th century drive to abolish slavery. (Friends World Committee for Consultation, 2012)

Despite the connections that Kabarak could draw with Quaker tradition, Quaker engagement with environmental concern and environmental activism on a large scale is a relatively new development – arguably more so than the changes to marriage procedure and marriage recognition discussed in the previous chapter. It stems most obviously from the work on 'social testimony' in the twentieth century – the work that gave rise to texts such as 'Foundations of a True Social Order' (London Yearly Meeting 1918), to the formulation of 'testimony lists' expressing the systemic and all-encompassing character of Quaker insights, and to renewed political and social activism in various spheres. Thinking systemically about war and social injustice – and about the 'seeds' of war and injustice in individual lives – led, as environmental awareness grew in the wider population, to 'systemic' thought that included the non-human environment.[1]

As I have argued, this kind of 'systemic' thinking in Quaker thought and practice has deep and living theological roots – in the 'here and now' experience of being caught up in the innerhistorical movement of God's truth; in the call to 'answer' the Light of Christ both in oneself and in every other; and in the open-ended commitment to be guided and ordered by the Spirit. My earlier discussions suggested that even the Quaker testimony that looked very

---

1 For a fascinating account of the development and practice of environmental activism in a specific British Quaker meeting from the 1990s onwards – which connects this development both to the wider national picture and to the history of Quaker 'simplicity' – see Peter Collins, 2011, 'The Development of Ecospirituality among British Quakers', *Ecozone* 2/2, pp. 83–98. I am grateful to Helen Lee for discussions of this article in relation to her own ongoing research on Quaker environmentalism. As should be apparent, I would disagree with Collins' characterization of early Quaker simplicity as 'biblically based', which seems to me to underrate the complex interactions of scriptural interpretation, theological reflection and social protest that shaped 'negative testimony'.

individualized, peculiar and non-systemic – like Thomas Ellwood's hat or Margaret Fell's refusal to swear an oath – had significant theological and 'systemic' implications. In this chapter, I explore in more detail how Quaker environmental testimony arises and develops, not only from a recent emphasis on explicit social and political analysis but also from deeper currents in Quaker theological ethics.

First, though, I should note one possible further problem with connecting Quakers and environmentalism. It could be argued that Quaker environmentalism reflects in part a belated movement of collective repentance. While there were strong pressures on Quakers to avoid conspicuous (over)consumption, Quaker invention, organization and finance played a significant role in Britain's industrial revolution. Indeed, the material presence and power of Quakers in Britain and elsewhere today – the buildings, endowments and trusts from which Quaker testimony is supported – owes much to this industrial heritage. There has been relatively little reflection among Quakers on the ambiguous character of their specific shared past; but they are part of a wider movement of repentance or self-criticism in the global North. The specific contribution of Quakers seems trivial in the wider context of massive global inequalities, unsustainable systems of production and consumption in more or less all areas of life, and the patterns of environmental degradation that they create. Be that as it may, I think it is worth specifically acknowledging Quakers' part in sustaining a human-centred narrative of 'progress' that led to the unsustainable exploitation of natural resources. Quakers' beliefs in the presence of Christ to and in all, or their emphasis on the guiding power of God in history, did not automatically translate into uncritical belief in human progress – but occasionally they did.[2] The disturbing reminder from Nayler and others – to pay attention to the victims, to recognize and resist the 'persecuting spirit' even when it

---

[2] See on this Brian D. Phillips, 1989, 'Friendly Patriots: British Quakerism and the Imperial Nation 1890–1910', unpublished thesis, University of Cambridge. On the wealth of nineteenth-century British Quakers in relation to claims about 'simplicity', see also Collins, 2011, 'Development of Ecospirituality', pp. 87–8.

happens to say something we agree with or find convenient – was probably not heard often and clearly enough when Quakers were doing well out of industrial capitalism.[3] An alternative is reflected in the testimony of one of the best-known 'Quaker saints'.

John Woolman's simplicity

One Quaker figure above all stands out as a genuine precursor of the environmental movement – John Woolman. Widely recognized by Quakers and non-Quakers alike as one whose lived testimony was far ahead of his time – and arguably of all times since – Woolman presents a remarkable and durable image of holiness. He is frequently described as a 'saint', and not only by Quakers.[4] Woolman combined a persistent challenge to all forms of slavery – the testimony for which he is best known – with persistent critiques of ostentatious consumption, destructive and unsustainable patterns of farming, exploitative labour conditions and cruelty to non-human animals.

A primary locus of Woolman's testimony, which makes him of particular interest to Quakers in the contemporary North and West, was his resistance to expected patterns of *consumption*. He

---

[3] The problem of course went beyond the unsustainable use of natural resources, to more immediate questions of social justice. The Quaker Liberal MP John Bright's opposition to laws restricting and regulating child labour is talked about rather less than his anti-war speeches and his campaigns for the extension of the franchise. Isichei's verdict on Bright and other nineteenth-century Quaker 'voices of industry' is probably the fairest and most charitable that can be reached; they saw farther than most in some respects and were culpably blind in others. Elizabeth Isichei, 1970, *Victorian Quakers*, Oxford: Oxford University Press.

[4] For a striking and perceptive account of Woolman's significance for contemporary environmentalism, see Sallie McFague, 2013, *Blessed are the Consumers: Climate Change and the Practice of Restraint*, Minneapolis, MN: Fortress Press, especially Ch. 3. In a deliberately ecumenical book, McFague does not, in my view, give quite enough weight to Woolman's distinctive Quaker theology and spirituality. For a full biography, see Thomas P. Slaughter, 2008, *The Beautiful Soul of John Woolman: Apostle of Abolition*, New York: Hill & Wang. Jon Kershner's important recent work has focused on reading Woolman as a theologian, and on the deep connections between Woolman and the apocalyptic emphases of early Quakers – see Jon Kershner, 2013, 'The Valiant Sixty-First? John Woolman's (1720–1772) Abolitionist Theology and the Restoration of the Lamb's War', *Quaker Studies* 13, pp. 23–49.

TESTIMONY

is famous for refusing many of the minor luxuries of his Virginian colonial environment – sugar, silver cutlery, dyed clothes, horse-drawn transport – because they relied on slavery or on the exploitation of human and non-human labour. Somewhat less famous beyond Quaker circles are what might be called his proto-environmentalist writings. These reveal an astonishingly clear-sighted understanding of how consumption is inextricably linked to long-term social and ecological patterns, and these in turn to spiritual dis-ease that affects all members of the body politic.

In one of his last writings, *Conversations on the True Harmony of Mankind and How it May Be Promoted* (1772/1987), Woolman begins a dialogue between a 'labouring man' and a 'man rich in money' (note the equivocation of this attribution of 'riches') with a discussion of the rather practical and prosaic issue of interest rates. From a simple enquiry from the labouring man to the rich man about 'whether a way may not be opened for thee and thy family to live comfortably on a lower interest' (p. 5), Woolman draws lines both outward, to the social and ecological consequences of high interest, and inward, to the spiritual sickness that both produces and is produced by the demand for high interest. Outwardly, small farmers seeking to pay off debts by raising grain 'have by too much tilling ... robbed the earth of its natural fatness' (p. 6). The labouring man in the dialogue has 'known grain and hay so scarce that I could not anywhere near get so much as my family and creatures had need of', and has 'seen poor creatures [i.e. domestic animals] in distress ... when it did not appear to be in the power of their owners to do much better for them, being straitened in answering the demands of the wealthy' (p. 7).

In a second and more extensive dialogue (with a 'thrifty landowner'), Woolman turns his attention at greater length to the specific issue of global trade – and the exigencies created by the export of grain from the American colonies in order to import luxury goods and to acquire gold. He considers the use of monetary wealth to 'hire armies' – not, perhaps surprisingly, as a stand-alone argument that will convince the Quakers in his audience, but as part and parcel of the wider social and economic analysis (so, part of the problem with hiring armies is the further demands that their upkeep places on the poor). In a striking image he compares the apparent 'strength' of a society organized around excessive consumption and the accumulation of gold to a convulsive fit in the body politic – and fits 'though strong are only manifestations of disorder' (p. 14).

Like much of Woolman's written and lived testimony, however, the economic, social and ecological analysis cannot be separated from an analysis of the 'spirit' or spirits at work in the situation. At a key point in the dialogue he describes the daily physical toll on 'poor labouring men' caused by being required to work longer hours to purchase necessities – and then, scarcely missing a beat, he moves straight to an account of the spiritual costs of an economy based on extravagant consumption. On the one hand, there are those whose 'wandering desires' give them 'power to turn money into channels of vanity' (p. 8). On the other, there are those who are forced for the sake of earning a living to 'put forth [their] strength' in trades designed to 'support pride'. Work in the pride and vanity economy, work designed to support pride – even, from context, someone else's pride – means working for that which is 'opposite to Divine love'. It 'hath a tendency to weaken those bands which ... bind and unite my Soul in a holy fellowship with the Father and with his Son Jesus Christ' (p. 9). Bad work is – Woolman might equally have said, and meant it more seriously than most who use the expression now – soul-destroying.

The disordering force is named later in the dialogue as 'that spirit in which men receive honor one of another' (p. 15). This spirit is not a disembodied force – Woolman never talks about it apart from people's 'entanglement' with it or life 'in' it; but it needs to be named in order to identify the interconnectedness of individual and structural sins. As we have seen, the spirit of pride is set in direct contrast to the Spirit of love which draws the soul into the fellowship of God. In a tone far less apocalyptic than that of his seventeenth-century precursors, Woolman stages the world as a confrontation – between love and pride, and also between truth and the manifold but interconnected forms of falsehood. His testimony is both an explanation of his own conversion, away from the 'spirit in which men receive honor one of another', and an urgent call to others to convert. And the conversion he seeks is simultaneously individual, local and interpersonal, and global in its effects.

The civil and gentle tone of Woolman's dialogues, and of his other essays (on slavery and poverty), does not detract from the importance of what is at stake. In fact, as should by now not be surprising, the choice and use of a peaceful and non-confrontational rhetorical style is itself integral to what Woolman is doing. For Woolman as for Nayler and others, to speak about God and the ways of God in a form that does not reflect the love of God is not to speak truthfully at all.[5] And, while it is much easier for a twenty-first-century reader to approach Woolman through his writings, his contemporaries would have been drawn to them by his life and actions – including, as his fame spread and he travelled widely, by his distinctive dress and appearance. They would have read them as a further manifestation of the lived testimony Woolman gave, not as free-standing tracts. The writing – its style and approach as well as its content – is part of Woolman's testimony, not simply the explanation or background justification for it.

The confrontation between truth and falsehood in Woolman's work, the scene of testimony, is strikingly practical and mundane. It is found, for example, in the decisions people make about what to farm on a plantation. Woolman's labourer is in favour of keeping sheep, whose 'looks are modest, their voice is soft and agreeable' and who 'supply us with matter for warm and useful clothing' (p. 5); the temptation to regard this as a quaint and idiosyncratic preference is quickly suppressed when we remember that the

---

5 The interconnection between speaking the truth and speaking in love is reflected in Woolman's various accounts of Quaker business meetings. His journal for 1760 records an occasion when he spoke in a business meeting about his conviction that 'the spirit of lotteries was a spirit of selfishness ... and that pleading for it in our meetings, set apart for the Lord's work, was not right': '[I]n the heat of zeal I once made reply to what an ancient Friend said, which when I sat down I saw that my words were not enough seasoned with charity, and after that I spake no more on the subject.' John Woolman, 1970, *The Journal and Major Essays of John Woolman*, ed. Phillips P. Moulton, Richmond, IN: Friends United Press, p. 110.

SUSTAINABILITY AND SIMPLICITY

alternative to keeping sheep was exporting grain, and importing cloth that the 'labouring man' could ill afford. The systemic character of the 'spirit' of pride means, for Woolman, that it is encountered at every turn of ordinary life. His journal records not only a dramatic experience of conversion, but many small 'conversions' of aspects of his life and behaviour – most of them with inevitable social and public consequences. He documents meticulously his transition to wearing undyed cloth (and his decision that it was best to continue wearing the dyed clothes he already had until they had worn out); he describes his negotiations with individual neighbours and acquaintances over his refusal to draft wills that treated 'negroes' as property. He experiences a deep and disturbing sense of 'concern' in matters that his neighbours – including his Quaker neighbours – took for granted.

The 'everydayness' of Woolman's testimony has important implications for how we read his life. By the time of his late writings, his life and thought appears as a complete whole, and his theological and spiritual reading of society, economy and ecology has a compelling coherence. But this coherence is not given to him all of a piece, as a single rational programme to be implemented. He works it out, step by step, in response to the circumstances in which he finds himself. At any one time he is *both* embroiled in 'hurtful' habits and assumptions *and* living in conformity with the guidance of the Holy Spirit. Although he is clearly a child of the Enlightenment, with a deep-seated optimism about the prospects for a better social and economic order, he is the very antithesis of an armchair theorist. He does not claim that his insights and suggestions are innovative, only that they are not being put into practice. He is, in his own way, an heir of the Quaker 'Cynics' as well as the saints and martyrs; he repeatedly calls into question the value of the social currency.[6]

---

6 As well as the literal currency; the *Conversations* also contain a fascinating 'naive' discussion of the relative value of gold and other metals such as iron and steel, with the labouring man concluding that the benefit to himself of an increased circulation of gold (as opposed to metals with greater use value) is dubious at best.

TESTIMONY

When simplicity becomes complicated: seeing with a single eye

An obvious way to describe Woolman's life and mission is in terms of *simplicity*. The gift he seeks and finds is, in his own terms, a 'single eye', referring to Matthew 6.22: 'The light of the body is the eye; if therefore thine eye be single, thy whole body shall be full of light.'[7] It is the capacity to see things clearly as they are in truth, which also means under the judgement of God and in the universal love of God. The 'single eye' does not *simplify* reality, but it simplifies desire, perception and judgement. It gives a way of living and perceiving that relies only on the worth accorded by God and not on the many and conflicting ways of according 'honor' from other people; that directs love to God and the neighbour rather than into a confusing mass of 'wandering desires'; and that orders individual and social life as a single interconnected whole rather than a mass of conflicting interests and power struggles.

If anything, Woolman's simple living and single-eyed knowing makes his world more complex. It means that he cannot allow his immediate wishes or partisan interests to limit his field of vision and responsibility. It means, for example, that he sees the suffering of non-human animals and has to deal with it; most of his contemporaries (and perhaps most of ours) could keep things simple by ignoring the rather clear evidence before their eyes when, for example, animals' 'eyes and the emotions of their bodies manifest that they are oppressed'.[8] Here, as in many other cases, Woolman's insight restores a sense of the *real* complexity of the world – and of the real evils caused by people's inability to face that complexity.

At several points in this book the relationship between simplicity and complexity in Quaker testimony has emerged as an issue. Woolman in many ways brings the issue to a head. When he considers things with his 'single eye', he shows that the truth people try

---

[7] King James Version; the word *haplous*, 'single', poses known difficulties for translation, carrying connotations of wholeness but also of sound function and of sincerity.

[8] Woolman, 'A Plea for the Poor', in *The Journal and Major Essays*, p. 238.

SUSTAINABILITY AND SIMPLICITY

to avoid is generally more complicated than the lies they live by. If I am honest, I would probably have hated to work with Woolman, or to have him in my Quaker meeting – because his scruples and concerns and refusals to compromise always make things so much more complicated. But at the same time, when I attend to his scruples and concerns, I see that he makes things no more complicated than they really are. And I also see that the genuinely damaging complications are the ones caused by trying to maintain self-deception, by desperately trying to hold together a simple story that does not do justice to how the world is.

Woolman's life and work also further illuminate the 'double negative' character of testimony. On the one hand, his testimony is centred on negations and refusals. He wears *un*dyed cloth, he does not take sugar or travel in horse-drawn carriages. He refuses to write wills that treat people as property. He frees himself, and attempts to free his neighbours, from superfluity and 'cumber'. So his saintliness, his holiness, is achieved by negation and the creation of boundaries – by separating himself from the ordinary concerns of the world and from the problematic habits that permeate everyday life. He stands firmly, and self-consciously, in the Quaker tradition of 'testimonies against'; in his day, he was one of the most peculiar specimens of a (still) peculiar people.

At the same time, though, Woolman stands out as a figure of extraordinary *integrity* – in the sense of wholeness or completeness, not simply of stubborn adherence to principles. His various small denials and refusals give him not a restricted and conflicted life but a coherent life – a life in which, over and over again, a 'way becomes open' for new forms of relationship and action, and a life that makes a deep kind of sense both to himself and to those who encounter him. So his holiness is also about wholeness. It is about the 'single eye' that leaves nothing out; and it is about a kind of integrity that reflects and responds to the unity of divine love. All that has been denied with the various small negations is, Woolman suggests, various kinds of pointless cumber, various obstacles to an integrated life.

TESTIMONY

Moving forward: new Quaker testimony on environmental concern

John Woolman provides the obvious starting point for thinking about contemporary Quaker environmental activism. He is, as I noted above, frequently cited by Quakers as a key precursor for this emerging strand of Quaker testimony. This does not make him a good basis on which to claim a long history of Quaker environmental concern; he was ahead of, and out of joint with, his time, as much among his fellow Quakers as among society at large. However, what we can reasonably do is read Woolman's testimony, alongside other Quaker testimony, as a clue to what might be distinctive about Quaker environmental concern, and what it might tell us about Quaker approaches to theological ethics.

One obvious recent example of Quaker testimony in relation to environmental concern is the collective commitment expressed by Britain Yearly Meeting in 2011 to become 'a low-carbon, sustainable community'.[9] But this collective statement of intention – or aspiration – is rather unusual in Quaker terms, in that it seems to require a specific (although not fully defined) programme of action that had, at the time of writing, hardly commenced. It promises to do something. As many Quakers were quick to point out beforehand and afterwards, such a statement means nothing if it does not connect with a wider body of testimony – of patterns of collective action and speech, undertaken in faithfulness to the leadings of God that directly challenge and transform their context. So we should expect to learn more by looking at the rather small-scale individual and local actions of Quakers: at local gardening and microgeneration projects; at decisions about transport, catering, development and use of buildings; and more often than not, at decisions about changed or reduced consumption. As with every area of testimony we have discussed, there is a wide range of individual practice; there is internal debate and conflict; there are spoken and unspoken differences in relation to class, age, gender

---

9 Britain Yearly Meeting, 2011, minute 36 of Yearly Meeting held at Canterbury. The text is available http://www.quaker.org.uk/minute-36.

SUSTAINABILITY AND SIMPLICITY

and location; but it is reasonable to claim, in the early twenty-first century, that there is a coherent body of Quaker testimony that responds to the present reality and future threat of humanly created environmental crisis.

As we might expect by now, the practice of challenging and changing an environmentally destructive way of life is more widespread and more unified among Quakers than is the explanation for why they are doing this. One core group of ideas that do often appear to shape Quaker thought on the issue are those around responsible stewardship – a key concept for much, though by no means all, contemporary Christian environmentalism, including much within the historic peace church traditions.[10] In particular, in recent texts of Quaker environmentalism, there is a repeated critique of behaviour, policies and statements that imply human ownership of or sovereignty over the non-human creation.

In other words, there is a double negative, a denial of lies – in this case, the denial of the false and misguided implicit anthropology of unconstrained consumerism, the vision of human life that makes (a minority of) humanity the owners and sole disposers of the goods of creation, and that instrumentalizes the non-human creation for humanity's good. Thus, the most recent form of British Quakers' *Advices and Queries* states, 'We do not own the world, and its riches are not ours to dispose of.' A recent statement from British Quakers, on climate change, affirms 'The Earth is God's work and not ours to do with as we please';[11] alongside the positive declaration that the earth is 'God's work', the emphasis of the statement as a whole falls on the critical-negative consequence. There is specific reference to a systematic enacted falsehood that needs to be challenged: 'prevailing social values have obscured what it means to live authentically on this Earth'.[12]

---

10 On this, see Willis Jenkins, 2008, *Ecologies of Grace: Environmental Ethics and Christian Theology*, New York: Oxford University Press, Ch. 4.

11 Statement on climate change by Meeting for Sufferings, June 2009.

12 Meeting for Sufferings (Britain Yearly Meeting), 2009, 'A Quaker Response to the Crisis of Climate Change', http://www.quaker.org.uk/quaker-response-crisis-climate-change.

TESTIMONY

In the present situation, then, testifying that the earth is God's work entails all manner of 'testimonies against' – resistance to patterns and structures of life in which everyone, at least in the global North, is deeply and differentially implicated. The corporately agreed statements of Quaker groups are primarily intended to provoke, as well as to reflect on, individual and collective action. They do not present a fully developed and distinctive theology of stewardship, of creation, or of humanity's place among the creatures. Indeed, claims like 'We do not own the world', read out of context, lend themselves to non-theological as well as theological readings – we do not own the world because future generations have a claim on it; we do not own the world because we are only one among millions of interdependent species; we do not own the world because 'ownership' makes no sense when we are talking about the natural environment. Quaker collective statements do generally place these claims in theological contexts – the quotation just given goes on to call on readers to 'rejoice in the splendour of God's continuing creation'. But, as we might expect, theological coherence is very rarely prioritized over the effective expression and generation of active commitment. The emphasis in the positive injunctions is on the verbs rather than the nouns; 'rejoice in the splendour of God's continuing creation' is about rejoicing, rather than about the rather complex issues raised by the idea of 'continuing creation'.

The relative lack of explicit attention to theological coherence in Quaker writings about the environment is, I want to suggest, not surprising and not a problem. It is unsurprising not just because 'liberal unprogrammed' Quakers are in fact theologically diverse but also because, as I have been arguing, testimony sets theology in motion. New ways of understanding and expressing the relationship between God, self and world emerge over time through practices of 'denying lies'. A community can be united and confident in what they deny, while being diverse, provisional and experimental in what they affirm.

Besides 'stewardship', an obvious candidate for the guiding principle of Quaker environmental concern is one that springs

SUSTAINABILITY AND SIMPLICITY

to mind as a description of Woolman's testimony – simplicity. Woolman's attempts to get rid of 'superfluity' and 'cumber' place him in an ongoing Quaker ethical tradition that is also an aesthetic – the tradition described by Peter Collins as 'plaining', the conscious avoidance or removal of ornament. The drive to simplify has, historically, shaped many aspects of life – dress, speech and rhetoric, furniture, vocabulary. Particularly in the seventeenth century, the drive towards plaining or simplicity was linked to the role of ornament – sartorial, rhetorical, architectural – as a signifier of wealth or status. However, again as Collins demonstrates in his ethnographic study of a contemporary Quaker community, it would be a mistake to restrict its significance to this original social context. Plaining or simplicity, as an aesthetic as well as an ethical imperative, is deeply embedded in the habitual formation of Quaker perceptions and practices. Plaining, unconsciously as well as consciously, shapes how Quakers see and judge things. The architecture of purpose-built Quaker meeting houses through the centuries – generally emphasizing simple form without ornament – provides good evidence of the durability and pervasiveness of the 'plain' aesthetic, and also a clue to one of the ways in which it is transmitted and maintained.

We have already noted how, over many centuries, 'plain' dress and 'plain' speech were among the peculiarities that most clearly distinguished Quakers from their non-Quaker neighbours; and I suggested that these 'peculiarities' needed to be understood not only negatively (as maintaining a boundary between the community and 'the world') but also positively – clearing a space for spiritual and social formation. The problem with turning plainness into a code was that it lost the dynamic character of testimony – its responsiveness to particular cases on the one hand, and its capacity to be transformative of social contexts, on the other. By contrast, Woolman's testimony was both deeply traditioned – in that he was able to draw on a history of 'plaining' or simplicity among Quakers in order to explain his decisions about dress and lifestyle – and highly innovative, in that his practices of simplicity were directly confronting and challenging the complex social and economic problems of his day. He was not simply advocating 'plainness' as a rule of life; he was actively 'plaining' the life and context of a middle-class American, and inviting his neighbours, Quaker and non-Quaker, to join him in the exercise.

Contemporary Quaker environmental concern advocates a similar exercise of active simplicity – in the context of human-made environmental crisis. The aim is not self-denial for its own sake, but refusing to be part of specific 'hurtful' practices. The *telos* of this action is not world-denying but to the highest degree world-affirming – affirming the interdependence essential to creaturely life, creating the possibility of the mutual flourishing of the human and non-human creation. Environmental action is, in fact, perhaps the clearest contemporary example of how testimony's double negative, the denial of lies, is not *just* negative. It is the hopeful and faithful affirmation that the world both is and can be otherwise. People who act to challenge existing and destructive patterns of economic organization and consumption are compelled to seek alternatives that are more, not less, realistic – and more, not less, conformed to the movement of God's love. Any specific negation (say, for a very trivial contemporary example, not eating air-freighted food) gives rise to numerous possible 'affirmations' (eat seasonal or local foods, grow food, preserve food).

This is not to deny the genuine sense of restriction, constraint and sheer frustration – as well as added complexity – that negative testimony produces, both in the person who adopts it and in those who relate to or depend on them. How is Woolman going to travel without horse-drawn transport, and how am I going to travel without taking an aeroplane?[13] One important effect of the communal statements, which claim this contemporary exercise of simplicity as shared Quaker testimony, is that they recognize an implication of the fact that individual actions have social and ecological effects – one person cannot change much, even about her own life. It is hard to act differently as an individual without

---

13 For the record, I do fly sometimes. On at least one occasion I took a plane in order to attend a conference about ecology and theology. The bitter irony is rarely lost in these situations.

SUSTAINABILITY AND SIMPLICITY

at least the beginnings of a 'different' social context, without some shared space in which to experiment with more realistic forms of organization and patterns of consumption, and in which to speak about and think through what is happening. Even Woolman – who is easy to represent, with some justification, as a lone hero – needed people to travel with, to stay with, to worship with and on occasion to argue with.

This – the need for a community as the context for testimony, particularly around environmental and ecological problems – sounds like an obvious practical point. In fact, it says something important about the embodied and historical character of testimony – and about how following the leading of the Holy Spirit requires genuine openness to the complexity of history. If testimony were simply a case of maintaining personal integrity and sticking to one's predetermined and fixed principles at all costs, it would be much easier to imagine as an individual exercise, much harder to distinguish from a sanctified ego trip – and much less likely to be properly responsive to 'what love requires'. In the end, it would tend towards a lie, because it would set the individual person up as self-sufficient and self-founding and deny her dependence on other people – even for the formation and testing of her cherished principles. But testimony as 'doing truth', within and in response to the ways of God with the world, always refers to and draws on a much wider context – not only because the truth it enacts goes beyond individual integrity, but because the realities it responds to are complex, interdependent and globally connected.

The situation of contemporary Quakers is, however, very different from that of at least some earlier experiments in simplicity. Quakers are not only not alone in recognizing the environmental crisis and attempting to respond to it, but also not even particularly advanced or distinctive. There is plenty of advice available, especially to the global North's middle classes, on how to 'plain' their lives. For at least some subcultures to which many Quakers belong (say, educated liberal professionals) it is not very 'counter-cultural' to be concerned about the environment and to be attempting, with whatever degree of seriousness or success, to change your lifestyle accordingly. Many Northern Quakers do not have to work out for themselves – like Woolman thinking through the implications of his dyed clothes – how existing patterns of activity and consumption are socially and ecologically destructive. They can join a broad stream of activists, 'ethical consumers' and groups of concerned people – and they can bring what they learn in this broader stream of environmental concern back into the Quaker context to be reflected on and integrated into ongoing thought about what contemporary simplicity or plaining might look like.

The upshot of all this so far seems to be that, while Quaker communities and the history of Quaker testimony provide a hospitable context for environmental concern, they do not obviously have a brand-new set of practical imperatives to offer the environmental movement. This, once again, is not necessarily a problem. There is no reason why Quaker distinctiveness should become apparent in every context. In fact, as we have seen in other cases (for example, the history of Quaker testimony against oaths), the point about negative testimony is that it discloses a truth that makes sense. It can be taken up and accepted by people who do not come from the same theological or ecclesial starting point. A multi-sourced shared text like the Kabarak Call, even though it is primarily directed at Quakers worldwide (already a very diverse community), can reach out to many different groups, among and beyond the Christian churches.

Conclusion: beyond success or failure

So is there anything specific or distinctive that Quakers offer to environmental ethics? I make one suggestion. Looking at environmental concern within the framework of Quaker testimony highlights, and helps us to think through, one of the key and understated issues for environmental ethics and environmental theology – the question of success. Do we engage in environmental activism, in environment-related testimony, because it is effective? Or do we do this because it is the right thing to do, regardless of effectiveness or the prospect of success?

SUSTAINABILITY AND SIMPLICITY

One of the interesting features of the 'stewardship' paradigm for Christian environmental ethics, as it is sometimes enunciated, is that it seems to apply regardless of the effects of the action taken.[14] If responsible care for the natural environment is a matter of obedience to divine command, or of the fulfilment of a God-given mandate, or of living a life of Christ-like sacrificial love, then it is a path set down for Christians to follow even if – perhaps especially if – there is no reasonable prospect of averting or mitigating environmental disaster. As with Christian pacifism in the (broadly) Anabaptist tradition, the question of success or effectiveness simply does not arise.

Clearly this idea, that simplicity and the transformation of patterns of consumption is required not because of its effects but as a matter of obedience to vocation, is also an important dimension of Quaker thinking on environmental activism. It is an important corrective to the approaches and assumptions that are likely to be present in at least some non-religious environmental groups – and an important coda to Quakers' use of data and recommendations on the present environmental crisis. The dominant public account of global climate change (in particular) focuses on the likely catastrophic effects of inaction – or rather, of continued action along present lines – and the possible positive effects of specific changes. Debates around environmental policies focus, necessarily and rightly, on their effectiveness and their prospects of success. In this context, it is very useful to call to mind the determined *in*effectiveness of generations of Christian pacifists – who, in obedience to their vocation, deliberately refused to claim the power to shape the future through their actions, and were extremely clear-eyed about their very limited prospects for success or flourishing.

Having said that, and as in the case of the 'peace testimony', it is not quite clear that Quakers want to, or should, be entirely indifferent to whether their actions make a difference to the rest of the world. The experiments in simplicity or 'plaining' in which Quakers have begun to engage are not just attempts to follow a

---

14 See the discussion of this in Jenkins, 2008, *Ecologies of Grace*, Ch. 4.

command to care for the earth (which might equally end in abject failure as in conspicuous success). As those who create them might read them, they are small-scale experiments in world transformation, in life shaped by the 'quickening Spirit' of God, in being effective signs of the in-breaking reign of God.

There are obvious risks here of triumphalism – and of the sanctification, with a thin veneer of theological language, of an activist desire to fix everything or to be seen to be doing some good. But these risks should not prevent us from following through the implications of Quaker claims about the Spirit 'guiding into all truth'. On the basis of what I have said so far, we would *expect* good testimony to make sense, and to find resonances beyond the specific theological and ecclesial contexts that give rise to it. We would also expect it to make some small difference in the world – not because the people who live out the testimony are particularly clever or well intentioned, but because they are caught up in the movement of the Spirit, the movement of love that draws the world to fullness of life.

Given its character as 'testimony against' dominant patterns of falsehood and violence, we would also, of course, expect good testimony to look very odd and rather threatening (like John Woolman in his undyed clothes); and we would not expect its success, or any of its effects, to be immediately apparent. It is not obvious that centuries of Christian pacifism, even allied to various kinds of pragmatism and 'middle space' experimentation, have done much to reduce the dominance of militarism, the everyday presence of violence and the suffering caused by war. It is also, at the time of writing this, genuinely far from obvious whether Quakers or anyone else can do anything that will make a difference to the next few decades of anthropogenic environmental disaster. The best reason for persisting in the face of a very limited chance of success is probably not just 'We should give it a try' or 'We can't just do nothing'. Nor, in Quaker terms, is it just 'We must, in any case, live in accordance with the commands of God'. It is more like 'We must, in each case, live truthfully', or 'We must, in each case, do what love requires'.

SUSTAINABILITY AND SIMPLICITY

This in turn reminds us that effective and faithful testimony is a matter of case-by-case judgements, none of which start from nowhere, but rather few of which are fully determined by precedent. 'What love requires' is – as we saw in the discussion of *Towards a Quaker View of Sex* and its critics – a very vague prescription. The paradigmatic way for Quakers to turn this sort of vague prescription into specific action is not by reducing 'love' to a formula or a set of rules, but by a process of discernment – informed by the history of testimony, by the needs of the present situation, and by openness to surprise.

One surprising element that Quakers and other church communities engaged in environmental activism might bring to the present situation is joy. There is, if we are realistic, little basis for optimism in the face of climate chaos. As successive generations of Christians have been reminded in different ways, however, the injunction to 'rejoice always' (1 Thessalonians 5.16) is not conditional on the belief that things are about to get better. It is also not conditional on taking oneself 'out of the world' or ignoring what is going on. The 'joy' expressed in recent Quaker statements on environmental concern seems to have more to do with the joyful experience of being called *and* equipped, collectively, to meet the requirements of the call – of being 'gathered' out of a desperate situation and enabled to do things differently. It also resonates with the apocalyptic–prophetic vision that sees and responds to the work of God in situations of loss and failure – as in the 'oceans' vision of George Fox quoted in the Prologue to this book, or in a frequently cited letter dating from the years of persecution:

> Sing and rejoice ye children of the Day and of the Light, for the Lord is at work in this thick night of darkness that may be felt . . . the seed Christ is over all and doth reign. And so be of good faith and valiant for the Truth . . . in the seed Christ stand and dwell, in whom you have life and peace. (Fox 1698; *QF&P* 20.23)

Whatever can be said about the future of the environmental crisis and the future of Quaker and other responses to it, there must be

TESTIMONY

a space for the joyful confidence that the 'negative testimony' to which individuals and communities are urgently summoned is a *double* negative. Against all appearances, the course being followed leads to 'life and peace'. This is the potential contribution to environmental movements that Quakers 'know experimentally' from their history – and appear ready to take forward in new 'experiments' now.

Afterwords

Quakers and theological ethics: making a holding minute

Quaker meetings for business, or for 'church affairs', are conducted as meetings for worship. The matter to be considered is introduced and the meeting falls silent. When it works well, spoken contributions are offered as ministry – for the sake of the meeting and the process of discernment in which it is engaged, rather than to advocate an individual's point of view. The point is to find the right way forward. The point is to see what is really going on. The point is to hear and feel and respond to the leadings of the Spirit of God. The point is to 'give over thine own willing' and receive a new and 'quickening spirit'. When it works well, just as in a meeting for worship, the spoken words are only part – and not the most important part – of what is going on. Spending time in meetings for business one learns not only the odd jargon and unusual expressions that surround the process, but some of the norms and expectations that are linked to the basic commitments shaping it. Speakers can assume that they have been heard. Those waiting to speak can ask themselves whether their speaking is (still) necessary. The same point is rarely made twice. There is room, and need, for the voice of the expert. There is also room, and need, for the voicing of a not yet fully formulated anxiety. When it works well, it is extremely difficult for a majority to impose its will on a minority, or for a vocal minority to sway the centre. The only way to 'win' is to reach a decision that the whole meeting can own.[1]

---

1 There are many fuller expositions of Quaker business method; for a recent extended reflection, on this and related Quaker traditions, by a former clerk of Britain Yearly Meeting, see Peter J. Eccles, 2009, *The Presence in the Midst: Reflections on Discernment*, London: Quaker Books. See also the introductory essay for an ecumenical audience by Eden Grace, 2000, 'An Introduction to Quaker Business Practice', paper presented to Special Commission on Orthodox Participation in the World Council of Churches, Damascus, available at http://www.edengrace.org/quakerbusiness.html.

TESTIMONY

In Quaker business process, surprises are frequent – and not only the sort of unpleasant surprise that comes from lack of preparation. Even with the best preparation, issues brought to a Quaker meeting for business tend to change shape, over the course of a meeting. The few questions that are posed as yes/no dilemmas – should our Friend John Archdale swear an oath in order to take up his seat in Parliament? – still often (though perhaps not in that case) turn out to have answers other than yes or no. It is very risky; it takes a long time; it can be enormously frustrating. The slowness of the Quaker decision-making process is the subject of many self-deprecating jokes. On the plus side, decisions made in this way tend to be effective.

The clerk of a meeting for business writes and offers minutes of its deliberations. Minutes – like the examples quoted at various points in this book – are heard and agreed by the meeting as a whole; the consideration does not end before a minute is accepted. The very long minutes of yearly meetings (such as those conveying the decisions on recognizing same-sex marriage and on sustainability) are unusual, but not exceptions to any rule; they have also been accepted, word for word, by the whole meeting. The characteristic grammar of Quaker minutes, as it has developed, gives important clues about the process and what it means. Minutes in the contemporary British Quaker context generally use the first person plural – the 'we' – and the present or the present-perfect tense. *We have heard this report. We welcome it. We ask the committee to carry out its recommendations.*[2] They are not a record of what was said, but an expression of the point that has been reached – and the shared action that results. What makes a minute 'acceptable', and enables the consideration of this particular item to end, is (mostly) what the minute *does* – or what the meeting

---

[2] This use of the present or present-perfect tense is not common in early Quaker minute books and it is not clear when it originated. However, the emphasis on recording collective decisions and actions rather than individual contributions can be seen from seventeenth-century minute books.

AFTERWORDS

'does' through accepting the minute. Is it the right thing to do, now, to welcome this report?[3]

Minutes in a Quaker business meeting are offered as possible or plausible interpretations of a group process – including, but not limited to, what has been said and what individual experience and expertise has been offered. And most minutes are interpretations that take the form of action; 'We have heard' this, we have sat with it together, we have waited, and the action we now take is our response to what we have heard – our way of 'making sense' of it, shaped by an experimental trust in the Spirit's making sense of all things. Typically, Quaker minutes do not just describe what has happened or report what is going on; they carry it forward and make the next move.

An acceptable minute is not claiming, or claimed, to be the *only* possible interpretation of the issue presented, the words spoken, and the situation the meeting finds itself in – as if the whole exercise were about solving a mystery, to which clues were gradually unveiled and we had to guess at the right solution. Claiming to be guided by the Spirit of Christ to particular actions – as Quakers do – is not like claiming to have gained privileged access to a celestial book of answers. At the start of the meeting, and even at the end, many ways forward might be open – there might be many possible ways of reading and responding to what has happened. What concludes the process is not 'the right answer', but an acceptable answer – a minute that 'answers' the situation.[4]

Nor, however, is Quaker business method easy to redescribe simply as a consensus-finding process for resolving disputes – of a kind that has been quite successful in non-Quaker and non-church contexts.[5] At least in Quaker terms, doing 'Quaker business

---

[3] This incidentally helps to explain why Quaker minutes are often clearer on ethics than on theology. Theology – at the level of wording – takes longer to agree, and does not change what the minute does. The theology sometimes has to be filled in later.

[4] Theological categories of 'fittingness' or *convenientia*, work well here; minutes reflect answers, conclusions or agreed actions that are not necessary or compelled, but that work.

[5] It has been studied sympathetically and at length as a method for decision-making applicable beyond Quaker circles; see for example Michael J. Sheeran, 1996, *Beyond Majority Rule: Voteless Decisions in the Religious Society of Friends*, Philadelphia, PA: Philadelphia Yearly Meeting.

TESTIMONY

method' well, and especially in difficult or non-routine matters, requires faith – not as assent to particular doctrines, but as active 'giving over' of one's work to the work of God. It goes beyond any exercise of seeking, balancing or claiming power – even the kind that works by compromise or uneasy consensus. An observer who did not enter into the faith of the participants could, of course – as with any form of liturgy – describe what was going on in psychological or sociological (or other) terms without reference to the idea of being 'guided by the Spirit'; and it is important to resist the temptation to find a clear piece of evidence that there is 'really' something different, special or extra going on. Quakers do not need to claim that their business process is special or miraculous in order to be able to say that it is a core expression and source of their faith – the place from which they are gathered and guided, and the place where they learn to make sense of the world.

The process of putting this book together has sometimes felt like clerking a very large and very long meeting for business. Perhaps this is because of the importance of collective statements – from the 1660 'Declaration of the Harmless and Innocent People' onwards – in the history of Quaker theological ethics. I have had the sense of responsibility to come up with a plausible interpretation of a complex whole, composed of many voices, much testimony and a great deal of silence. As part of that larger responsibility I have felt obliged, for example, to listen to the different voices; not to be swayed by the particularly eloquent or particularly appealing; not to gloss over differences; to be only too aware of the many voices I have been able to include; but still to bear in mind that *something* must be said, or done, as a result of all this.

That is the problem and the point at which the analogy breaks down. Minutes *do* something. Even books or extended statements written by groups of Quakers – at least as I have read and interpreted them here – are actions, interventions, exercises in 'speaking truth to power' or in opening up conversations. An individual writer, on the other hand, while she might possibly do something by writing a book, cannot possibly 'do' something *on behalf of* the great cloud of witnesses. There is no way for one person to create an acceptable minute – both because she cannot ask the meeting to accept it and because there is no shared action involved. This is not just a comment about a writing process – it says something important about how Quaker theology, and especially Quaker theological ethics, works. To interpret testimony you have to do something with it; when it starts to dissolve into vague generalities, the solution is not to come up with more precise wording, but to bring it into a specific situation. We might see in the Good Samaritan parable – and its framing in the young man's question – a similar response to problematic ethical vagueness; the neighbour is not clearly specifiable in advance, the neighbour is waiting for you somewhere on the road, and the intolerably vague commandment will make perfect sense when you meet him.

Even if I could offer a minute to my imagined Quaker gathering – extended across time and space – it is not clear what it could possibly say. There are many pressing global concerns demanding the attention of Quakers worldwide (and the Kabarak Call names some of them); the global concerns have their national and local manifestations, and at national level there are in each case additional pressing problems; meanwhile, there are the multiple ethical challenges of everyday life, not just 'ethical consumerism' or well-defined ethical dilemmas, but living well or badly with our neighbours from day to day.[6] And the interpretation-into-action of Quaker tradition goes on all the time, whether we write about it or not; ignoring some strands of the history, reworking and revivifying others, undertaking local and contingent 'experiments' on the basis of experience. It goes on against a background of deep differences – even in the present, even before we start to engage with history – about theological language, about political and ethical stances, and about the specific vocation of a small number of Quakers in a world facing more and more new crises.

---

6 These are the sorts of 'ethics' with which the New Testament authors seem very concerned, and courses on 'ethics' have often seemed much less concerned – featuring boring virtues like self-control and generosity, and irritatingly non-sexy vices like gossiping and avarice.

TESTIMONY

If the book is a Quaker business meeting, all that can be offered at the end is a holding minute. The holding minute is normally used when no decision has been taken and no clear way forward found – but where there is still an intention to return to the issue, and the trust that something will come of it. It is not a way of agreeing to disagree or of deciding to do nothing; the matter under consideration is not intractable, but needs more time and more space. The 'holding minute' – and the group that agrees it – holds questions open, and holds the various voices that have already been heard and the points on which clarity has emerged. The meeting that makes a holding minute does not fix anything and does not give up on anything. It holds persistent complexities and stubborn conflicts; it holds on to the guidance and formation that it has already received; it 'holds together' in the intention to continue shared reflection and worship; and it holds all of this (to use another common Quaker phrase) 'in the Light' and in prayer.

The 'holding minute' says something rather important about the temporality of Quaker ethics and Quaker testimony. The early Quakers' thought is often described as displaying a realized eschatology – an experience, to quote the title of an influential book, of 'heaven on earth', the present reality of the reign of God. Looked at in this way, subsequent developments – like the formalization of shared 'peculiarities' and the development of a behavioural creed – tend to look like the abandonment of this sense of present and real transformation – capitulation to the idea of an interim ethic or the loss of an eschatological narrative altogether.[7] But the holding minute says both 'We trust in the presence of the Spirit of God, at work in history and already experienced among us' and 'This work happens in and through people, by entreaty and not by force – so it has to take time'.

A 'holding minute' also suggests holding to what Quakers are already doing. The stubbornness of Quakers – and the bewilderment

---

[7] This is roughly the line of development traced in Pink Dandelion, 2005, *The Liturgies of Quakerism*, Aldershot: Ashgate. I acknowledge numerous helpful discussions of Quaker 'realized eschatology' (or not) with Janet Scott.

AFTERWORDS

and frustration that it occasionally causes, not least to other Quakers – has emerged as a sub-theme at several points in this book. The reason General Monck was worried about the large number of Quakers in the army in the 1650s was not that they were committed to nonviolence (at that point, many of them were not) but that they ignored the chain of command and would not be told what to do; they were 'neither fitt to command nor obey'.[8] My argument in this book has been that Quaker stubbornness is not just the result of inherent bloody-mindedness (hard though this sometimes might be to believe). At its best, it is the result of a refusal to sacrifice truth to power – combined with the knowledge, confirmed from Quaker historical experience read in the light of scriptural testimony, that living in conformity with the Spirit of Christ is rarely a formula for quick success.

At the same time, Quaker 'stubbornness' locates itself in the public square rather than behind closed doors or (at least these days) in a separate space where peculiarity can be maintained; it hopes in the long run to persuade, to gain 'by entreaty', to answer and to find an answer. Paradoxically, there is also something impatient – or, better, expectant – about Quaker approaches to theological ethics. The transformative action of the Spirit of God is supposed to be 'here and now'; and testimony expects to 'answer that of God' in its hearers. The experiment is based on a confident and outward-looking faith.

Looking beyond Quaker theological ethics

The image of the 'holding minute' for this book will not quite do, for another reason. I have attempted throughout the work to bring out some of the implications of Quaker thought and practice for theological ethics more generally. Several of the key ideas and frameworks I have used to interpret Quaker theological ethics may well have wider relevance. Among them are 'experimental' ethics

---

8 George Monck, letter to Oliver Cromwell, 21 March 1656, in John Thurloe, 1742, *A Collection of the State Papers of John Thurloe*, Vol. 6, London.

that both begins from experience and proceeds through faith; the interpretation and continuation of the testimony of Christ through action in the here and now; sustained ethical refusals as the 'double negative', which opens up space for social and political transformation and for attending to the complex present needs of the world; speaking truth to power, not as an exercise of power but as a way of confronting power; and the call to understand the connections between individual 'conscientious' action and wider systemic concerns.

One question that has been left largely implicit so far relates to how theological ethics is done – and the place of theological ethics in wider public and academic contexts. Thinking about this issue in the light of my discussion brings me to two specific suggestions, from a Quaker perspective, about the form and approach of theological ethics. I take them both as rather chastening suggestions for myself. First and most importantly, theological ethics should avoid defending the system – even and especially the theological system – while blaming the victim; and second, theological ethics should be willing to acknowledge where it comes from.

The first of my suggestions relates back to the discussion of James Nayler, Mary Dyer and the part that compassionate identification and (in Dyer's case) enacted solidarity with victims of injustice played in their testimony and their theology. In relation to Nayler, I identified a challenge posed back to Quakers – whether the reading of Nayler at the time and since had tended to defend the Quaker organization at the expense of Nayler, who had already suffered public humiliation and torture for his controversial action. In order to find a comparable challenge for theological ethics more broadly, I turn once again to John Woolman – this time to the complex and justly famous account of his near-death 'conversion experience'. Seriously ill and 'so near the gates of death that I forgot my name', he first sees a 'mass of matter' consisting of 'human beings in as great a misery as they could be', and is informed that 'I was mixed with them'. He then hears the voice of an angel singing 'John Woolman is dead' – and, while still wondering what that means,

> I was then carried in spirit to the mines, where poor oppressed people were digging treasures for those called Christians, and heard them blaspheme the name of Christ, at which I was grieved, for his name to me was precious. I was then informed that those heathens were told, that those who oppressed them were followers of Christ; and they said among themselves, 'if Christ directed them to use us in this sort, then Christ is a cruel tyrant'. (Woolman 1970, p. 186)

Woolman's first instinct when he hears the complaints of the 'oppressed people' against Christ is to defend the name of Christ and condemn the blasphemy. Faced with an obvious and glaring wrong, his first reaction – which is natural enough for one to whom the 'name of Christ was precious' – is grief and shock at the suggestion that the 'name of Christ' has anything to do with it. The vision ends after he receives his 'information' about the enslaved miners' view of Christ, so there is no specific comment on his reaction to the suggestion that, for the victims of Christian civilization, 'Christ is a cruel tyrant'. He does, on recovery from his illness, start refusing to eat from silver vessels (from the mines he saw in his vision); and he finds himself temporarily unable to speak in meetings for worship, where his 'mind was very often in company with the oppressed slaves' (p. 187). It seems, then, that he does not spring to the defence of the 'name of Christ'; he looks for ways to redress the injustice caused by the misuse of the name of Christ. For the moment, he seems to accept the accusation, or at least to recognize its force. Christ has in this case been made into a tyrant. The way to defend him – it appears from Woolman's response – is not to try to argue the accusation down (as might have been possible, by saying that the slave-holders were not 'really Christians' or that the slaves had misunderstood Christ), nor to abandon the 'name of Christ', but to change and challenge the patterns of behaviour that make Christ a 'tyrant' and to place oneself alongside the victims of Christian power. And at the centre of Woolman's vision is an experience of union with Christ (quoting 'I live, yet not I, but Christ liveth in me').

TESTIMONY

It is difficult for anyone to whom the name of Christ is 'precious' to hear accusations against 'Christianity' in general – to be told that 'Christianity' is, for example, responsible for perpetuating racism or racial injustice, or part of the 'roots of our ecologic crisis', or colluding in violence against women. A natural reaction is to take it either as a personal attack or as an attack on a friend, and to enter into apologetic mode – either the apology in the sense of a defence of Christianity ('That is not really Christianity, you have misunderstood everything about Christianity'), or an apology as the response to a guilt-trip. The alternative response – which is suggested, I think, by Woolman's vision in the context of our earlier discussion of Dyer, Nayler and others – is to start by seeing what is going on; by acknowledging both the wrong done and the part played in it by Christianity, by asking seriously whether Christ has become a 'cruel tyrant'.

The next step, for theological ethics, certainly will involve an account of what the true 'testimony of Jesus' might look like once the wrongs of Christianity have been acknowledged. It probably will not, however, centre on the attempt to out-argue or out-narrate the critics of Christianity (even when, as is very often the case, the most vocal critics are *not* particularly close to or particularly closely identified with the 'victims' they purport to speak for). The only way to defend the name of Christ against blasphemy, having seen Woolman's silver mine, is to close down the mine – which might entail a theological critique of slavery, but not a story about how Christianity is the only effective response to slavery. The only way to defend the name of Christ against blasphemy, in the face of the Christian perpetrators of the Rwandan genocide, is to begin work for reconciliation – which will also require extensive theological critique and reconstruction.[9]

---

9 I am grateful to Jolyon Mitchell, David F. Ford, Karen Kilby and Kevin Ward for various discussions of theological 'reconstruction' in Rwanda, based on their experiences and conversations in that context. Much has been written on the churches' role in the genocide; for a theological 'strong reading', see Ephraim Radner, 2012, *A Brutal Unity: The Spiritual Politics of the Christian Church*, Waco, TX: Baylor University Press. On this point, that is, the need to name Christian complicity in violence for what it is, I agree with Radner against his critics, although elsewhere in the book I query various specific points of his diagnosis and prescription.

AFTERWORDS

The point here is not simply about 'admitting error' or about taking the gravity of sin seriously – although the role of communal confession of sin in theological ethics deserves further development and exploration.[10] It is about seeing the task of theological ethics as faithful response to 'reality as it is in God' rather than advocacy or defence of a Christian viewpoint – or even defence of the 'name of Christ', of a particular way of understanding and speaking of Christ. Theological ethics must involve articulating what Christians – 'as to our own particulars', in the words of the 1660 declaration – are called to do, and how this calling is understood; but this does not mean closing off alternative voices, nor denying justice to the victims of Christian and Christianized systems of power.

The same applies, without question, for Quaker theological ethics – which, certainly as practised in this book, betrays a tendency to justify Quakerism not only over against its critics but also over against the victims of its self-justifying errors. There is, as far as I can see, no theological reason for Quakers to try to prove that Quakers have the best answers, or have always been right; and every theological and ethical reason to think that this is a very bad idea. The great early Quaker apologists, like Barclay and Bathurst, wrote vindications of *truth* and apologies for *true Christian divinity*; their commitment to defending the 'particulars' of Quaker practice and identity arose from, and made no sense without, a wider commitment to truth.

So theological ethics needs to be done in a way that sits light to the defence or justification of a particular communal identity – in particular, of Christian identity. The other side of this is that theological ethics, and ethicists, should acknowledge where it comes from. It is not always clear how and why the 'ethical' questions in

---

10 On which, see Jennifer M. McBride, 2011, *The Church for the World: A Theology of Public Witness*, New York: Oxford University Press. McBride's account of ethics as 'confession unto repentance' owes much to the later theology of Dietrich Bonhoeffer; see for example Dietrich Bonhoeffer, 2005, *Ethics* (*DBWE* 6), ed. Ilse Tödt et al., trans. Reinhard Krauss et al., Minneapolis: Fortress Press, pp. 134–45. Note also the significance accorded to repentance in the Kabarak Call (Friends World Committee for Consultation, 2012).

theological ethics arise and become important; for whom they are important, and to whom the responses are addressed. However, we have seen at various points in my discussion how the reading of an ethical text can shift once we acknowledge the specific experiences that animate it, and the community (historical and present) on which it draws.

Calling for critical attention to location and context in theological ethics is, of course, nothing new. Feminist and (in particular) womanist ethicists are among those who in recent years have called for theological ethics to be grounded in specific experiences of embodied struggle for justice and for human flourishing.[11] The implications of this work have not, however, always been taken on board by theological ethicists whose personal and institutional location is more privileged. It is not always acknowledged, let alone performed, that *all* work in theological ethics is 'particular' and partial; experimental, at least in the sense of drawing from experience; and experimental in a forward-looking sense in that it affects the communities from and into which it speaks. Quaker theological ethics simply puts again, from a different direction, the challenge to ethicists to reflect faithfully on the specific 'experimental knowing' on which they can draw, the 'experiments' in which they are engaged and the concerns that make specific questions pressing.[12] This does not (the Quaker sources suggest) mean giving up on any claim to truthfulness; it means, rather, being more truthful about the context and motivations of our work, just because the truth of God comes about in and through the 'particulars' of historical and embodied life.

If this attention to 'particulars' had no other effect, it might at least open up possibilities for serious and open-ended deliberation across differences. The wider public conversation around

---

11 A *locus classicus* is Emilie M. Townes, 2006, *Womanist Ethics and the Cultural Production of Evil*, New York: Palgrave Macmillan.

12 This draws on Peter Ochs' approach (influenced by C. S. Peirce) to rereading philosophical texts, attending to the underlying dilemmas or concerns – the 'real doubts' or the 'suffering' in a social or intellectual context – that motivate a discussion, often without being explicitly voiced. Peter Ochs, 2005, *Peirce, Pragmatism and the Logic of Scripture*, Cambridge: Cambridge University Press.

theological ethics – and to some extent academic discussion about theological ethics – seems increasingly to be characterized by rhetorical power struggles between irreconcilable sides (the 'religious' and the 'secular', the 'liberal' and the 'conservative'), which can simultaneously be very aggressive towards individuals and very inattentive to nuance and context. Quaker theology, and theological ethics, emerged in a highly combative rhetorical space – and often entered it with an equally combative tone. My suggestion, however, has been that the commitment to experimental engagement with 'that of God in every one' allowed a way of speaking truth that, while it addressed and challenged 'power', did not simply repeat the dominant account of power or the expected ways of winning a rhetorical power game.

It is also possible – in theological ethics as in a Quaker business meeting – that stopping to think about where we speak from, and what we are called to attend to *now*, might end up changing the agenda or shifting the questions. In the course of writing this book, for example, I have begun to ask myself why, as a theologian and ethicist concerned with matters of gender and sexuality, I have spent very little time (relatively) answering the questions raised by the resurgent misogyny and normalization of sexual violence – as well as the homophobia – encountered by my students in the specific contexts of British university life.[13] Theological ethicists, at least those of us who are located in the centres of academic power, might need to pay less attention to which existing or well-established arguments we are winning, and more attention to the concerns and questions that emerge when we attend to a wider range of voices and silences around us. This is worth doing – even if all we can come up with for the moment, on any given matter, is a holding minute.

---

13 A recent indicative example from my own local context was the use of descriptions of sexual violence (along with excessive alcohol consumption) to advertise a student nightclub in 2013: http://www.independent.co.uk/student/news/leeds-freshers-violation-club-to-close-following-intense-student-pressure-8985678.html. Attempts to dismiss this and similar incidents – of which there have been many since – as manifestations of 'lad culture' are almost as worrying as the incidents themselves.

Bibliography

Where two publication dates are given, page references in the text are to the later edition.

Primary Quaker sources

American Friends Service Committee, 1955/2012, *Speak Truth to Power: A Quaker Search for an Alternative to Violence – A Study of International Conflict*, Philadelphia, PA: American Friends Service Committee.
Anonymous (sometimes attributed to George Fox), 1654, *The Glorie of the Lord Arising, Shaking Terribly the Earth, and Overturning All . . . Also a Testimony from the Lord against Swearing, with a Word to the Heads of the Nation, and the Judges of Life and Death, by those whom the world calls Quakers*, London: Giles Calvert.
Beth Allen, 2007, *Ground and Spring: Foundations of Quaker Discipleship*, London: Quaker Books.
Sydney D. Bailey, 1993, *Peace is a Process*, London: Quaker Home Service.
Elizabeth Bathurst, 1691, *Truth Vindicated by the Faithful Testimony and Writings of the Innocent Servant and Hand-maid of the Lord, Elizabeth Bathurst* (posthumous publication of 'Truth's Vindication'), London: Sowle.
Gervase Benson, 1656, *The Cry of the Oppressed from Under their Oppressions*, London: Giles Calvert.
Joseph Besse, 1753, *A Collection of the Sufferings of the People Called Quakers*, London: Hinde.
Hester [Ester] Biddle, 1655, *Wo To Thee Town of Cambridge*.
George Bishop, 1661, *New-England Judged*, London: Sowle.
W. C. Braithwaite, 1921/1961, *The Second Period of Quakerism*, 2nd edn, Cambridge: Cambridge University Press.
Rachel Brett, 2012, *Snakes and Ladders: A Personal Exploration of Quaker Work at the United Nations*, London: Quaker Books.
Howard H. Brinton, 1943, *Guide to Quaker Practice*, Wallingford, PA: Pendle Hill.
Britain Yearly Meeting, 1994, *Quaker Faith and Practice: The Book of Christian Discipline of the Yearly Meeting of the Religious Society of Friends (Quakers) in Britain*, London: Britain Yearly Meeting. References in text as *QF&P*.
Britain Yearly Meeting, minutes from 2008, 2009, 2011.
Britain Yearly Meeting, 2014, *This Light that Pushes Me: Stories of African Peacebuilders*, London: Britain Yearly Meeting.

BIBLIOGRAPHY

Luke Cock, 1721/1842, 'The Weeping Cross', sermon reproduced in *The Friend: A Religious and Literary Journal*, 15/35, 7th day, 5th month, pp. 278–9.

Anne Docwra, 1683, *An epistle of love and good advice to my old friends and fellow-sufferers in the late times*, London.

Mary Dyer et al., 1659/1841, *Narrative of the Martyrdom at Boston of William Robinson, Marmaduke Stevenson, Mary Dyer and William Leddra*, Manchester: John Harrison.

William Dyer, 1659/1902, letter to the magistrates at Boston, reprinted in *The Friend*, 6 September 1902, Philadelphia.

Peter J. Eccles, 2009, *The Presence in the Midst: Reflections on Discernment*, London: Quaker Books.

William Edmundson, 1676/1834, Epistle from Newport, 15th day, 7th month 1676, reprinted in *The Friend, Or, Advocate of Truth*, 3/1, Philadelphia, p. 9.

Thomas Ellwood, 1714/2011, *The History of the Life of Thomas Ellwood, Written by Himself*, ed. Rosemary Moore, New Haven, CN: Yale University Press.

Katharine Evans et al., 1715, *A Brief History of the Voyage of Katharine Evans and Sarah Cheevers*, London: Sowle.

Margaret Fell, 1666, *Womens Speaking Justified, Proved and Allowed of by the Scriptures*, London.

Margaret Fell [Fox], 1694, 'The testimony of Margaret Fox concerning her late husband', in George Fox, *A Journal*, London: Thomas Northcott, pp. i–ix.

Samuel Fisher, 1660, *Rusticus ad Academicos: or, The Country Correcting the University and Clergy*, London.

Samuel Fisher, 1661, *One Antidote More Against That Provoking Sin of Swearing*, London: Robert Wilson.

Simon Fisher, 2004, *Spirited Living: Waging Conflict, Building Peace*, London: Quaker Books.

George Fox, 1658, *A Warning to All the Merchants in London, And Such as Buy and Sell*, London.

George Fox, Richard Hubberthorn et al., 1660, *A Declaration from the Harmless and Innocent People of God*, London.

George Fox, 1694/1952, *Journal*, ed. J. L. Nickalls, Cambridge: Cambridge University Press.

George Fox, 1698, *A Collection of Many Select and Christian Epistles*, London: Sowle.

Friends World Committee for Consultation, 2012, *The Kabarak Call for Peace and Ecojustice*, http://www.saltandlight2012.org/call.pdf.

Eden Grace, 2000, 'An Introduction to Quaker Business Practice', paper presented to Special Commission on Orthodox Participation in the World Council of Churches, Damascus, http://www.edengrace.org/quakerbusiness.html.

Alistair Heron et al., 1963, *Towards a Quaker View of Sex: An Essay by a Group of Friends*, London: Friends Home Service Committee.

Ellis Hooks, 1661, *The Spirit of Christ and the Spirit of the Apostles and the Spirit of the Martyrs is Arisen, which bears testimony against swearing and oaths*, London: Giles Calvert.

TESTIMONY

Francis Howgill, 1672, 'Testimony Concerning the Life, Death, Tryals, Travels and Labours of Edward Burrough', in Edward Burrough, *The Memorable Works of a Son of Thunder and Consolation*, London.

London Yearly Meeting, 1861, *Extracts from the Minutes and Epistles of the Yearly Meeting*, London: Friends' Book Depository.

London Yearly Meeting, 1918, 'Foundations of a True Social Order', *Proceedings of London Yearly Meeting*, pp. 80–1.

London Yearly Meeting, 1960, *Christian Faith and Practice in the Experience of the Society of Friends*, London: Headley Brothers.

Meeting for Sufferings (Britain Yearly Meeting), 2009, 'A Quaker Response to the Crisis of Climate Change', http://www.quaker.org.uk/quaker-response-crisis-climate-change.

James Nayler, 1656, *An Answer to a Book Called the Quakers' Catechism*, London.

James Nayler, 1660/1716, 'His last testimony', in *A Collection of Sunday Books, Epistles and Papers Written by James Nayler*, London: Sowle.

Isaac Penington, 1662, *To All Such as Complain they Want Power . . .*, London.

Isaac Penington, 1681, *The Works of the long-mournful and sorely-distressed Isaac Penington . . .*, London: Benjamin Clark.

William Penn, 1682/1867, letter to Gulielma Penn née Springett, in Maria Webb (ed.), *The Penns and Peningtons of the Seventeenth Century*, London: F. Bowyer Kitto, pp. 340–3.

William Penn, 1682/1981, *No Cross No Crown*, London: Sessions.

William Penn, 1696, *Primitive Christianity Revived in the Faith and Practice of the People Called Quakers*, London.

William Penn and Richard Richardson, 1675, *A Treatise of Oaths, containing several weighty reasons why the people call'd Quakers refuse to swear*, London.

Norman Penney (ed.) (Friends Historical Society), 1686/1928, *Record of the Sufferings of Quakers in Cornwall 1655–1686*, London: Friends Book Centre, p. 52.

John Punshon, 1980, *Testimony and Tradition*, London: Quaker Home Service.

John Punshon, 1987, *Encounter with Silence: Reflections from the Quaker Tradition*, London: Quaker Home Service.

Janet Scott, 1980, *What Canst Thou Say? Towards a Quaker Theology*, London: Quaker Books.

Helen Steven, 2005, *No Extraordinary Power: Prayer, Stillness and Activism*, London: Quaker Books.

George Whitehead, 1664, *The Conscientious Cause of the Sufferers Called Quakers Pleaded*, London.

John Woolman, 1772/1987, *Conversations on the True Harmony of Mankind and How it may be Promoted*, ed. Sterling Olmsted, Philadelphia, PA: The Wider Quaker Fellowship.

John Woolman, 1970, *The Journal and Major Essays of John Woolman*, ed. Phillips P. Moulton, Richmond, IN: Friends United Press.

BIBLIOGRAPHY

Other sources

A Complete Collection of State Trials and Proceedings upon High Treason and Other Crimes and Misdemeanours, Vols 2 and 6, 1730 and 1816, London.

An Account of the Proceedings and Debates on the Tithe Bill, 1737, London: J. Roberts.

Nicholas Adams, 2006, *Habermas and Theology*, Cambridge: Cambridge University Press.

Paul Anderson, 2013, *Following Jesus: The Heart of Faith and Practice*, Newberg, OR: Barclay Press.

Stephen W. Angell and Pink Dandelion (eds), 2013, *The Oxford Handbook of Quaker Studies*, Oxford: Oxford University Press.

Sarah Apetrei, 2009, 'The Universal Principle of Grace: Feminism and Anti-Calvinism in Two Seventeenth-Century Women Writers', *Gender & History* 21, pp. 130–46.

Hugh S. Barbour, 1985, *The Quakers in Puritan England*, Richmond, IN: Friends United Press.

Richard Bauckham, 2007, *The Testimony of the Beloved Disciple: Narrative, History and Theology in the Gospel of John*, Grand Rapids, MI: Baker.

Richard Bauman, 1983, *Let Your Words Be Few: Symbolism of Speaking and Silence among Seventeenth-Century Quakers*, New York: Cambridge University Press.

David Blamires, 2012, *Pushing at the Frontiers of Change: A Memoir of Quaker Involvement with Homosexuality*, London: Quaker Books.

Dietrich Bonhoeffer, 1943/2010, 'What is Meant by "telling the truth"?', in *Conspiracy and Imprisonment* (*DBWE* 16), trans. Lisa Dahill, Minneapolis, MN: Fortress Press.

Dietrich Bonhoeffer, 2005, *Ethics* (*DBWE* 6), ed. Ilse Tödt et al., trans. Reinhard Krauss et al., Minneapolis, MN: Fortress Press.

Constance Braithwaite, 1995, *Conscientious Objection to Compulsions under the Law*, York: Ebor Press.

Thomas Brown, 1760, *Works of Mr Thomas Brown, serious and comical*, Vol. 2, London: Henderson, pp. 7–8.

Michael Budde, 2011, *The Borders of Baptism: Identities, Allegiances and the Church*, Eugene, OR: Cascade.

Michael Budde and Karen Scott (eds), 2011, *Witness of the Body: The Past, Present and Future of Christian Martyrdom*, Grand Rapids, MI: Eerdmans.

Thomas Carlyle, 1836, *Sartor Resartus*.

Jeremy Carrette, 2013, 'The Paradox of Globalization: Quakers, Religious NGOs and the United Nations', in Robert Hefner et al. (eds), *Religions in Movement: The Local and the Global in Contemporary Faith Traditions*, London: Routledge.

Jeremy Carrette and James Bernauer, 2004, 'Beyond Theology and Sexuality: Foucault, the Self and the Que(e)rying of Monotheistic Truth', in Jeremy Carette and James Bernauer (eds), *Michel Foucault and Theology: The Politics of Religious Experience*, Aldershot: Ashgate, pp. 217–32.

TESTIMONY

William Cavanaugh, 1998, *Torture and Eucharist: Theology, Politics and the Body of Christ*, Oxford: Blackwell.

Noam Chomsky, 1969, *American Power and the New Mandarins*, New York: Random House.

Noam Chomsky, 2000, *Chomsky on Miseducation*, ed. Donaldo Macedo, New York: Rowman and Littlefield.

David Colclough, 2005, *Freedom of Speech in Early Stuart England*, Cambridge: Cambridge University Press, especially pp. 77–119.

Peter Collins, 2009, 'The Problem of Quaker Identity', *Quaker Studies* 13/2, pp. 205–19.

Peter Collins, 2011, 'The Development of Ecospirituality among British Quakers', *Ecozone* 2/2, pp. 83–98.

Jackson I. Cope, 1956, 'Seventeenth-Century Quaker Style', *PMLA* 71/4, pp. 724–54.

Maurice A. Creasey, 1956, 'Early Quaker Christology', PhD thesis, University of Leeds (https://www.woodbrooke.org.uk/data/files/CPQS/Summaries/Maurice_A_Creasey.pdf).

Eveline Cruikshanks and Stuart Handley, 2002, 'John Archdale', in D. Hayton, E. Cruikshanks and S. Handley (eds), *The History of Parliament: The House of Commons 1690–1715*, Martlesham: Boydell and Brewer.

Leo Damrosch, 1996, *The Sorrows of the Quaker Jesus: James Nayler and the Puritan Crackdown on the Free Spirit*, Cambridge, MA: Harvard University Press.

Pink Dandelion, 1996, *A Sociological Analysis of the Theology of Quakers*, Lewiston, NY: Edwin Mellen.

Pink Dandelion, 2005, *The Liturgies of Quakerism*, Aldershot: Ashgate.

Pink Dandelion, 2007, *An Introduction to Quakerism*, Cambridge: Cambridge University Press.

Jeffrey Dudiak, 2010, 'Response to Muers and Wood', *Quaker Religious Thought* 115, article 5.

Christopher Durston, 1989, *The Family in the English Revolution*, Oxford: Blackwell.

Melvin B. Endy, 1973, *William Penn and Early Quakerism*, Princeton, NJ: Princeton University Press.

James Fodor, 2004, 'Postliberal Theology', in David F. Ford with Rachel Muers (eds), *The Modern Theologians*, 3rd edn, Oxford: Blackwell.

David F. Ford and C. C. Pecknold, 2006, *The Promise of Scriptural Reasoning*, Oxford: Blackwell.

Michel Foucault, 1961/2001, *Madness and Civilisation: A History of Insanity in the Age of Reason*, trans. Richard Howard, London: Routledge.

Michel Foucault, 1983/2001, *Fearless Speech*, ed. Joseph Pearson, Los Angeles: Semiotext(e).

Michel Foucault, 1984/2011, *The Courage of Truth*, ed. Frédéric Gros, trans. Graham Burchell, New York: Palgrave Macmillan.

Robin Gill, 2006, *A Textbook of Christian Ethics*, 3rd edn, London: T&T Clark.

Philip Goodchild, 2002, *Capitalism and Religion: The Price of Piety*, London: Routledge.

BIBLIOGRAPHY

Jonathan Griffiths, 2009, 'Christ as the personal "word of the oath" in Hebrews 6:13—7:28', paper presented at British New Testament Society seminar on the Catholic Epistles, University of Aberdeen.

Douglas Gwyn, 1986, *Apocalypse of the Word: The Life and Message of George Fox*, Richmond, IN: Friends United Press.

Douglas Gwyn, 2011, *Conversations with Christ: Quaker Meditations on the Gospel of John*, Philadelphia, PA: Quaker Press.

Mark Haddon, 2003, *The Curious Incident of the Dog in the Night-Time*, London: Jonathan Cape.

Thomas Hamm, 2003, *The Quakers in America*, New York: Columbia University Press.

Daniel W. Hardy, 2001, *Finding the Church*, London: SCM Press.

Charles Harris, 1932, 'Liturgical Silence', in W. K. Lowther Clarke (ed.), *Liturgy and Worship*, London: SCM Press, p. 778.

Stanley Hauerwas, 2002, *With the Grain of the Universe: The Church's Witness and Natural Theology*, London: SCM Press.

Stanley Hauerwas, 2004, *Performing the Faith: Bonhoeffer and the Practice of Nonviolence*, Grand Rapids, MI: Brazos.

Tom Heron, 1977, *Call it a Day*, St Ives: Ark Press.

Mike Higton, 2008, *SCM Core Text Christian Doctrine*, London: SCM Press.

Mike Higton and Rachel Muers, 2012, *The Text in Play: Experiments in Reading Scripture*, Eugene, OR: Wipf and Stock/Cascade.

Christopher Hill, 1964, *Society and Puritanism in Pre-Revolutionary England*, New York: Schocken.

Christopher Hill, 1975, *The World Turned Upside Down: Radical Ideas During the English Revolution*, London: Pelican.

David Hilliard, 1997, 'The Religious Crisis of the 1960s: The Experience of the Australian Churches', *Journal of Religious History* 22/1, pp. 209–27.

Gene Hillman, 2002, 'Quakers and the Lamb's War: A Hermeneutic for Confronting Evil', *Quaker Theology* 7.

Alison Duncan Hirsch, 1994, 'A Tale of Two Wives: Mythmaking and the Lives of Gulielma and Hannah Penn', *Pennsylvania History* 61/4, pp. 429–56.

Elaine Hobby, 2012, 'Hester Biddle', in Marion Ann Taylor and Agnes Choi (eds), *Handbook of Women Biblical Interpreters: A Historical and Biographical Guide*, Grand Rapids, MI: Baker, pp. 69–72.

Stephen R. Holmes, 2012, *Baptist Theology*, London: T&T Clark International.

Craig Hovey, 2008, *To Share in the Body: A Theology of Martyrdom for Today's Church*, Grand Rapids, MI: Brazos.

Craig Hovey, 2010, 'Narrative Proclamation and Gospel Truthfulness: Why Christian Proclamation Needs Speakers', in Chris K. Huebner and Tripp York (eds), *The Gift of Difference: Radical Orthodoxy, Radical Reformation*, Winnipeg, MB: CMU Press, pp. 87–103.

Craig Hovey, 2011, *Bearing True Witness: Truthfulness in Christian Practice*, Grand Rapids, MI: Eerdmans.

TESTIMONY

Balthasar Hübmaier, 1524/1905, *On Heretics and Those Who Burn Them*, in Henry Vedder (ed.), *Balthasar Hübmaier: Leader of the Anabaptists*, New York: Putnam's.

H. Larry Ingle, 1994, *First Among Friends: George Fox and the Creation of Quakerism*, New York: Oxford University Press.

Elizabeth Isichei, 1970, *Victorian Quakers*, Oxford: Oxford University Press.

Willis Jenkins, 2008, *Ecologies of Grace: Environmental Ethics and Christian Theology*, New York: Oxford University Press.

David L. Johns, 2013, *Quakering Theology: Essays on Worship, Tradition and Christian Faith*, Aldershot: Ashgate.

David Jones, 1999, *Conscience and Allegiance in Seventeenth-Century England: The Political Significance of Oaths and Engagements*, Rochester: University of Rochester Press.

Emmanuel M. Katongole, 'Threatened with Resurrection: Martyrdom and Reconciliation in the World Church,' in Budde and Scott (eds), *Witness of the Body*, pp. 190–203; quoting Julia Esquivel, 1982, *Threatened with Resurrection*, Elgin, IL: The Brethren Press, pp. 59–61.

N. H. Keeble, 2002, *Cultural Identity of Women in the Seventeenth Century*, London: Routledge, p. 117.

Thomas C. Kennedy, 2001, *British Quakerism 1860–1920: The Transformation of a Religious Community*, Oxford: Oxford University Press.

Stephen A. Kent, 1983, 'The Quaker Ethic and the Fixed Price Policy: Max Weber and Beyond', *Sociological Inquiry* 53/1, pp. 16–32.

Jon Kershner, 2013, 'The Valiant Sixty-First? John Woolman's (1720–1772) Abolitionist Theology and the Restoration of the Lamb's War', *Quaker Studies* 13, pp. 23–49.

Mark Knights, 2011, *The Devil in Disguise: Deception, Delusion and Fanaticism in the Early English Enlightenment*, Oxford: Oxford University Press.

Barry Levy, 1988, *Quakers and the American Family: British Settlement in the Delaware Valley*, Oxford: Oxford University Press.

Andrew T. Lincoln, 2000, *Truth on Trial: The Lawsuit Motif in the Fourth Gospel*, Grand Rapids, MI: Baker.

John Locke, 1689/2003, 'A Letter Concerning Toleration', in Ian Shapiro (ed.), *Two Treatises of Government and a Letter Concerning Toleration*, New Haven, KT: Yale University Press, pp. 211–55.

Pam Lunn, Betty Hagglund, Edwina Newman and Pink Dandelion, 2009, '"Choose Life!" Quaker Metaphor and Modernity', in Elaine Graham (ed.), *Grace Jantzen: Redeeming the Present*, Aldershot: Ashgate, pp. 91–110.

Alisdair MacIntyre, 1991, *After Virtue: A Study in Moral Theory*, London: Duckworth.

J. L. Martyn, 1968, *History and Theology in the Fourth Gospel*, Louisville, KY: Westminster John Knox.

Jennifer M. McBride, 2011, *The Church for the World: A Theology of Public Witness*, New York: Oxford University Press.

James W. McClendon, Jr, 2002, *Ethics: Systematic Theology*, Vol. 1, 2nd edn, Nashville, TN: Abingdon Press.

BIBLIOGRAPHY

Sallie McFague, 2013, *Blessed are the Consumers: Climate Change and the Practice of Restraint*, Minneapolis, MN: Fortress Press.

Elizabeth T. McLaughlin, 1967, 'Milton and Thomas Ellwood', *Milton Quarterly* 1/2, pp. 17–28.

Charlotte Meredith, 2014, 'Jeremy Paxman Brands Conscientious Objectors of WW1 "Cranks"', *Huffington Post*, 2 February, http://www.huffingtonpost.co.uk/2014/02/04/jeremy-paxman-britains-great-war-cranks-n-4721895.html.

Rosemary Moore, 2000, *The Light in their Consciences: The Early Quakers in Britain 1646–1666*, University Park, PA: Pennsylvania State University Press.

Charles C. Moskos and John Whiteclay Chambers II, 1993, 'The Secularisation of Conscience', in Moskos and Chambers (eds), *The New Conscientious Objection: From Sacred to Secular Resistance*, Oxford: Oxford University Press, pp. 3–21.

Rachel Muers, 2010, 'Levinas, Quakers and the (in)visibility of God: Responses to Jeffrey Dudiak and Corey Beals', *Quaker Religious Thought* 114, article 6.

Rachel Muers, 2014, 'The Ethics of Stats: Some Contemporary Questions about Telling the Truth', *Journal of Religious Ethics* 42/1, pp. 1–21.

Andrew R. Murphy, 2003, *Conscience and Community: Revisiting Toleration in Early Modern England and America*, University Park, PA: Penn State University Press.

Anne G. Myles, 2001, 'From Monster to Martyr: Re-presenting Mary Dyer', *Early American Literature* 36/1, pp. 1–30.

Yasuharu Nakano, 2008, 'Elizabeth Bathurst's Soteriology and a List of Corrections in Several Editions of her Works', *Quaker Studies* 13/1, pp. 89–102.

Edwina Newman, 2007, 'Children of Light and Sons of Darkness: Quakers, Oaths and the Old Bailey Proceedings in the Eighteenth Century', *Quaker Studies* 12/1, pp. 73–88.

H. Richard Niebuhr, 1932, 'The Grace of Doing Nothing', *Christian Century*, 23 March 1932.

Reinhold Niebuhr, 1932, 'Must We Do Nothing?', *Christian Century*, 30 March 1932.

Peter Ochs, 2005, *Peirce, Pragmatism and the Logic of Scripture*, Cambridge: Cambridge University Press.

R. B. Outhwaite, 1995, *Clandestine Marriage in England, 1500–1850*, London: Hambledon.

Brian D. Phillips, 1989, 'Friendly Patriots: British Quakerism and the Imperial Nation 1890–1910', unpublished thesis, University of Cambridge.

Gay Pilgrim, 2008, 'British Quakerism as Heterotopic', in Pink Dandelion and Peter Collins (eds), *The Quaker Condition: The Sociology of a Liberal Religion*, Cambridge: Cambridge Scholars Press, pp. 53–68.

Rebecca Probert, 2009, *Marriage Law and Practice in the Long Eighteenth Century: A Reassessment*, Cambridge: Cambridge University Press.

John Punshon, 2006, *Portrait in Grey: A Short History of the Quakers*, 2nd edn, London: Quaker Books.

J. Ben Quash, 2005, *Theology and the Drama of History*, Cambridge: Cambridge University Press.

Ephraim Radner, 2012, *A Brutal Unity: The Spiritual Politics of the Christian Church*, Waco, TX: Baylor University Press.

TESTIMONY

Paul Ramsey, 1967, *Deeds and Rules in Christian Ethics*, New York: Scribner.
Randi Rashkover, 2005, *Revelation and Theopolitics: Barth, Rosenzweig and the Politics of Praise*, London: T&T Clark.
Paul Ricœur, 1967, *The Symbolism of Evil*, Boston, MA: Beacon Press.
Paul Ricœur, 1980, *Essays on Biblical Interpretation*, ed. Lewis Mudge, Minneapolis, MN: Fortress Press.
Eugene F. Rogers, 1999, *Sexuality and the Christian Body: Their Way into the Triune God*, Oxford: Blackwell.
Nancy Black Sagafi-nejad, 2011, *Friends at the Bar: A Quaker View of Law, Conflict Resolution, and Legal Reform*, Albany, NY: SUNY Press.
Paul Salzmann (ed.), 2000, *Early Modern Women's Writing: An Anthology 1560–1700*, Oxford: Oxford University Press.
Jackie Leach Scully and Pink Dandelion (eds), 2007, *Good and Evil: Quaker Perspectives*, Aldershot: Ashgate.
Timothy W. Seid, 2001, 'Samuel Fisher: 17th-Century Quaker Biblical Scholar', *Quaker Religious Thought* 97, article 7.
Michael J. Sheeran, 1996, *Beyond Majority Rule: Voteless Decisions in the Religious Society of Friends*, Philadelphia, PA: Philadelphia Yearly Meeting.
Thomas P. Slaughter, 2008, *The Beautiful Soul of John Woolman: Apostle of Abolition*, New York: Hill & Wang.
Carole Dale Spencer, 2007, *Holiness: The Soul of Quakerism: A Historical Analysis of the Theology of Holiness in the Quaker Tradition*, Milton Keynes: Paternoster Press.
John Spencer and Rhona Flin, 1993, *The Evidence of Children: The Law and the Psychology*, London: Blackstone.
J. P. M. Sweet, 1981, 'Maintaining the Testimony of Jesus: The Suffering of Christians in the Revelation of John', in William Horbury and Brian McNeil (eds), *Suffering and Martyrdom in the New Testament*, Cambridge: Cambridge University Press, pp. 101–7.
John Thurloe, 1742, *A Collection of the State Papers of John Thurloe*, Vol. 6, London.
Emilie M. Townes, 2006, *Womanist Ethics and the Cultural Production of Evil*, New York: Palgrave Macmillan.
Allison Trites, 1977, *The New Testament Concept of Witness*, Cambridge: Cambridge University Press.
UK Parliament, 2013, *Proceedings of the Public Committee hearings on the Marriage (Same-Sex Couples) Bill*, Thursday 14 February.
T. L. Underwood, 2001, *Primitivism, Radicalism and the Lamb's War: Baptist–Quaker Conflict in Seventeenth-Century England*, Oxford: Oxford University Press.
Max Weber, 1905/1930, *The Protestant Ethic and the Spirit of Capitalism*, trans. Talcott Parsons, London: Unwin Hyman.
Samuel Wells, 2004, *Improvisation: The Drama of Christian Ethics*, Grand Rapids, MI: Brazos.

BIBLIOGRAPHY

Ludwig Wittgenstein, 1980, *Culture and Value*, ed. G. H. von Wright, trans. Peter Winch, Oxford: Blackwell.

William M. Wright, 2009, *Rhetoric and Theology: Figural Reading of John 9*, Berlin: de Gruyter.

Edith Wyschogrod, 1998, *An Ethics of Remembering: History, Heterology and the Nameless Others*, Chicago, IL: University of Chicago Press.

Index

Advices and Queries (1994) 183
aesthetics 82, 185
Africa 8, 148
Anabaptism 12–14, 19, 69–70, 105, 114, 119–20, 122–3, 140, 147, 189
Anglicanism 42
animals, non-human 175–6, 180
apocalyptic 32–3, 38, 71, 177, 191
apophatic theology 56, 59, 79
Appleby, Charles and Mary 153–4, 161
Archdale, John 109, 119, 126, 194
Arendt, Hannah 63
asceticism 56, 59, 69, 89, 158, 170
attention (in worship) 77–8, 161
authority 2, 11, 36–7, 45, 87, 92–3, 102, 116, 154, 160, 169

Baptists 38, 105, 123
Barclay, Robert 71, 78, 203
Bartlet, Michael 94n18
Barth, Karl 13
Bathurst, Elizabeth ix, 73–4, 203
Bauman, Richard 82, 118–19
Baxter, Richard 131–2, 141
behavioural creed 26, 27, 198
Benson, Gervase 113
Bible, biblical interpretation 3, 11, 20, 28, 29–42, 45, 47, 50, 85, 114, 116–17, 132, 139, 161, 172
Biddle, Hester 34
Blamires, David 164
blasphemy 51–2, 201–2
Bonhoeffer, Dietrich 62–3, 146–7
Book(s) of discipline, *see* Christian Faith and Practice, Quaker Faith and Practice
Braithwaite, William 110, 121
Brinton, Howard 17, 24, 25
Britain Yearly Meeting 29, 149, 161–2, 182
Budde, Michael 136
business method 193–6, 205

capitalism 27, 85, 175
Carlyle, Thomas 92

INDEX

Cavanaugh, William 117
Chomsky, Noam 93, 95
Christian Faith and Practice in the Experience of the Society of Friends (1959 Book of Discipline) 23
Christology 13, 42, 72, 115–16
Civil War, English 8, 12
Clarendon Code 9
class 143, 167, 182, 186–7
climate change 27, 183, 189
clothing 179, 181, 190, *see also* hat honour, plain dress
Cock, Luke 101
Collins, Peter 82, 185
Commonwealth 12, 131
communion 12, 75, 90
conflict 2, 9, 12, 50, 54, 56, 62, 65, 67, 70, 78, 97, 105, 126, 130, 139, 142, 146, 148, 160, 182
conscience 21, 34, 84, 95, 106, 109, 111, 118, 121–9, 131–4, 143–4, 171, 200
conscientious objection 21, 106, 122, 125–7
consensus 129, 195–6
consumerism 134, 183, 197
consumption 27, 174–7, 182, 186–9
conversion 16, 18, 40–1, 178–9
convincement 16, 20, 43, 102, 116
Creasey, Maurice 42
creation 76, 183–4, 186

Cromwell, Oliver 147
Cynics 88–91, 179

Damrosch, Leo 139
Dandelion, Pink 4, 26, 27
Declaration of the Harmless and Innocent People of God ('Peace Testimony') 55, 58, 68, 97, 196, 203
dialogue 149–50, 152
discernment 27, 48, 50–2, 79, 97–8, 101, 109, 125, 128–9, 151–2, 172, 191, 193
disownment 129
doctrine 140, 147, 149, 196
Docwra, Ann 73
double negative 21, 58, 64, 73, 181, 183, 186, 192, 200, *see also* negative testimony
Dyer, Mary 21, 134–9, 142–5, 148–9, 167, 200, 202

ecclesiology 9, 11
economics 24–5, 67, 85, 157–8, 172, 176–9, 186
Edmundson, William 47
Ellwood, Thomas 83–4, 86, 91–2, 94, 102, 104, 174
Endy, Melvin 41
environment 22, 172–6, 182–92
equality 22–3, 25, 162, 172
eschatology 198
Esther 143
experimental knowing 15–20, 67, 69, 150–1, 162, 192, 197, 204–5

Fell, Margaret (later Fox) 36, 50, 123–4, 126, 132, 143, 146, 174
festivals 55, 133
First World War 24, 125
Fisher, Mary 94
Fisher, Samuel 33, 104
Foucault, Michel 81, 86–91, 94
Foundations of a True Social Order (1918) 24, 173
Fox, George 5, 9, 15, 19, 36, 41, 50, 55, 92, 100, 106, 111, 146, 151, 156–9, 162, 191
freedom 21, 109, 119, 122–5, 127, 130–9, 142–5, 149, 168, 171

gathered 10–12, 20, 34–5, 53, 74–5, 92, 104, 111, 124, 130, 133, 145, 151, 156, 168, 191, 196–7
Genesis, Book of 35, 72–3
Goodchild, Philip 77
Good Samaritan 197
Gospel 40, 44, 126
gospel order 147, 151–2, 168
grammar 14, 22, 194
Gregory, Brad 140
'Guide', inner 100–1, 134, 149

Haddon, Mark 60
hagiography 137
Hardwicke Act 155
Hardy, Daniel W. 76
hat honour 83–4
Hauerwas, Stanley 13, 62, 69

Hebrews, Epistle to 115–16
hermeneutic 33, 38
Heron, Tom 78, 164–5
Higton, Mike 30
holding minute 193, 198–9, 205
holiness 11, 75–6, 158, 160, 175, 181
homophobia 167, 169, 205
homosexuality 164, 166, 168
Hooks, Ellis 115, 123
Hovey, Craig 14, 87, 90, 119–20, 136
Howgill, Francis 10–11, 53
Hübmaier, Balthasar 140
Hutchinson, Anne 143

Identity 2, 4–6, 18, 24, 38, 82, 91, 125, 127, 142, 157–8, 170, 203
Integrity 23, 25, 81, 84, 106, 172, 181, 187

James, Book of 110–11
Jesus Christ 12–16, 20, 32, 36, 38–9, 41, 43–52, 56, 68–9, 73, 80–1, 85, 95, 100, 103, 106, 111, 113–8, 120, 123–4, 131, 158, 172, 177, 202
John, Gospel of 35, 40–8, 56, 63, 81, 98, 115
Johns, David 137
Jones, Rufus 42
joy 191–2
Judson, Sylvia Shaw 135, 137, 145
justice 108, 143, 172, 203–4

INDEX

Kabarak Call for Peace and Ecojustice (2012) 172–3, 188, 197
Kamara, Abdul 148–9
knowing experimentally, *see* experimental knowing

Lamb's War 54
language 6, 10, 11, 13, 18, 20–2, 24, 27, 31–3, 35, 37, 42–4, 50, 56, 58, 63–4, 71, 79, 81–94, 98–101, 103, 108, 110–13, 149, 157, 159, 166, 168, 170, 182, 185, 190, 197
leadings 37, 99, 130, 182
Levy, Barry 159
liberal, liberalism 2, 4–5, 22, 25–6, 29, 30, 33, 42, 131, 152, 167, 184, 187, 205
Light 20–1, 36, 40–5, 48, 54, 85, 98, 100, 124, 126, 131–2, 139, 141, 149, 157, 166, 173, 191, 198
Lincoln, Andrew 45–6
liturgy 15, 67, 111, 159, 196
Locke, John 120
London Yearly Meeting 24, 173

Marcellin, Sizeli 43, 53
Marian martyrs 140–1
marriage 22, 152–63, 166–7, 169–71, 173
martyrs 21, 52, 120, 129, 134, 136–42, 146–7, 158, 179
Matthew, Gospel of 110, 114–6, 180
McBride, Jennifer 64

McClendon, James 13, 19–20, 38, 146–7
meeting houses 185
Methodists 160
minutes 194–9, 205
modernity 12
Monck, George 199
Moskos, Charles C. 125
mysticism 20, 38, 42, 72, 90

narrative 15, 21, 23, 33, 35, 43–5, 143, 164, 174, 198
Nayler, James 21, 51–3, 103–4, 129, 131–2, 134, 139–42, 145–9, 174, 178, 200, 202
negative testimony 21, 55–6, 58–60, 62, 64, 66–9, 71–2, 80–1, 97, 105, 134, 168, 170, 186, 188, 192
Niebuhr, H. Richard 65–6
Niebuhr, Reinhold 66
Nonconformists 9, 109, 155, 157
nonviolence 21, 54, 58, 62, 64–70, 72, 86, 96–9, 105, 128, 136, 139, 199

oats 1
oaths 9, 21, 55, 57–8, 105–27, 131–2, 188
openness 21, 27, 127, 187
Owen, John 34

pacifism 54, 65–7, 96–9, 146–7, 189–90
Parliament 51–2, 108–9, 111, 194

parrhesia 87–90, 94, 96, 99
particularity 18–19
peace 2, 13–14, 19, 22–5, 54–5, 64, 66, 70, 68, 97, 113, 115, 118, 125, 128, 148–9, 151–2, 154, 161, 169, 170–3, 178, 189, 191–2
peace churches 13–14, 19, 70, 125, 127, 183
'Peace Testimony', *see Declaration of the Harmless and Innocent People of God*
peculiarity/peculiar people 10, 55, 57, 133–4, 138, 174, 181, 185, 198–9
Penington, Isaac 71–2, 74
Penn, Gulielma 170–1
Penn, William 39, 80, 98, 109, 111–12, 127, 170–1
persecution 9–10, 34, 52, 107, 130, 140–2, 154, 157, 159–60, 191
plain dress 82, 185, *see also* clothing
plainness 81–4, 185–6
plain speech 21, 81–4, 86, 108, 111, 185
pluralism 131–2
prayer 27, 78, 132, 198
primitive Christianity 38–9
politics 2–3, 6, 8, 23, 27, 32, 40, 64–5, 69, 71–2, 77, 86–8, 97, 106, 110, 114, 116–17, 119–22, 124, 126–7, 132, 134, 136, 140, 142, 146–7, 150, 159, 170, 173–4, 176, 197, 200
prophetic 2, 33–4, 36–8, 64, 66, 72, 85, 90, 99, 105, 124, 191
Protestant 9, 13, 85
Punshon, John 24
Puritan 9, 12, 33, 42, 156, 160

Quaker Act (1662) 107–8
Quaker Faith and Practice (1994 Book of Discipline) 3, 23, 106–7, 146
Quaker Peace Network Africa 148
Quaker Women's Group 166
quaking 9
quietism 20, 70–1, 75, 119

race, racism 202
Radical Reformation 13–14, 19
Ramsey, Paul 164
redemptive love 100
Reformation 11–12, 16, 140, 154, 156
Reformation, Henrician 117
repentance 64–5, 96, 101, 144, 174
Restoration, of the English monarchy 9, 130, 154
resurrection 38, 47, 49, 73, 103
revelation 20, 37, 41, 44–6, 56–7, 103, 132, 142, 144
Revelation, Book of 35, 46, 54
Rich, Robert 146

INDEX

Ricoeur, Paul 43, 45
Robinson, William 139
Rogers, Eugene 158, 170
Rustin, Bayard 93–4, 97–8
Ruth 158
Rwanda 43, 70, 202

Said, Edward 94
salvation 16, 45, 48–50, 102, 113, 122
same-sex marriage 22, 152–3, 161–3, 169–71, 194
science 17–18, 166
Scripture, *see* Bible
Scully, Jackie Leach 2n1
sectarianism 48
Seekers 9–10, 74
sexuality 22, 25, 152–3, 163–4, 166–8, 170, 205
Sierra Leone 148
silence 9–11, 21, 71, 74–9, 82, 135, 145, 196, 205
Simmonds, Martha 51, 146
simplicity 22–3, 25, 27, 82, 172, 175, 180, 185–92
slavery 47, 55, 98, 173, 175–6, 202
Speak Truth to Power (1955) 93, 96, 98–100, 104
speech, *see* language
Springett, Gulielma, *see* Penn, Gulielma
Stevenson, Marmaduke 139
stewardship 23, 172, 183–4, 189

Stuart, Charles 161
Sturge, Joseph 94–5
success 67–8, 85, 99, 101, 149, 188–91, 199
sustainability 23, 25, 117, 172, 194

tithes 9, 55, 57, 133
Towards a Quaker View of Sex (1963) 163–9, 191
truth 13, 18–19, 21–3, 36–7, 44–8, 50, 53–4, 56–8, 60–4, 68–70, 77, 79, 80–106, 111, 113–15, 116–22, 124, 126, 131–2, 135–6, 138, 142–7, 149, 160, 162–3, 167, 170, 173, 177–8, 180, 187–8, 190–1, 196, 199–200, 203–5

United Nations 70
universality 19–20, 40–3, 72–3, 100, 126, 132, 150, 157, 180
Universal Light 21, 149
unprogrammed worship 4, 21, 29, 30, 76, 78–9, 95, 104, 151, 184

virtue 15

West African Quaker Peace Network 148
Whitehead, George 126, 133, 150
Williams, Roger 123
witness 13–14, 150

Wittgenstein, Ludwig 58–9
Woolman, John 175–82, 185–8, 190, 200–2
womanism 204
Word of God 32
words, *see* language
worship 1, 4, 6, 9, 11–12, 18, 21, 26, 29, 42, 51, 56, 74–9, 92, 95, 104, 106, 109, 123–6, 130–6, 138, 145, 149, 151, 156, 161, 171–2, 187, 193, 198, 201

Wyschogrod, Edith 61–2

Yoder, John Howard 13, 69